WHY WE'RE WRONG ABOUT NEARLY EVERYTHING

WHY WE'RE WRONG

ABOUT NEARLY

EVERYTHING

A Theory of Human Misunderstanding

BOBBY DUFFY

BASIC BOOKS

New York

Basic Books
Hachette Book Group
1290 Avenue of the Americas, New York, NY 10104
www.basicbooks.com

Printed in the United States of America

Originally published in 2018 by Atlantic Books in Great Britain

First US Edition: November 2019

Published by Basic Books, an imprint of Perseus Books, LLC, a subsidiary of Hachette Book Group, Inc. The Basic Books name and logo is a trademark of the Hachette Book Group.

The Hachette Speakers Bureau provides a wide range of authors for speaking events. To find out more, go to www.hachettespeakersbureau.com or call (866) 376-6591.

The publisher is not responsible for websites (or their content) that are not owned by the publisher.

All figure sources and data are available from www.perils.ipsos.com except the following: 'Trends in birth rates per 1000 females aged 15–19 by ethnicity in the US' (page 62): www.hhs.gov/ash/oah/adolescent-development/reproductive-health -and-teen-pregnancy/teen-pregnancy-and-childbearing/trends/index.html

'Do you feel closer to a particular party than all other parties?' (page 148): European Social Survey 2002–2016

'Key moves in public trust over time' (page 223): Ipsos MORI Veracity Index

Print book interior design by Amy Quinn.

The Library of Congress has cataloged the hardcover edition as follows:
Names: Duffy, Bobby, author.
Title: Why we're wrong about nearly everything : a theory of human misunderstanding / Bobby Duffy.
Other titles: Perils of perception
Description: First US edition. | New York : Basic Books, 2019. | "Originally published in 2018 by Atlantic Books in Great Britain." | Includes bibliographical references and index.
Identifiers: LCCN 2019018610 (print) | LCCN 2019021210 (ebook) | ISBN 9781541618091 (ebook) | ISBN 9781541618084 (hardcover)
Subjects: LCSH: Knowledge, Sociology of. | Ignorance (Theory of knowledge) | Perception. | Truthfulness and falsehood.
Classification: LCC HM651 (ebook) | LCC HM651 .D84 2019 (print) | DDC 306.4/2—dc23
LC record available at https://lccn.loc.gov/2019018610

ISBNs: 978-1-5416-1808-4 (hardcover), 978-1-5416-1809-1 (ebook)

LSC-C

10 9 8 7 6 5 4 3 2 1

CONTENTS

PERILS EVERYWHERE

I hated my psychology classes at college. As I remember them now, they were taught by a succession of super-smart, suave professors who all looked the same, closer to snake-hipped rock stars than fusty academics. They were all tall and slim, with haircuts that didn't play by professorial rules. They wore all-black clothes or, rarely, paisley shirts, and shoes that were just that bit too pointy. (I admit, jealousy may be clouding my own perceptions a little; in fact, I think I've just described Russell Brand.) The students, of both genders, swooned—partly because of the professors' rebellious looks, partly because they seemed to know so much about how we thought. There's nothing more attractive to most confused young adults than someone who *really* understands them.

But I had a problem with that. I hated the cognitive tricks that demonstrated we nearly all fall into the same mistaken ways of thinking. They'd set us up with questions or experiments that were custom made to elicit a particular answer and show how typical our brains were. At that insecure but arrogant age, I wanted to be special and unpredictable—but my answers were just like everybody else's.

Take this example, from a professor at the University of Maryland:

> You have the opportunity to earn some extra credit on your final grade. Select whether you want two points or six points added onto your final paper grade. But there's a small catch: if more than 10 per cent of the class selects six points, then no one gets any points, not even the people who chose two points.[1]

Here is a very direct and teachable moment, a lesson in the 'tragedy of the commons'—where individuals try to obtain the greatest benefit from a particular resource, taking more than their equal or sustainable share, and therefore ruin it for everyone, including themselves. Of course, the class conformed to type, and failed. Around 20 per cent selected six points, so they all got nothing. In fact, only one class in one semester over the eight years the professor had been conducting his mildly cruel experiment had actually managed to get the extra points.

Given my lingering sensitivity to psychological tricks, it's not without irony that a lot of my working life has been focused on running similar tests. I spent twenty years at opinion research firm Ipsos MORI, designing and dissecting research from around the world to help understand what people think and do, and why. I'm now a (definitely not snake-hipped) professor at King's College London, focusing on the same challenges of public delusion, and what they mean for public policy. Across these roles, I've run hundreds of surveys on public misperceptions—what we call the 'Perils of Perception'—investigating a range of social and political issues, from sexual behaviour to personal finance, across a large number of countries. We now have over 100,000 interviews, across forty countries on some questions, allowing us to weigh up our perceptions against reality. This is a unique and fascinating source of data on how we see the world, and why we're often so wrong about it. Previous work has tended to focus on one issue or sphere of life, and few get beyond a handful of countries. You can dig into the full set of Ipsos studies at www.perils.ipsos.com

Across all the studies and in every country, people get a lot wrong on nearly every subject we've covered, including immigration levels, teen pregnancy, crime rates, obesity, trends in global poverty, and how many of us are on Facebook. But the key question is 'Why?'

Let's start off with a question that's got very little to do with the sort of social and political realities we'll look at later, but helps to highlight why there might be this gap between perceptions and reality: 'Is the Great Wall of China visible from outer space?' What do you think? If you're anything like the population in general, there's about a 50–50 chance that you answered 'yes', as surveys show that half of people say they believe the Great Wall is visible from space.[2] They're wrong—it's not.

At its widest, the Great Wall is only nine metres across, about the size of a small house. It's also built of rock that is similar in colour to the surrounding mountains, so it blends in with the landscape. When you take a bit of time to think about it, the idea that the Great Wall is visible from space is actually slightly ridiculous, but there are some very good reasons why you might have thought it is.

First, it's not something you'll have pondered on a lot. Unlike me, you probably haven't looked up the width of the Wall or its distance from outer space (and then got caught up in endless forum discussions about the claim). You don't have the pertinent facts readily available to you.

Second, you may have vaguely heard someone say it when you weren't paying much attention. You may even have seen it in print or heard it on the television. For years, Trivial Pursuit had it as an (incorrect) answer. You're less likely to have seen it in Chinese school textbooks, but it's still noted as a fact in those. However, you've likely seen it somewhere, probably more than once, and haven't seen anything to contradict the assertion, so it settled in your head.

Third, you almost certainly answered the question quickly, wanting to get on with the rest of the book—the sort of 'fast thinking' popularised by the Nobel Prize–winning behavioural scientist Daniel Kahneman that relies on mental shortcuts. You may therefore have confused different measures of scale. We know that the Great Wall of China is extremely 'big'—in fact, it's one of the largest man-made structures on earth. But that is mainly due to its length, which isn't the property that will make it visible from outer space.

Most important, your answer was also perhaps more emotional than you might think for such a mundane trivia question. Spend some time researching the answer, and you'll discover that even *astronauts* argue over it. (For the record, Neil Armstrong says it's not visible, which is good enough for me.) You'll even find photos from seemingly reliable sources purporting to show the Great Wall as seen from space. (In at least one case, the photo was of a canal.) With something as big as the Great Wall, we *want* to believe that astronauts, aliens, even gods, can see our handiwork. We want it to be true because it's impressive—and this emotional response alters our perception of reality.

Drawing on faulty prior knowledge, answering a different question than the one we are asked, juggling comparisons across different scales, relying on fast thinking, and missing how our emotions shape what we see and think are just some of the perils of perception we face every day. The Great Wall of China is a real, physical thing, an object that can be measured. Imagine now how the same problems of perception wreak havoc when we are contemplating complex and disputed social and political realities.

But there is a final point. Now I've pointed out that the best evidence suggests that the Great Wall is not visible from space, you probably believe me, and if you had a vague idea it was, you've probably changed your mind. Of course, this is not a highly charged debate, tied up with your identity and tribal connections, so it is easier to shrug and update your view. But still the point remains that we have the ability to adapt our beliefs in the face of new facts.

Having started with (literally) a trivia question, it is worth emphasizing that this is firmly *not* the focus of the book, fascinating and satisfying as (other people's) factual ignorance and belief in the absurd can be. We love to smirk at the one in ten French people who still believe the earth may be flat; the quarter of Australians who think that cavemen and dinosaurs existed at the same time; the one in nine Brits who think the 9/11 attacks were a US government conspiracy; or the 15 per cent of Americans who believe that the media or government adds secret mind-controlling signals to television transmissions.[3] Our main interest is not niche stupidity or minority belief in conspiracies, but much more general and widespread delusions about individual, social, and political realities.

Let's look at one very basic question about the state of society that is much closer to our focus: 'What proportion of the population of your country is aged sixty-five or over?' Think about it yourself. You may have heard that your country has an ageing population, or that it even faces a demographic 'time bomb', that the population of older people is getting too large for the younger people in your country to support in their retirement. The media frequently highlight the pressures on the economy of supporting a growing elderly population, particularly in countries such as

Italy and Germany. There have even been stories on how, in Japan, adult nappy sales are set to overtake baby nappy sales. These stories may be apocryphal, but they provide such a vivid image that they stick with us.

So, what would you guess?

When we asked members of the public in fourteen countries, in every single country the average guess was much higher than the actual proportion. In Italy the actual figure is 21 per cent, whereas in Japan it's 25 per cent. These are big numbers—one in five and one in four of the whole population, and roughly double the proportion compared with the actual figures a generation or two ago. Yet the average guesses were around twice the actual population figures. People in Italy thought 48 per cent of the population—about half—were sixty-five or older.

Q. What proportion of the population of your country is aged sixty-five or over?

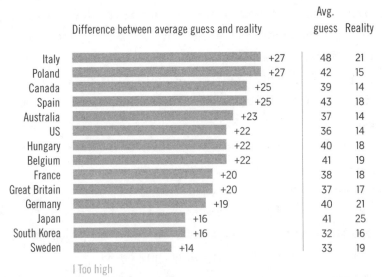

	Difference between average guess and reality	Avg. guess	Reality
Italy	+27	48	21
Poland	+27	42	15
Canada	+25	39	14
Spain	+25	43	18
Australia	+23	37	14
US	+22	36	14
Hungary	+22	40	18
Belgium	+22	41	19
France	+20	38	18
Great Britain	+20	37	17
Germany	+19	40	21
Japan	+16	41	25
South Korea	+16	32	16
Sweden	+14	33	19

| Too high

Figure 1. All countries hugely overestimated the proportion of their population aged 65 or over.

As you can see from this one, very simple example, our delusions are not just driven by the particularly febrile political moment we're living through. There are no massive misinformation campaigns by automated bots on Facebook or Twitter trying to convince us that our populations are older than they really are, but we're still very wrong. Our misperceptions are wide, deep, and long-standing. Political ignorance has been a concern from the very dawn of democracy, with Plato's grousing that the general public were too ignorant to select a government or hold it to account.

It is hard to prove that delusions have been widespread for a long time, because measuring them requires representative surveys, and social scientists started conducting rigorous public opinion polls only relatively recently. In the middle of the twentieth century, surveys of people's perception of social realities were rare, limited primarily to simple political facts—for example, which party was in power, what their policies were, and who the leaders were. But some of these early questions, first posed as far back as the forties, have been asked again in recent studies, and, as we'll see, the responses suggest that nothing much has changed.[4] People were as likely to be wrong back then as they are now, long before 2016, when 'post-truth' (the idea that objective facts are less influential in shaping public opinion than appeals to emotion and personal belief) was named 'Word of the Year' by Oxford Dictionaries.

That's not to say that our current, ideologically driven discourse and the explosion of social technology have no effect on our perceptions of reality, or that we're not living in particularly dangerous times. In fact, those technological shifts are particularly terrifying in their effect on our accurate view of the world or key issues—because the quantum leap in our ability to choose and others to push 'individual realities' at us plays to some of our deepest biases, in preferring our existing worldview and in avoiding conflicting information.

But that's exactly the point—if we only focus on what's *out there,* what we're told, we'll miss a key element of the problem: it's partly *how we think* that causes us to misperceive the world.

This raises an important point about the findings of the Perils of Perception surveys—the focus of these studies is not primarily to root out *ignorance* so much as to discover *delusions.* It seems a fine distinction, and drawing a clear line between the two is often difficult in practice, but the principle is essential.

Ignorance means literally 'to not know' or to be unacquainted with. Delusions and misperceptions, however, are a positive mis-understanding of reality, or, as Brendan Nyhan, a professor of government at Dartmouth College in New Hampshire, and his colleagues put it, 'misperceptions differ from ignorance insofar as people often hold them with a high degree of certainty . . . and consider themselves to be well informed'.[5] Few of the people we've surveyed think of themselves as ignorant; they are answering what they believe to be true.

In practice, rather than a neat delineation, there is a spectrum of false belief from ignorance to delusion. People are moveable and unsure of their certainty in many cases. The distinction shows us how difficult it is to change people's delusions simply by giv-ing them more information, as though they are an empty vessel just waiting to be filled with facts that will fix their mindset and behaviour.

An investigation of delusion instead of ignorance shifts the fo-cus from public opinion as a blank slate to be written on, to a sense of a range of people holding a range of opinions and beliefs moti-vated by many of the same, underlying ways of thinking. It raises the vital question of *why* we believe what we do—this is the real value in understanding the perils of perception. Our delusion can provide clues to what we're most worried about—and where we're not as worried as we should be. As we'll see, attention-grabbing stories of teenage pregnancies or terrorist attacks make us think these phenomena are more common than they really are, whereas our own self-denial leads us to underestimate obesity levels in the population as a whole.

Our delusion also provides more subtle lessons. What we think others do and believe—that is, what we think the 'social norm' is—can have a profound effect on how we ourselves act, even when our understanding of that norm is hopelessly misguided. For example, many of us are saving too little into our pension pots to support a decent lifestyle when we retire—but we think this is more common than it actually is. Given we instinctively feel there is safety in being in the 'herd', this delusion that it's normal not to save could negatively impact our own behaviour.

More than that, when we compare what we think *others* do with what we say *we* do, we get a hint of how we view those behaviours—for instance, what things we do that we're ashamed of. Sometimes what we're ashamed of is surprising—and enlightening. As we'll see in the first chapter, it seems we're more ashamed of overeating sugar than of not exercising. Realising that we're more likely to lie to ourselves about how much sugar we consume is a vital step to improving our health—as individuals and as a society. There are lessons for each of us, even if we feel pretty well-informed about the world. Our errors aren't about gross stupidity: we're all subject to personal biases and external influences on our thinking that can distort our view of reality.

We can classify all the varied explanations of our misperceptions into two groups: how we think and what we're told.

HOW WE THINK

We have to start with how our brains grapple with numbers, mathematics, and statistical concepts. Given that we're often asked to quantify the world and our perceptions of it, numeracy plays a large part in how well we understand the world overall. The statistics about data growth are themselves impossible for us to fully grasp: incredibly, over 90 per cent of the data on the In-ternet was created in the last two years; 44 billion gigabytes of data were created on the Internet *every day* in 2016, but this is projected to grow to 463 billion gigabytes a day by 2025.[6] With the exponential growth in data being created and communicated about many of the things that concern us, the issue of numeracy is ever more vital.

Dealing with the types of calculations we now need to make doesn't come completely naturally to many of us. MRI studies of the brains of humans (and monkeys!) indicate that we have a built-in 'number sense', but we are particularly attuned to the num-bers one, two, and three, and, beyond that, to detecting large (not small) differences in comparing numbers of an object.[7] We often fall back on these evolutionary number skills.

But much of life involves calculations that are more complex than comparing the relative size of small numbers. A century ago the great science fiction writer H. G. Wells said,

> Endless social and political problems are only accessible and only thinkable to those who have had a sound training in mathematical analysis, and the time may not be very remote when . . . for complete initiation as an efficient citizen of one of the new great complex world-wide States that are now develop-ing, it is as necessary to be able to compute, to think in averages and maxima and minima, as it is now to be able to read and write.[8]

Wells's reference to how important mathematical understand-ing is to 'endless social and political problems' seems made for our times, but we've got a long way to go before we'll completely satisfy his vision. Countless experiments show that around 10 per cent of the public don't understand simple percentages.[9] Many more of us have problems understanding probability. The French scholar

Pierre-Simon Laplace called probabilities 'common sense reduced to a calculus', but that doesn't make most of us any better at calculating them.[10] For example, if you spin a coin twice, what's the probability of getting two heads? The answer is 25 per cent, because there are four equal-probability outcomes: two heads, two tails, heads then tails, and tails then heads. Worryingly, only one in four people in a nationally representative survey got this right, even when they were prompted with multiple-choice answers.[11] This may seem a rather abstract test of our ability to understand key facts about the world, but, as we'll see, probabilistic thinking is the foundation for building an accurate sense of social realities.

So it is concerning that we don't seem to be that bothered about our lack of basic mathematical fluency. In a study we conducted for the Royal Statistical Society, we found that, contrary to Wells's vision, the public put much more importance on words than we do on numbers (which was a bit depressing, both for me and the Royal Statistical Society). When we asked people what would make them prouder of their kids, being good with words or being good with numbers, only 13 per cent said they would be most proud about their child's mathematical ability, with 55 per cent saying they'd be most proud of their child's reading and writing ability. (The other 32 per cent said they wouldn't be proud about either, which seems particularly mean-spirited tiger parenting!)[12]

Our delusions are very far from all being about our less-than-perfect knowledge of probabilistic statistics. Over the past decades, pioneers in the fields of behavioural economics and social psychology have conducted thousands of experiments to identify and understand other mistakes and shortcuts commonly made by the human mind—what are called 'biases' and 'heuristics'. They have explored our bias towards information that confirms what we already believe, our focus on negative information, our susceptibility to stereotyping, and how we like to imitate the majority. Daniel Kahneman and his long-time collaborator Amos Tversky hypothesized that our judgements and preferences are typically the result of so-called fast thinking, unless or until they are modified or overridden by slow, deliberate reasoning.[13]

One common mental error that is worth flagging up front, both because it may be less familiar and because it is so crucial to many delusions that we'll discuss, is 'emotional innumeracy', a theory which proposes that when we're wrong about a social reality, cause and effect may very well run in both directions: our concern means we overestimate the prevalence of an issue as much as the prevalence causing our concern. For example, say that people overestimate the level of crime in their country. Do they overestimate crime because they are concerned about it, or are they concerned about it because they overestimate it? There are good reasons to think it's a bit of both, creating a feedback loop of delusion that is very difficult to break.

Finally, there is the possibility that our delusions are almost entirely shaped by instinctive workings in our brain—an idea born out of the field of psychophysics (the study of our psychological reactions to physical stimuli). This has only just started to be applied to social issues, and analyses by David Landy and his graduate students Eleanor Brower and Brian Guay at Indiana University suggest that a significant portion of many of the errors we make in estimating social realities might be explained by the sorts of biases they see in how people report physical stimuli. For example, we underestimate loud sounds and very bright light, and overestimate quiet sounds and low lights, in a quite predictable way—a pattern we also see in the data about how we perceive the state of social and political realities. We hedge our bets towards the middle when we're uncertain, which may mean that our underlying view of the world is not as biased as it might seem.

However, unlike sound and light, the realities we'll look at are often socially mediated, and our explicit estimates have meaning to us, that we defend, and are related to other attitudes. Despite this, I find psychophysics an encouraging addition to our understanding of our delusion: we may not always be as wrong as we think, or, rather, our errors may not represent such a biased view of the world.

WHAT WE'RE TOLD

The second group of factors influencing how and what we think about the world is external in origin.

First, there is the media. Whenever I present any findings from the Perils of Perception surveys at conferences, without fail the very first 'question' I get—sometimes shouted from the audience while I'm still speaking—is, 'That'll be the *Daily Mail* effect!' (if I'm in the UK) or 'That'll be the Fox News effect!' (if I'm in the United States) or 'That'll be the fake news effect!' (when I'm presenting, well, anywhere).

'Fake news' as a concept quickly gained incredible traction in 2017, being named 'Word of the Year' by at least one dictionary publisher. But I think it's a pretty unhelpful term, and it has only passing relevance to the types of delusion we're interested in here, for a couple of reasons.

Properly defined, it's way too small a concept. Our key delusions do not have their roots in entirely fabricated stories, created sometimes as clickbait to earn money for the creators and publishers or for more sinister reasons, as we'll explore.

Even this limited use of the term has been undermined, mainly by the locus of many of the 'real' fake news stories, Donald Trump, as he has helped turn it into an attack phrase for both the media in general and individual reports that opponents do not agree with. The '2017 Fake News Awards' hosted on the website of the Republican National Committee, for example, featured a perplexing array of 'winners', from actual errors in reporting, tweets from a journalist's personal account that had been retracted and deleted, photographs that showed crowds as smaller than they really were, supposed faux pas on how to feed koi carp, rebuffed handshakes that turned out to be accepted—all the way up to a denial of collusion with Russia during the 2016 presidential election.

As we will see, our delusions are far from being just a 'fake news effect'—although we will look at the incredible reach and frightening levels of belief in a few of the highest profile examples of actual fake news, to highlight the broader challenge of disinformation.

While there is going to be relatively little simplistic media-bashing in our explanations, it is still a vital actor in the system creating and reinforcing delusion. However, the media more generally is not actually the most important root cause of our delusion, though it is influential: we get the media we deserve, or demand.

These days, information technology and social media present even more challenges to our understanding of the world around us, given the extent to which we can filter and tailor what we see online, and how it is increasingly done without us even noticing or knowing it. 'Filter bubbles' and 'echo chambers' incubate our delusion. Unseen algorithms and our own selection biases help create a personalized view of the world, tailored to our own individual realities. The pace of technological progress that is allowing this splintering is frightening, but also so apparently complex and unstoppable that it's numbing. A very few years ago the suggestion that we would each be experiencing our own individual realities online would have seemed like a *Black Mirror* episode, but now it's accepted with a shrug. That is dangerous because it plays to some of our deepest psychological quirks—our desire to have our already held views validated and our instinctive avoidance of anything that challenges them.

In 2018, Facebook was caught supplying the data of around 87 million of its users to political consulting firm Cambridge Analytica to target communications during the 2016 US presidential campaign and the EU Referendum vote in Britain. However, the signs are that even this shocking example did not lead to wholesale rejection of our 'filtered world': even at the height of coverage, and the #deletefacebook campaign, technology monitoring firms reported the worldwide usage of Facebook remained within normal, expected ranges.[14]

Politics and political culture also feed directly into our delusion. Few of us have regular, direct personal contact with serving politicians, so much of what we're told by politicians and the government comes via the media, and the statements made by politicians gather a disproportionate amount of media coverage, particularly during key election campaigns. And in recent years we've had a glut of key campaigns. Both Donald Trump's election in America and the Brexit vote in the UK were widely called out as the apogee of deceptive communications, giving birth to new phrases, such as 'alternative facts'. Yet, of course, there has never been a golden age when political communications were 100 per cent accurate, in any country. For example, in France in the mid-1600s, during the Civil War, an infamous series of pamphlets provided an outlet for justified outrage at royal suppression, alongside entirely fake accusations that Louis XIV's chief minister, Cardinal Mazarin, had committed a whole series of sexual transgressions, including incest.[15]

Of course, it is increasingly the case that politicians do communicate directly with people through social media, with President Trump's tweets becoming so central to his communications that his press secretary confirmed they were official announcements. As a result, some Twitter users tried suing for being blocked from seeing them, and there have even been calls to add them to the National Archive. We can rest easy: 'covfefe' will be preserved for future generations.[16]

Finally, there is that thing we call real life—what we see directly ourselves; what we hear from family, friends, and colleagues; what we confront when we're out and about in the world. Not all of our views about social realities are created from television or Twitter. But as we'll soon see, there are significant risks from assuming that our own experience is completely typical.

A SYSTEM OF HUMAN DELUSION

Listing the different drivers of our delusions, as I have done above, may create the impression that these are separate effects that operate and can be assessed individually. This is not how it works in practice. In reality, there are myriad interactions and feedback loops between them, that together create a system of delusion.

It's not just my list-making that encourages this false sense of separation—much of the existing evidence and analysis reinforces that view.

'How we think' effects are often examined individually in psychology experiments. This makes sense, as these experiments are set up to test highly specific hypotheses about the causes of our biases. And such experiments are essential to our understanding of the importance of different explanations of our faulty thinking and behaviour—but it also encourages us to think of our biases and heuristics as discrete phenomena, when they're not.

Of course, the academics working in the field are well aware of this, and many do study interactions, but when the often striking results grab popular attention, they are generally presented in isolation or as checklists of distinct human quirks. This research is helpful, but it can't tell us how human delusion works in real life. Real-life contexts are complicated, and our thoughts are often susceptible to multiple, simultaneous effects: intent, values, and identity all matter. For example, when we massively overestimate the prevalence of teen pregnancy in our countries, we're overweighting negative, vivid stories that catch our attention and play on our susceptibility to stereotypes and misunderstanding of social norms. Researchers, academics, and authors (including me!) also have their own motivations to keep it simple: single, striking messages draw attention, bringing sales, accolades, more funding, and more book deals!

We more intuitively understand that the 'What we're told' effects, such as political, media, and social media communications, interact with each other. There are glaringly obvious examples of partisan media outlets parroting messages from politicians on their side of the debate, or trashing opponents. Many of us are also aware of media tycoons or organisations in turn influencing political agendas. But even beyond these extreme examples, we understand how the content and tone of public debate can be set by one influencing the other, with each in pursuit of their own ends of power, popularity, or money. We naturally group them together, as part of the same misleading environment: it's no coincidence that politicians, journalists, and social media outlets often jostle with each other for the accolade of the least trusted group in many societies.

The interactions between how we think and what we're told are not as well recognised, however. Almost all existing analysis tends to focus on one side or the other: on our fallible human brains *or* a manipulative information environment that leads us astray. This echoes our human need for simplicity and solutions: we want to see problems as caused by one thing or another, providing a clear focus for blame and a single answer. We therefore miss the real issue—that we live in a system that, by default, breeds delusion.

Excellent books that focus mainly on our own mistaken thinking largely ignore that there are actors in politics and communications that have vested interests in pushing a particular worldview at us. Other excellent analysis—for example, the many recent books on how we're living in a 'post-truth' age—bases its explanations almost entirely in the current political and media environment, ignoring our own biased ways of thinking about realities.

The much more frightening reality is that one reinforces the other. Politicians, media, and social media achieve the reaction they desire by, for example, emphasising vivid, negative, stereotypical stories—because the reality is, we are influenced more by these than by accurate but dry statistics. Politicians, journalists, and content creators understand this intuitively because they are human too (despite what some think). They are subject to the same biases as the rest of us, so even where this is not part of a dastardly plan, their own delusions drive their actions. But this is also then reinforced in feedback loops of achieving political results, and increasingly instantaneous ratings of popularity, such as number of views, clicks, shares, or 'likes'. The delusion can easily become the reality for vast swathes of the population.

This systemic view explains why the delusions we'll explore appear so intractable—why they are pretty constant across time, and why they exist in all countries and across a very wide range of issues. This is not a strange or new phenomenon of our post-truth age. The fact that we're so surprised by the scale of our delusions, as reflected in the gasps and laughter at how wrong we are whenever I present the results (and, to be honest, my own reaction at the findings in every new study I do), shows we naturally underestimate how baked-in it is.

Even if these problems are fundamental, leveraging them is not excusable. People who exploit the system of human delusion for their own gain present a real social risk. They need to be held to account. Equally, we as individuals have a responsibility to do all we can to resist the temptation to fall into lazy, flawed thinking—and there are some simple tactics we can employ to help, as we'll see.

In fact, it's more important than ever that these collective responsibilities are taken seriously—because our new, constantly evolving information environment presents an accelerating threat to a reality-based view of the world. The early days of the creation of the Internet, and then social media platforms, were filled with hope about their power to inform and connect. We largely ignored the systemic risks of the opposite effects, of misleading and dividing people—precisely because we were insufficiently focused on how our biases and heuristics would interact with this new information environment. We were blinded by the technological advances and forgot the flawed, motivated, and manipulative (in short, human) aspects of how we produce and consume information in practice.

We need to have these interactions much more in mind for the inevitable next evolutions of our media and political communications. Machine learning and artificial intelligence tools mean that political campaigns can already test 100,000 variations of a message *every day*, to identify the most effective tweaks, targeted at individuals based on detailed profiling.[17]

But as we'll see, this is only the start. The need for actions to both control what we're told and help equip people better to challenge how we think is more urgent than ever.

———

In the following chapters I'll take you on a tour of what we think and how we think about some of the biggest decisions facing us today, from how much money to save for retirement and how to respond to concerns about immigration, to how to encourage people to engage with global poverty. As we look at where we get things wrong, we'll also consider how we can get things right—both as individuals and as a society. It is possible to become more aware of the realities on which our decisions rest. We don't have to fall prey to our delusions. To help understand that further, we'll look at which countries have the most—and least—accurate view of their own societies, and the lessons this points to for dealing with our delusions (spoiler: we all need to move to Sweden).

Keep in mind these five points as you read through the chapters that follow and we explore our delusions and the reasons behind them:

1. Many of us get a lot of basic social and political facts very wrong.
2. What we get wrong is as much about how we think as what we're told—which means, as much as we'd like to, we can't merely blame the media, social media, or politicians for our mistaken beliefs; we need to look at the whole system, including our own faulty thinking.
3. Our delusions are often biased in particular directions, because our emotional responses influence our perceptions of reality. Our delusions therefore provide valuable clues that we shouldn't just laugh at or ignore.
4. More than this, our delusions can in turn shape social and political realities. They have serious consequences for so many aspects of our lives, from political outcomes, social cohesion, to our own health and finances.
5. Acknowledging the complexity and scale of the problem is our only real chance to deal with our delusions, individually and collectively.

I feel privileged to have worked on such a variety of fascinating studies, to be able to understand our delusions from many different points of view. I have no vested interest in ascribing the source of our delusions to one particular cause, or to conclude that only one particular action will solve it. The reality is the causes are multiple, as are the actions required. Many recent writers, from Philip Tetlock to Nate Silver, have drawn on Isaiah Berlin's famous essay on the distinction between philosophers who think like hedgehogs and those who think like foxes. According to Berlin, hedgehogs know one big thing that they stick to as an explanation for everything. In contrast, foxes know lots of things and constantly update their view, realising that a full understanding of the world is beyond them. This book is for foxes.

One point is worth emphasizing: I passionately believe that facts still matter and have a role to play in forming our views and behaviour. It is *not* okay to create or encourage delusions just because it suits our purposes or taps into something people *feel* is true. We need to recognize that our emotions and patterns of thinking are important parts of the explanation—a fuller understanding of why we are wrong is our only chance to move us closer to reality. And that is the aim: to hold on to a fact-based understanding of the world.

There is also plenty of hope.

The reality of how the world is now and how it has changed are both better than we tend to think. There has been remarkable progress across so many of the social issues we'll look at. That's not the same as saying things are perfect, or that we couldn't have done more, but a sense of optimism is justified by many measurable facts.

Although much of the evidence I'll focus on from social psychology vividly outlines our biases, this should not lead us to conclude that we're automatons, immune to reason and new information. Maybe not surprisingly, I haven't entirely given up my suspicion (from my student days) of people or theories that imply that the human mind is utterly predictable. I hope this book lays out a balanced view: I show some startlingly wrong perceptions of the world, and how many of the reasons for that are due to how we think—but also that there is more hope than there may at first seem, and facts still matter in that.

One of the most fascinating aspects of our delusion studies, for me, has been gathering information on the realities across a wide range of social issues among many countries. It provides a great reminder of not just how worrying or encouraging reality can be, but also of the huge diversity of behaviours and views across different nations. One of our built-in biases is to assume that other people are more like us than they really are. This data on social realities shows how wrong that assumption often is. If nothing else, I hope this book will show you what a varied and extraordinary place the world really is.

CHAPTER 1

A HEALTHY MIND

There is no lack of advice on how to be healthy. New diets and workout regimens promise us instant health, and a never-ending stream of 'superfoods' purport to cure all ills. Yoga with goats is actually a thing, with classes available from Oregon to Amsterdam.[1]

However, the challenges to healthy living are not just spurious fads. Frankly, people deserve to be confused if they think that spirulina, chia seeds, goji berries, and activated almonds are all they need to be healthy. It's not even just about the latest dietary evil picked out by tabloid headlines, twisting serious research to play to our sense that the world has gone mad: 'Now baby food and biscuits are linked to cancer', sighs the UK's *Daily Mail*.[2]

No, there are also shifts to official guidelines, as we continually learn more about how our bodies work. As recently as 2005, US dietary guidelines were almost exclusively focused on reducing total fat consumption, with no distinction made between saturated and unsaturated fats. In the current guidelines, Americans are warned for the first time that they are 'eating and drinking too much added sugar'. The same applies to physical activity, with an array of different guidelines over time and around the world on how often, for how long, and at what intensity we should exercise.

There are libraries full of well-researched books, few of which fully agree with each other, because the facts are complex, uncertain, and shifting. It's nearly impossible to isolate the effect of individual nutrients on the body, and diet and exercise also affect people differently—genetics influence how we metabolize the foods we eat. More basically, much of the data about diet is flawed: as we'll see, controlling and measuring what people actually eat (as opposed to what they say they eat) is very difficult. There are also vested interests pushing a particular view of the reality: industry groups, politicians, media, and campaigners each have their own, selective take. Even with this apparently most scientific of issues, the roots of our delusion are systemic, with motivated actors leading us astray.

It's the same, or worse, with happiness, with endless serious and spurious studies showing what's *really* important in achieving life satisfaction. One thing that does seem to be clear is that health and happiness are connected, more so than we're often aware. A study in the UK showed that eliminating depression and anxiety would reduce misery by 20 per cent, compared with just 5 per cent if policy makers managed to eliminate poverty.[3]

It's little wonder, then, that people are confused, as responses to our surveys clearly show. Our misperceptions paint a picture of denial and self-delusion, combined with a dangerous focus on eye-catching scare stories.

FOOD FOR THOUGHT

Identifying delusions about our health is important. Doing so forces us to look at the realities of how we take care of ourselves, and in many cases, the actual health statistics are shocking. This is especially true when it comes to our weight and diet.

Across the thirty-three countries we surveyed in one particular study, an average of 57 per cent of adults were overweight or obese. That is truly terrifying—that nearly six in every ten people are heavier than the medical profession says they should be for their own health.

In the United States, 66 per cent of the population is overweight or obese; in the UK, the figure is 62 per cent. In Saudi Arabia, the proportion is even higher, at 71 per cent. Only two countries in Western Europe—France and the Netherlands—can boast that less than half of their population are overweight or obese, but they aren't exactly models of health, since the proportion in each is 49 per cent.

As important for our purposes, people in each of these countries greatly underestimated the percentage of people who are struggling to maintain a healthy weight. Saudi Arabia is an extreme example: Saudis believed that only 28 per cent of people in their country were overweight or obese. People in Turkey, Israel, and Russia all on average guessed that the proportion of overweight or obese people was about half the actual level. Of the countries surveyed, only three (India, Japan, and China) overestimated how many people were overweight or obese, and only one (South Korea) got it right.

How can so many of us get it so wrong about one of the most basic elements of our health? There are a number of explanations.

First, the definition of being 'overweight' or 'obese' is not at all intuitive. These terms refer to classifications according to the Body Mass Index (BMI), which was developed in the mid-1800s, and is calculated by dividing our weight in kilograms by our height in metres squared. It's a simple calculation, yet it's not one many of us can do in our heads. The number is mostly a collective shorthand for comparing populations or is used in a clinical setting to raise the issue of diet with a patient. The dividing line between

Q. Out of every 100 people aged 20 years or over in your country, how many do you think are either overweight or obese?

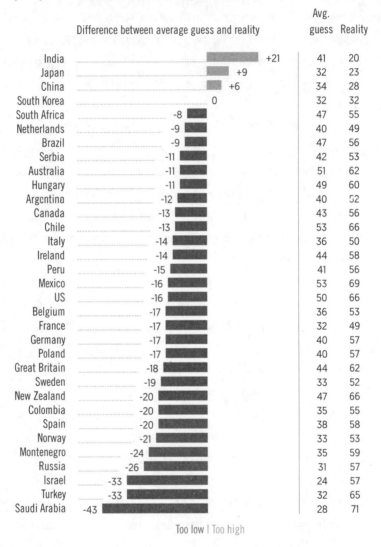

	Difference between average guess and reality	Avg. guess	Reality
India	+21	41	20
Japan	+9	32	23
China	+6	34	28
South Korea	0	32	32
South Africa	-8	47	55
Netherlands	-9	40	49
Brazil	-9	47	56
Serbia	-11	42	53
Australia	-11	51	62
Hungary	-11	49	60
Argentina	-12	40	52
Canada	-13	43	56
Chile	-13	53	66
Italy	-14	36	50
Ireland	-14	44	58
Peru	-15	41	56
Mexico	-16	53	69
US	-16	50	66
Belgium	-17	36	53
France	-17	32	49
Germany	-17	40	57
Poland	-17	40	57
Great Britain	-18	44	62
Sweden	-19	33	52
New Zealand	-20	47	66
Colombia	-20	35	55
Spain	-20	38	58
Norway	-21	33	53
Montenegro	-24	35	59
Russia	-26	31	57
Israel	-33	24	57
Turkey	-33	32	65
Saudi Arabia	-43	28	71

Too low | Too high

Figure 2. On the whole, people greatly underestimated the percentage of people who are either overweight or obese.

'normal', 'overweight', and 'obese' is also somewhat fluid: the Hospital Authority of Hong Kong, for instance, says that patients with a BMI of 23 to 25 are overweight, whereas in the United States, UK, and EU they would be classified as normal.[4] The fact that the BMI measure itself is a contested concept, not just because of the blurry lines between categories but whether it is that accurate a measure of how fat we are,[5] points to the bigger issue for our delusions: how difficult it is for the general population to have a clear view of realities when the apparently most basic metrics are complex. But BMI remains an important, if flawed, indicator of a reality. A study across 195 countries showed there were about 4 million extra deaths associated with being overweight or obese globally in 2015—nearly 7 per cent of all deaths that year.[6] In total, 120 million disability-adjusted life years (the number of years lost due to ill-health, disability, or early death) were lost to being too fat. But the crucial point is that nearly *half* of those years lost were due to being overweight, *not* obese.

It could be that some people in the survey were only thinking of obesity when they estimated the number of people in their country who were overweight or obese. This is sometimes the figure that the media focus on, and will be what some people will be familiar with. In several countries, the estimates do seem to split the difference: for example, the 50 per cent average guess for the United States population is exactly halfway between the actual figures for overweight and obese combined (66 per cent) and obese alone (33 per cent).

This is just one example of a wider set of explanations for why we're so often misguided about who and what are unhealthy, that reflect engrained biases in how we think. When asked to make judgements of these sorts, we rely on what behavioural scientists call the 'availability heuristic', a mental shortcut whereby we reach for information that's readily available, even if it doesn't quite fit the situation or give us the full picture. The availability heuristic was described by behavioural psychologists Daniel Kahneman and Amos Tversky in 1973. In their classic experiment, they asked people to listen to a list of names and then recall whether there were more men or women on the list. Some people in the experiment were read a list of famous men and less famous women, whereas others were read the opposite. Afterwards, when quizzed by the researchers, individuals were more likely to say that there were more of the gender from the group with more famous names. Later researchers have linked this effect to how easily people could retrieve information: we tend to develop an overreliance on what we can remember easily when coming to decisions or judgements.[7]

When it comes to weight, we reach for similarly ready benchmarks, generalizing from a faulty image of ourselves and drawing on what we've observed about those around us. And we really do have a very faulty image of ourselves. In a study in the UK, for example, only one in five men with grade 1 obesity—the lowest level, with a BMI of 30 to 34.9—classified himself as obese. More shockingly, only 42 per cent of those with grade 2 or 3 obesity— sometimes called 'severe' or 'morbid' obesity, with a BMI of 35 or higher—considered themselves to be obese. To give you an idea of how far in denial the other six in ten were, a 5-foot, 10-inch (1.8-metre) man would need to be *at least* 17 stone (108 kilograms; 239 pounds) to have a BMI this high. To the extent that people use themselves as the benchmark by which to judge others, it's no wonder they underestimate the general problem.

As physician Nicholas Christakis and political scientist James Fowler have shown in their research, people also tend to surround themselves with people like themselves and, over time, they tend to mimic each other's behaviour—including around activities like eating and exercising.[8] Social norms get set—and the average level of health among the group shifts as a result. We want to fit in, so we imitate the majority; we have a 'herding bias'. This means that a person who is overweight or obese is more likely to have friends and family who are also overweight or obese. These two effects taken together—our own sense of denial and false belief that we are more normal than we really are, based on our skewed comparison set—blind us to the scale of the issue and mean we are not as worried as we should be.

SHAME AND SUGAR

Our delusions about our dietary health extend to how differently we see key aspects of healthy living. We surveyed people in six countries—the United States, the UK, France, Germany, Canada, and Australia—about sugar consumption and exercise. The survey described the guidelines for what constitutes 'too much sugar', as well as the minimum recommended level of physical activity per week. The participants were then asked whether they met those guidelines, or whether they ate too much sugar or got too little exercise. Once they'd assessed their own behaviours against the guidelines, they were asked what percentage of the total population in their country ate too much sugar and exercised too little.[9]

The survey showed an intriguing result: respondents thought other people were just as likely (40 per cent) to meet their government's physical activity guidelines as they were themselves (also 40 per cent), but more people thought *others* were overeating sugar (66 per cent) compared with those who said they *themselves* had too much sugar in their own diet (40 per cent).

This provides a fascinating clue to how people view these activities, particularly when compared with the other activities they were asked about in the survey. The responses for sugar consumption were very similar to what they said when they were asked about illegal and immoral activities, like tax evasion or taking a sick day from work when they weren't really sick. We are much more likely to say these are activities that others do than admit to doing them ourselves. Of course, 'immoral' activities vary country by country. People in the United States were pretty happy to admit

Perceived social norm

Q. Out of every 100 people in your country, how many do you think eat more sugar than the recommended daily limit?

Own behaviour

Q. Do you think you eat more sugar than the recommended daily limit?

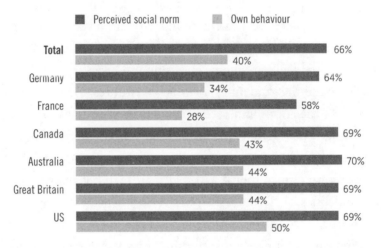

Figure 3. In every country a gap exists between our average guess at how many other people eat too much sugar (the perceived social norm of sugar consumption) and what we admit to ourselves (own behaviour).

they took bogus sick days—37 per cent said they personally did it, compared with just 6 per cent of the French[10]—which probably reflects the social acceptability of 'duvet days' in a country where people get very little official holiday entitlement. While hardly any French people said they personally took a 'sickie', they thought four in ten other French people did.

Why is there this gap for sugar consumption and other activities but not exercise levels? Shame may be a big part of the explanation. With recent shifts in nutrition guidelines to focus on sugar consumption and the introduction of sugar 'sin' taxes, sugar has become the latest dietary pariah, supplanting fat. The mental image is of overweight kids guzzling super-sized soft drinks—not something we want to associate ourselves with. The implications of this 'shame gap' are significant: in the near future, manufacturers of foods with high levels of added sugars are likely to see even stricter regulations—because we don't protect what we're ashamed of. The 'sugar tax' on high sugar drinks in the UK, France, Norway, and some US cities is a case in point: despite extensive lobbying from the industries affected, public reaction at the time of its introduction was generally muted and has been near silent since. Warning labels, even more prohibitive taxes, and outright bans in some circumstances, like we see on tobacco and alcohol products, could be in the cards—and our delusions suggest there may continue to be little public outrage at these measures. Indeed, many manufacturers are already reacting to both consumer preferences and the threat of more drastic government intervention by frantically reformulating their products to reduce sugar levels, cutting portion sizes, or developing alternatives that are sugar-free.

Now that we've seen the guesses from the public, you might be wondering what the reality is. There is official data for physical activity across all the countries surveyed that suggests that we're overly pessimistic about ourselves as well as other people. While 40 per cent of people thought they got enough exercise, and that 40 per cent of the population as a whole got enough exercise, diary-based surveys of physical activity suggest that actually 64 per cent of people were meeting these guidelines.

Yet we also have very good reasons to distrust these diary measures. It has been shown time and again that people are bad at recording what they actually do. In one experiment, researchers compared how active people said they were in a diary with accelerometer data taken from measurement devices that they wore—medical-grade versions of Fitbits. The devices suggested that people had significantly overestimated their physical activity: they got around half as much exercise each week as they reported.[11] We're just bad at accurately recording what we do, and, even if it's not entirely conscious, we can't help kidding ourselves that we're more virtuous than we really are.

Similar diary reports on sugar consumption from the UK's National Diet and Nutrition Survey show that around 47 per cent of people ate too much sugar[12]—pretty close to what people admitted when surveyed, but below the proportion of 'other people' they thought consumed too much sugar. Again, there are good reasons to be sceptical about the accuracy of this official data. A study by the Behavioural Insights Team in the UK, using different sources of data, including analyzing national accounts to understand what we actually buy, indicates that we may be consuming 30 per cent to 50 per cent more calories than official survey measures suggest.[13] If our sugar consumption mirrors this overall uplift, our guess for the public in general could be pretty close to the (somewhat depressing) truth.

THE DANGERS OF OUR HERDING INSTINCT

It seems we may be in denial on our personal consumption of sugar, and we're definitely underestimating how fat we are. But there remains the key question of whether better communicating the huge scale of our health challenges to people actually helps shift behaviour. It seems obvious that knowing the truth is an important first step to taking action—but is it? American social psychologist Robert Cialdini's work suggests there are pitfalls for legislators and communicators trying to scare people into action.[14] In particular, when we hear a message that there's an obesity or inactivity 'epidemic', we hear that this behaviour isn't merely a concern, but that it's *common*. And the more common a problem is, the more likely we are to accept it as the norm—and norms have a powerful effect on us, pulling us towards them and implying that the behaviour is socially acceptable or even necessary.

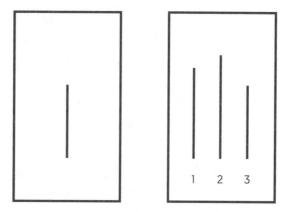

Figure 4. Solomon Asch's experiment to measure the effects of group pressure on individual judgement.

Experiments in the fifties by psychologist Solomon Asch remain the classic demonstrations of the power of this effect.[15] For these studies a line was drawn next to three other numbered lines—one that was shorter, one that was longer, and one that was the same length.

The experiment subjects were asked to simply indicate which numbered line matched the unnumbered one. If the subject was alone, they invariably gave the right answer. However, in another experiment, five other people entered the room, all of them actors, and all were witnessed giving the same wrong answer. After some quizzical looks and shaking of heads, one-third of the subjects followed the stooges' lead and also answered incorrectly. It seems absurd, but there is a very good reason so many of us follow others' leads—evolution has taught us that our survival is helped when we stay in the herd.

Of course, this lab test is a very artificial situation, and even here we should remember that two-thirds didn't fall into the trap. Still, they do not point out that while calling something 'normal' may be an effective tool for getting attention, it's a double-edged one.

The dangers from this normalization are perhaps reflected in our huge overestimation of diabetes in our population, as we saw in another study. As Figure 5 shows, there are some truly absurd answers. In India, Brazil, Malaysia, and Mexico, the average guess was that 47 per cent of their populations have diabetes! The actual figures are extremely high in some of these countries—around one in five of the population in Malaysia, and one in ten in the others—but not deserving of these huge overestimations.

In general, comparisons across the countries show how unrelated to incidence our guesses are: in the United States, the average guess was 34 per cent, whereas the actual proportion of the population suffering from diabetes was 11 per cent. Italians had a very similar guess, but the actual incidence was less than half the level we saw in America.

Diabetes presents a huge health concern for what is an extremely serious but largely avoidable condition, but more focus on the scale of such health issues alone is unlikely to be the answer. We may be too low in our assessment of how many of us are overweight, but we still recognize that it's a very large chunk of the population. Any more banging of the drum on the size of these issues will probably achieve very little on its own.

Our focus should instead be on individual behaviour and overcoming personal barriers to healthier choices, rather than on a societal epidemic. There are brilliant behavioural studies that do point to very practical things we can do, based on very well-evidenced advice, that work with our engrained biases, not against them: use smaller plates at home; sit far away from buffets when you're out, preferably with your back to the tantalising display of desserts; put the biscuits in an inaccessible cupboard; commit publicly to your exercise regimen and do it with friends—and many more.[16]

However, some health delusions need to be vigorously challenged for our own good and the health of those around us, like some views on vaccines.

Q. Out of every 100 people aged 20–79 in your country, about how many do you think have diabetes?

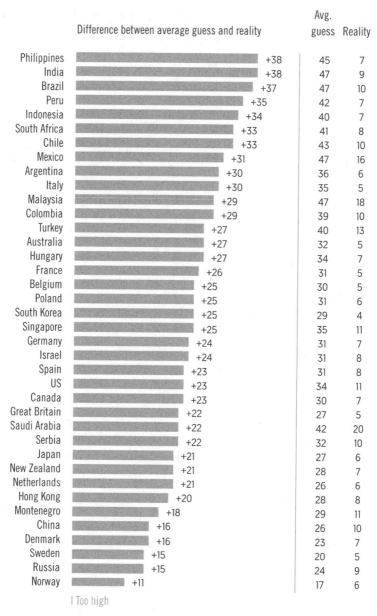

	Difference between average guess and reality	Avg. guess	Reality
Philippines	+38	45	7
India	+38	47	9
Brazil	+37	47	10
Peru	+35	42	7
Indonesia	+34	40	7
South Africa	+33	41	8
Chile	+33	43	10
Mexico	+31	47	16
Argentina	+30	36	6
Italy	+30	35	5
Malaysia	+29	47	18
Colombia	+29	39	10
Turkey	+27	40	13
Australia	+27	32	5
Hungary	+27	34	7
France	+26	31	5
Belgium	+25	30	5
Poland	+25	31	6
South Korea	+25	29	4
Singapore	+25	35	11
Germany	+24	31	7
Israel	+24	31	8
Spain	+23	31	8
US	+23	34	11
Canada	+23	30	7
Great Britain	+22	27	5
Saudi Arabia	+22	42	20
Serbia	+22	32	10
Japan	+21	27	6
New Zealand	+21	28	7
Netherlands	+21	26	6
Hong Kong	+20	28	8
Montenegro	+18	29	11
China	+16	26	10
Denmark	+16	23	7
Sweden	+15	20	5
Russia	+15	24	9
Norway	+11	17	6

| Too high

Figure 5. People in all countries hugely overestimated the extent of diabetes.

INOCULATING AGAINST IGNORANCE

It's April 12, 1955, ten years to the day from the death of President Franklin D. Roosevelt, the world's most famous polio victim. We're at the University of Michigan, waiting to hear the results of Dr Jonas Salk's trial of a polio vaccine.

Five hundred people are in the room, including 150 from the media, along with sixteen television cameras, some relaying the results to 54,000 physicians in cinemas across the country. People are listening on the radio in the United States and around the world, the results are broadcast on department store loudspeakers, and judges suspend trials so that people can listen. Paul Offit, the vaccine scientist, writes,

> The presentation was numbing, but the results were clear: the vaccine worked. Inside the auditorium Americans tearfully and joyfully embraced . . . church bells were ringing across the country, factories were observing moments of silence, synagogues and churches were holding prayer meetings, and parents and teachers were weeping. 'It was as if a war had ended', one observer recalled.[17]

Salk received a gold medal from President Eisenhower, and, in 1985, Ronald Reagan proclaimed that the country should celebrate 'Jonas Salk Day'.[18] Salk had ensured the impact of his discovery (and subsequent refinements) by not patenting the vaccine. When asked by an interviewer, 'Who owns the patent?' he replied, 'Well, the people I would say. There is no patent. Could you patent the sun?'[19]

Fast-forward to the present day, and the contrast between those scenes and how those currently working on vaccines are viewed by a section of the public could not be starker. Paul Offit is the inventor of the rotavirus vaccine, which is designed to prevent a disease that kills 600,000 children worldwide. He is also the author of *Autism's False Prophets* and a defender of vaccine safety. Offit regularly receives hate mail and death threats.

How did we get from there to here? It's a fascinating story to those who study conspiracy theories and how misinformation takes hold. And it's a global phenomenon. In the UK, vaccine concern was sparked by Andrew Wakefield's now completely discredited claims that the MMR vaccine caused leaks in the gut that went through the bloodstream to the brain. In the United States, it is more often linked to concerns about the levels of ethylmercury in vaccines and the supposed link from this to autism.

Most of the issues in this book measure discernible realities—things that can be counted. We can argue with the accuracy of this or that measurement, but conspiracy theories around medical outcomes are somewhat different—because we can never know the absolute truth with complete certainty. Scientific testing cannot, and should not be compelled to, prove a negative. It can only identify that no link can be found, and in the case of the vaccine–autism link, it has done exactly that for more than 1 million children—but it cannot guarantee that none exists, and it's in that space that misinformation takes hold.

The view from the National Autistic Society in the UK, a group that has no vested interest in cover-ups, is clear:

> Much research has explored whether there is an association between autism and vaccines, and the results have repeatedly shown there is none. This includes a *comprehensive 2014 review*[20] of all available studies in this area, using data from more than 1.25 million children. In addition, the original research linking the MMR vaccine with autism has been discredited and the author was struck off the medical register.[21]

A whole host of American celebrities and other high-profile individuals—from President Trump to Robert Kennedy Jr—are adding to public doubt. And this extends beyond America, notably to Italy, where Beppe Grillo and the Five Star Movement have consistently raised questions about vaccine safety—mostly in a more nuanced way than the extreme end of the anti-vax movement, but the effect is still insidious and likely to be part of the explanation for falling vaccination rates, and recent measles outbreaks, in Italy.

Has the belief stuck with the public more generally around the world? Our first ever multicountry study on vaccine delusions shows it's a varied picture, but, overall, around one in every five people still believes that 'some vaccines cause autism in healthy children', and 38 per cent are unsure whether it is true or not.

The proportions positively believing it is true ranged from an incredible 44 per cent in India and Montenegro, down to 8 per cent in Spain. The United States was in the middle of the range at 19 per cent, similar to the UK at 20 per cent.

Why do three in five of us feel unsure or believe that there actually *is* a link between some vaccines and autism in healthy children, despite the claim being so widely discredited? It has many of the ingredients of a conspiracy theory and is an excellent example

Q. True or false... some vaccines cause autism in healthy children?

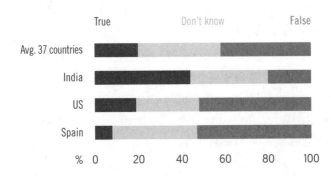

Figure 6. Across the countries surveyed, as a whole, three in five people were unsure or believed that there *is* a link between vaccines and autism in healthy children.

of how we think and what we're told can interact to blind us to realities.

First, it's a highly emotive issue: What could generate more emotion than the health of our children? We treat information differently when we are in highly emotional states, being more sensitized and less considered or rational.

Second, it involves an understanding of risk, which we really struggle with. In particular, as David Spiegelhalter, University of Cambridge professor and one of our best communicators on risk, explains, we need to understand the distinction between hazard, which is the potential for harm, and risk, which is the probability of that adverse outcome actually happening.[22] For example, there is an incredibly small but real chance that a vaccine could aggravate an underlying mitochondrial disorder, which has been linked to regressive autism in a tiny fraction of children. There are US court rulings that we could legitimately take as evidence of this being a hazard, but they are vanishingly rare, and the risk is therefore effectively nonexistent for nearly everyone. But that is a difficult point to communicate.

In addition, the communications we do see on vaccines are often actively unhelpful, with sections of the media keeping these stories alive. This does not just mean television shows or articles that give space to those who make the case for the vaccine–autism link without providing space for the counterclaims—articles in *Rolling Stone* magazine and regular segments on talk show *Larry King Live* in the United States have come in for those criticisms. No, there is a more subtle effect, even from 'balanced' reporting. This is where a media item says that every credible source disagrees with a position, but some others still believe it. A BBC *Horizon* episode—'Does the MMR Jab Cause Autism?'—reported both sides of the argument, including details of how Wakefield came to the claim, alongside medical professionals speaking out against him.[23] There is increasing evidence that this apparent balance actually serves to polarise. Cass Sunstein, in studies on re-actions to contradictory information on climate change, has called it 'asymmetric updating', where people take the information that fits with their views, even if it's on the marginalized side.[24] We'll come back to variations on this key bias—in which we only hear what we want to hear—throughout this book.

This doesn't just relate to mainstream media. The explosion of content online gives space to a wide variety of opinion, but it also makes it much harder to distinguish the reputable from the spurious. Anti-vaccine websites have respectable-sounding names, like the 'National Vaccine Information Center' or the even more impressive 'International Medical Council on Vaccination', which sounds like a UN agency but is in fact a campaigning organisation.

The narrative across all these sources is important. Stories stick with us, and there are a lot of individual case study claims in the vaccine–autism link. Jenny McCarthy, model, actress, and television presenter, is the highest profile 'autism mom' and regu-larly explains how she's told by 'thousands' of other parents how, following vaccination, 'I came home, he had a fever, he stopped speaking, and then he became autistic'. Elevating these stories to be on a par with scientific evidence, McCarthy says, without a hint of irony, 'parents' anecdotal information is science-based information'.[25]

In these environments, the story takes over. Paul Offit, the vaccine scientist, refuses to appear with McCarthy. He explains: 'Every story has a hero, victim, and villain. McCarthy is the hero, her child is the victim—and that leaves one role for you'.[26]

These medical delusions may be understandable, but they can have serious consequences, which are difficult to communicate in the same punchy way. First, with vaccinations there is something called a 'herd immunity threshold', where if vaccination rates drop below a certain level, infection spreads quickly among the un-protected. It differs for different diseases and vaccines, but with measles, for example, it's 90 per cent. And there have been very recent cases of significant measles outbreaks in communities where anti-vaccination sentiment has taken hold, such as in the Somali American community in Minnesota, in 2017.

Second, the focus on a disproved explanation for the condition distracts from developing a greater understanding of autism itself. The UK's National Autistic Society says,

> We believe that no further attention or research funding should be unnecessarily directed towards examining a link that has already been comprehensively discredited. Instead, we should be focusing our efforts on improving the lives of the 700,000 autistic people in the UK and their families.[27]

While our data shows that vaccine delusions are sticking with a section of the public around the world, the controversy around its reporting has at least encouraged some broadcasters to address the dangers of 'false balance'. For example, the BBC reinforced its guidelines on how to present discredited scientific views, so now it at least seems less likely that debunked claims like Andrew Wakefield's would be given the same space to take hold.[28]

ON TOP OF THE WORLD

In the past few decades, entire academic disciplines have been devoted to unravelling the ingredients of life satisfaction and well-being.[29] The United Nations, the World Bank, the Organisation for Economic Co-operation and Development (OECD), and a number of governments worldwide have joined in this pursuit of happiness. A few years ago in the UK, then prime minister David Cameron suggested adding national well-being as a key measure of the British economy, right alongside GDP growth.

Unhappily, well-being studies have gone a little quiet recently. It turns out that life satisfaction is often actually stubbornly stable when tracked over time at national levels, at least in more economically developed countries. In some ways, this relative stability should be reassuring: no matter what the circumstances, most people tend to end up being pretty happy most of the time. One classic study in 1978 showed that self-reported happiness didn't improve (beyond an initial bump) after a lottery win or decrease after a serious accident.[30] When life satisfaction does shift, it's difficult to definitively tie it to any actions that governments can take credit for or control.

I could write an entire book unpacking what happiness means and how it should be measured, but there are already quite a few very good books that do exactly that. However, one key complexity is that happiness is very hard to measure. And to understand that, we look to the distinction between what Daniel Kahneman calls the 'experiencing self' and the 'remembering self'.[31]

The experiencing self lives in the moment, whereas the remembering self tells a narrative of our lives to ourselves. We easily mix up these two selves, with the remembering self rewriting the behaviour and opinions of the experiencing self. Kahneman gives as an example one of his students who listened to a recording of beautiful music for twenty minutes. Then, at the very end, there was an awful screeching noise. In her view, the final moment had 'ruined the whole experience'. But Kahneman points out that, of course, the screech didn't ruin the *whole* experience; it simply changed how the experience was remembered. A story is most important to us in how it ends, and thus the ending affects how we remember it and its lessons for future decisions.

This may help explain the pattern we see when we ask people to estimate how many of their fellow citizens, taking all things together, are happy. In every single country we surveyed, people thought others were much less likely to report that they were happy. The least happy place across all forty countries surveyed was Russia, but, even there, 73 per cent said, taking all things together, they were very or rather happy. The happiest place was Sweden, where just about everyone—95 per cent—was happy. But the guess from Swedes for how many people in their country were happy was less than half that level.

In some countries, the gap between perceived happiness and reported happiness was massive. South Koreans thought that only 24 per cent of the people in their country would say they were happy, when in fact 90 per cent said they were happy just a few years earlier, as part of the comprehensive World Values Survey (WVS), which has been tracking happiness and life satisfaction in fifty-two countries since 1981. In this case, the gap might have been partly the result of a change in the political climate, as, by 2016, the news was filled with stories about the country's presidential corruption crisis and escalating nuclear tests being conducted by North Korea. Even the most accurate—Canadians—hugely underestimated their citizens' happiness: people thought only 60 per cent of their fellow Canadians would say they were happy, when 88 per cent said they were.

From having presented these results to people from many countries, I'm betting most of you are surprised that the actual reported level of happiness is so high in your country, rather than the guess being too low. That makes this an unusual example in our delusion studies—the quizzical looks and head-shaking in the audience are often because people see the guess as laughably wrong, but with this happiness question it's typically the actual results that throw people.

There are three likely explanations for the gap between reported and perceived happiness. The first is related to Kahneman's distinction between our remembering and experiencing selves. Our happiness question asked people for an overall assessment of their life, not about their in-the-moment delight. We can see how that long-term aggregate view would lead us to respond that 'yep, all things considered, I'm pretty happy'. That doesn't mean

Q. When asked in a survey, what percentage of people do you think said that, taking all things together, they were very happy or rather happy?

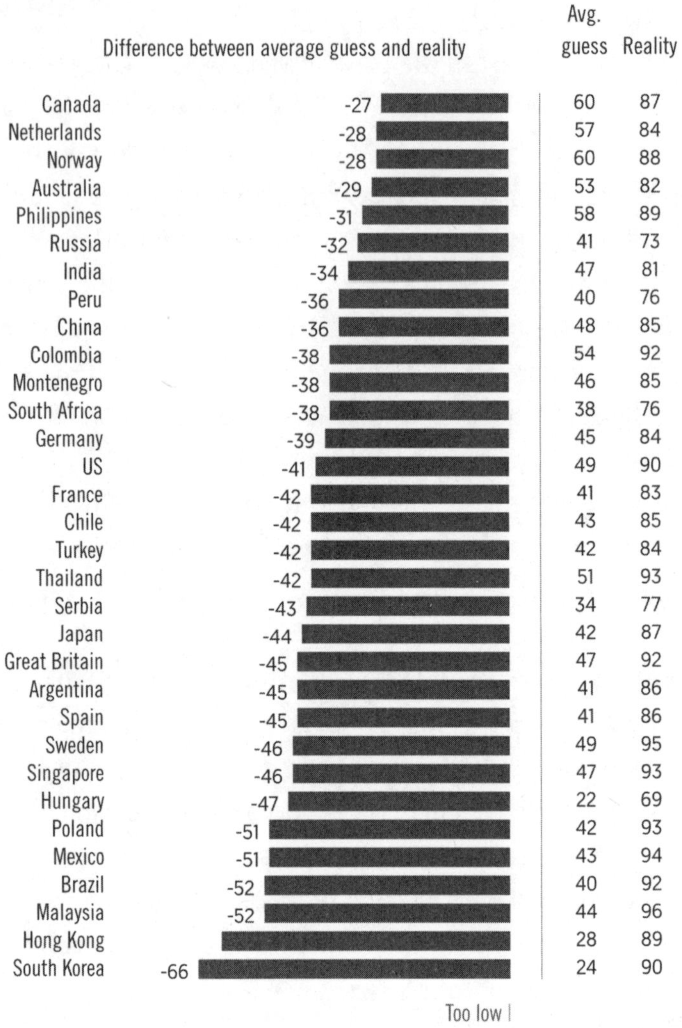

	Difference between average guess and reality	Avg. guess	Reality
Canada	-27	60	87
Netherlands	-28	57	84
Norway	-28	60	88
Australia	-29	53	82
Philippines	-31	58	89
Russia	-32	41	73
India	-34	47	81
Peru	-36	40	76
China	-36	48	85
Colombia	-38	54	92
Montenegro	-38	46	85
South Africa	-38	38	76
Germany	-39	45	84
US	-41	49	90
France	-42	41	83
Chile	-42	43	85
Turkey	-42	42	84
Thailand	-42	51	93
Serbia	-43	34	77
Japan	-44	42	87
Great Britain	-45	47	92
Argentina	-45	41	86
Spain	-45	41	86
Sweden	-46	49	95
Singapore	-46	47	93
Hungary	-47	22	69
Poland	-51	42	93
Mexico	-51	43	94
Brazil	-52	40	92
Malaysia	-52	44	96
Hong Kong		28	89
South Korea	-66	24	90

Too low |

Figure 7. Citizens of every country thought people were much less happy than they said they were.

we're walking around with constant grins on our faces, but that more immediate, arresting image of happiness may well be how people came to their guesses.

Second, more generally, we're unduly negative when assessing others. That is, we suffer from an 'illusory superiority bias': we tend to think that we're better than the average person when considering positive traits. Experiment after experiment has shown that we rate our relationship happiness, leadership skills, IQ, and popularity higher than we rate those of our peers. Eight in ten of us deem our driving ability to be better than average.[32] To see how pervasive the illusory superiority bias is, we took a large, representative sample of the population in one of our surveys and asked half of the people what *their* chances were of being involved in a road accident, as either a road user or pedestrian, in the coming year, and asked the other half what the *others'* chances were. As you've probably guessed, there was a big difference: 40 per cent in the first group picked the lowest probability option, whereas only 24 per cent in the second group picked that option for others. We like to think we're more careful and smarter than everybody else.[33]

There is evidence that this 'better-than-average effect' comes into play in our views of personal happiness, because, in our study, we asked people about not just others' happiness, but their own. In every single country, more people said that they themselves were happy than they said others were. For example, in South Korea, twice as many people said they were happy—48 per cent—than they guessed for the population as a whole. In Brazil, 67 per cent of respondents reported they were happy, but thought only 40 per cent of people in their country would answer the same way.

This highlights the third explanation for our error: people tended to report that they were less happy in the Ipsos surveys than they did in the WVS. As we saw above, in South Korea 90 per cent of people had told the WVS that they were happy, but only 48 per cent said the same to us; in Brazil, the WVS figure is 92 per cent, but only 67 per cent when we asked. Why was there a divergence?

The most likely explanation is that the difference has to do with *who* asks the question: Ipsos surveys people over the Internet (and an Internet survey is anonymous), whereas WVS has an interviewer ask the questions in person. Often, when there's a person asking the question, people respond differently.

This brings us to the other competing explanation for the gap between reported and perceived happiness: people may not always give a true account of their lives in surveys. When we answer questions about our own views or behaviour, we're not only trying to provide honest answers, we're also portraying an image of ourselves—whether we're completely conscious of it or not. We are subject to 'social desirability bias', a deep-seated need to make ourselves look good, to present a positive impression, or to give the responses we think are expected.

This social desirability bias is well recognized and studied in survey research, and is often most obvious in cases in which people are asked about illicit or embarrassing behaviour. For example, a review of a wide range of studies shows that 30 per cent to 70 per cent of those who test positive for cocaine or opiates deny having used the drugs recently.[34] Even with less obviously contentious issues, there can be a significant gap between what people say and what people do. When people are asked if they have voted in the most recent election, studies regularly find that around 20 per cent who claimed to have voted, didn't.[35] Yet, as the happiness surveys hint, social desirability bias is about more than hiding bad behaviour. Academics describe it as a form of 'impression management'—it's about projecting a positive image of yourself to others. Most of us don't want to be seen as unhappy, for our own sense of self-worth, in societies where that is clearly a positive goal and sign of success. Whenever we're looking at survey results, we should be particularly cautious with questions that involve self-image.

———

What do our delusions and miscalculations on health and happiness issues tell us about what we should do to improve our understanding of health and happiness?

Sadly, they firstly show how difficult a problem it is, as demonstrated by the fact that we keep getting fatter, despite the best efforts of so many people and organisations. The complexity and uncertainty of some health issues leave space for faulty leaps, based on emotion and stories. This heady combination of apparently conflicting and complicated information on something so close to us means we fall back on shortcuts: self-denial driven by the belief we're better or luckier than the average, and an equally powerful urge to follow a largely unhealthy norm.

But that leaves out the second half of the delusion equation: that we're also actively misled in what we're told, most obviously on vaccine safety, but also in myriad spurious health and happiness tips and scare stories. One feeds off the other, tapping into our emotions and colouring our view of the norm and ourselves.

How do we break this destructive cycle? It's futile to think we can entirely control our emotional reactions to such personal and vital issues as our own health and happiness, or, worse, the health of our kids. But we can challenge our subsequent thoughts and behaviours, using an array of tools that work with our biases rather than against them, nudging us to healthier choices.

Controlling misleading health information is even tougher, not least because it is complex, shifting and uncertain, and many sow doubt deliberately for their own purposes. But the history of mistakes that allowed false health information to take hold shows how we can do better in preventing and stopping health myths, through stronger editorial control, avoiding the trap of 'balanced' reporting of discredited ideas, and swifter challenge. And, of course, it's worth remembering that many major health trends have been positive. We're living longer than ever, and a lot of those additional years are healthy, productive ones—and that has a lot to do with the right health messages getting through.

CHAPTER 2

SEXUAL FANTASIES

Our brains are wired for sex. The survival of our species depends upon it. Yet sex is a minefield of misperceptions, mostly arising from the fact that we don't like to talk about it. Unlike some aspects of our health and happiness, where we can get a better idea of social norms from observation, sex tends to happen behind firmly closed doors (and the sex that is available for general viewing is not a fully accurate representation of the norm).

Because we don't have access to real-life comparative information, we turn to other 'authoritative' sources: playground or locker-room chat, old wives' tales, dubious surveys, and porn. Despite its (literal) centrality to life, there is a dearth of reliable information on sexual behaviour. Of all the subjects in this book, none proved more difficult to get robust 'actual' information for than sexual behaviour. Sure, there are endless dodgy surveys from condom manufacturers, beauty magazines, and pharmacies—they know that sex facts help sell stuff, even if they're spurious—but there is a shocking lack of high-quality, representative surveys around the world. Of course, it's not an easy subject to measure, and short of twenty-four-hour surveillance, we need to treat any information gathered with some caution (although the day can't be too far off when Alexa, Siri, or our 'smart' fridges tell the real truth about our sex lives!). Sadly, this lack of data is no doubt partly due to our still slightly embarrassed attitude towards sex.

It's in that space that delusions breed. For example, many of us still sniggeringly hold on to the belief that there is a link between shoe or hand size and penis size. Tragicomically, this became an actual discussion in the United States presidential campaign in 2016, with Donald Trump's supposedly small hands being linked to other physical 'inadequacies'. But he needn't have been so defensive: numerous serious academic studies have tried to find a link between penis size and hands, feet, ears, and a host of other body parts—and they haven't found any correlation.[1]

The largely unspoken importance of sex as a driver of our behavior and thoughts leads to widely believed but false claims about how much of our mental energy it takes up. For example, the trope that men think about sex every seven seconds is a commonly repeated claim, but think about it: that would require thinking about sex 500 times an hour, or 8,000 times during a waking day. Given that psychologists believe that people are generally incapable of genuinely 'multitasking'—that is, they can hold competing ideas in mind sequentially but not simultaneously—so many sexual thoughts would derail much other thinking. Although it is very difficult to identify precisely what we're thinking about a lot of the time, and counting it accurately is even more challenging, several academic studies have put it closer to around twenty times a day—which still sounds exhausting to me. To put that in perspective, one of the studies also asked men how often they thought about eating or sleeping, and the frequencies were much the same.[2]

There are rarer examples of more sinister sources of misinformation. For example, a study of Texas schools' sex education programmes found that some didn't contain a single fact at all, and instead covered pro-abstinence messages such as 'touching another person's genitals can cause pregnancy' and 'half of gay male teenagers tested positive for HIV'.[3]

As we'll see, we're confused enough about sex without officially sanctioned untruths.

WHAT'S YOUR NUMBER?

Let's start with that most basic of sexual questions: how many sexual partners have you had in your lifetime? What's your number? Or rather, what's everyone else's number? Feel free to think of your own number, and then guess for the rest of the population aged forty-five to fifty-four, separately for men and women.

We tried to keep this question simple for people: we didn't specify whether we are asking only about heterosexual partners or what we mean by a sexual partner—that is, the sexual acts that qualify someone as counting to your number. This may not seem like a big deal, but actually there is significant complexity in defining sex. Just think of Bill Clinton and Monica Lewinsky. Clinton notoriously denied that he had 'sexual relations with that woman', despite it coming out that he had received oral sex from her. This led to his impeachment for perjury in 1998, and to the definition of sexual relations becoming a national debate. As David Spiegelhalter outlines in his excellent book on the numbers behind our sex lives, this prompted researchers to rush out a paper based on a survey of Indiana University students asking what they considered as 'having sex'.[4] It turned out that the majority agreed with Clinton: only 40 per cent counted 'oral contact with genitals' as sex. While not representative of the American people overall, it did actually more or less predict how the Senate voted on Clinton's impeachment: forty-five senators thought he was guilty, fifty-five thought he wasn't, and he survived. For our purposes, though, Clinton would be in trouble. We'll follow the official definition used in most serious sexual behaviour surveys—that opposite-sex partners are anyone you've had oral, anal, or vaginal intercourse with.

It is depressingly difficult to get data that measures these activities in a robust enough way, and we actually only have good enough information for three countries—the United States, Britain, and Australia—but even these show some fascinating patterns.

First, people are actually rather brilliant at guessing the average number of partners reported by men, across all three countries.

Q. On average, how many sexual partners do you think men/ women aged 45–54 in your country have had?

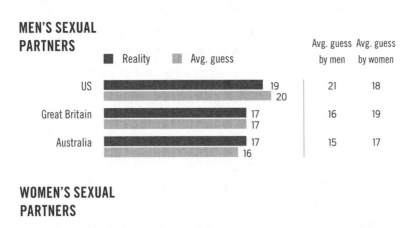

MEN'S SEXUAL PARTNERS	Reality	Avg. guess	Avg. guess by men	Avg. guess by women
US	19	20	21	18
Great Britain	17	17	16	19
Australia	17	16	15	17

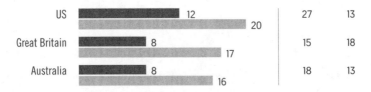

WOMEN'S SEXUAL PARTNERS	Reality	Avg. guess	Avg. guess by men	Avg. guess by women
US	12	20	27	13
Great Britain	8	17	15	18
Australia	8	16	18	13

Figure 8. Estimates of how many sexual partners people have had.

The actual figure in Australia and Britain is seventeen partners by the time people reach forty-five to fifty-four, and in the United States it is nineteen—and the average (mean) guesses are almost spot on. We've also split out what women and men guessed separately, and both genders are pretty good at guessing the number of partners men have had.

But it gets much more interesting with women. First, the standout pattern is with the 'actual' data—that the number of partners claimed by women is much, much lower than the number claimed by men. In fact, it's nearly half the level. This is one of the great conundrums of sexual behaviour measurement: it's seen again and again in high-quality sex surveys, but it's a statistical impossibility. Given that both men and women are reporting pairings, and they make up roughly equal proportions of the population, the numbers should roughly match. Of course, we've focused down on a slice of the age range, so some discrepancy could be explained by men having more partners outside this age range than women, but not at this scale. In any case, it's a pattern we see in all surveys, across all ages.

There are a number of posited explanations for this—everything from men's use of prostitutes to how the different genders interpret the question (for example, if women discount some sexual practices that men count). But it seems most likely to be a mix of men's rougher and readier adding up (the discrepancy in reported partners just about disappears when men are given a simpler task, like counting partners over just the last year) combined with men's conscious or unconscious bumping up of their figure, and women's tendency to go in the other direction.

There is evidence of the latter effect from a US study among students in which participants were split into three groups before asking them about their sexual behaviour. One group was left alone to fill out the questionnaire as normal. Another was led to believe that their answers could be seen by someone supervising the experiment. And the third was attached to a fake lie detector machine. I like to think my suspicious psychology student self would have guessed the game, but more likely I would have fallen for it, as the participants very clearly did in this study. The group of women who thought their answers might be seen claimed an average of 2.6 sexual partners, the standard anonymous questionnaire group said 3.4 on average, while those attached to the useless beeping machine said 4.4, which was in line with the men in the study.[5]

But that's not the most interesting pattern in our data. What's particularly fascinating is that our guesses for women are *identical* to our guesses for men. This makes us very wrong when we compare that with the actual reported number of sexual partners for women: the average guess in Australia is that women have had sixteen partners, when the reported number is eight; in Britain the guess is seventeen, when the actual reported is also eight; and in the United States the guess is twenty, when the actual reported is twelve. Of course, given what we've seen on our biases in reporting of our partner numbers between the genders—that someone is definitely lying, and probably both genders in opposite ways—it seems likely that the 'real reality' is we're better in our guesses than it seems. The most reasonable conclusion seems to be that men up their number a bit, women downplay theirs a bit more, and we actually reveal something close to the truth when guessing for 'other people'.

There is one final intriguing twist in the United States data—where men and women guess very differently for women. We don't see the same pattern in Britain or Australia, but American men think that American women have had twenty-seven partners *on average* (more than the twenty-one they guess for American men), but American women guess only thirteen.

This ludicrously high mean guess among men for US women is largely due to a small number of US men who think that US women have an incredible number of partners, rather than US men in general thinking that US women are very prolific. In fact, there were around twenty US men in our sample of 1,000 who went for numbers of fifty or (sometimes way) above, and that skews the data hugely.

So the overall picture is that beyond a handful of American men with a bizarre mental image of American women, we're actually surprisingly good at guessing the number of partners. But that's not the case for another 'what's your number' question: 'On average, how many times do you think men/women aged eighteen to twenty-nine in your country have had sex in the past four weeks?'

Again, you can think both of your own number (mine is a very quick calculation, and a very round number, given I've been writing this book pretty solidly for the last four weeks), and what you think the figure is for eighteen- to twenty-nine-year-olds. Sadly, we have even less 'actual' data here from reliable sources—just for the United States and Britain—but it's still a fascinating picture, and in this case, of a *very* wrong impression of how much sex other people have.

First, it is worth looking at the actual figures, as there are not the huge differences between what men and women report on frequency of sex that you see with sexual partners—the British figures are identical, and, whereas US women claim to have had more sex in the last month than men, it's not by a large amount. Basically, young people on average have sex once or one and a half times a week, which seems very believable, given the range of partner statuses and lifestyles at this age.

However, our guesses paint a completely different picture. For men, it's a very simple pattern—the average guess among both men and women for men is just way beyond reality. In both the United States and Britain, the guess is around fourteen sexual experiences in the last four weeks—ten more than the actual number. That means everyone in this age range is having sex every other day, around 180 times a year, compared with the more mundane reality of around 50 times.

But that's not the most remarkable error in our guessing— again it's men's views of women, this time in both the United States and Britain. Women go way too high in their guesses for women, but it is at least pretty consistent with their guesses for men—around twelve to fourteen times for both. But men think women are having an incredible amount of sex—twenty-two times a month! That's the equivalent of sex every weekday, plus twice on one special day each month.

While we don't have reliable 'actual' data for any other countries, we did ask our 'have a guess' question in Australia, Sweden, and Germany. We can't know for certain, but it seems unlikely that the actual level of four-week sexual activity is massively different among this age group in different countries. Given the consistency of the United States and British figures, we're probably

Q. On average, how many times do you think men/women aged 18–29 in your country have had sex in the last four weeks?

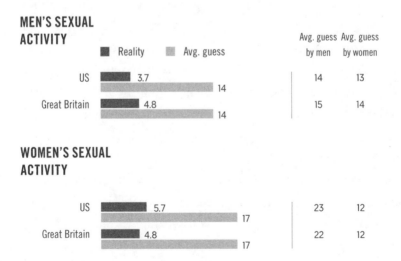

Figure 9. Estimates of how many times people have had sex in the last month.

very safe saying that the actual figures will be between three and eight times a month. That's a wide range—but the guesses in every single country are way over that, with each in double digits. The Swedes have a particularly strange mental image of their young people: the average guess is that men have sex twenty-seven times a month, and women twenty-four times a month!

Given this incredible view of the sex lives of young people across countries, it's perhaps no surprise that we're so wrong on how many (slightly younger) women get pregnant each year.

WHAT WERE YOU EXPECTING?

Teenagers showing off baby bumps in their school uniform make for compelling clickbait. It's very quick work in many countries to find examples of a screaming tabloid headline or a poignant talk-show interview in which the terrible plight of teenage mums is dissected: 'You got my sixteen-year-old daughter pregnant, then abandoned her' was the on-screen caption on one lurid talk show. However, we can't simply blame the media for putting undue attention on a glancingly small social phenomenon. Journalists are human, and they know we love vivid anecdotes, so that's what they give us.

In *The Storytelling Animal,* American scholar Jonathan Gottschall traced the evolutionary roots of our storytelling and story-making mind. We create narratives, linking causes to effects, in order to learn how to respond to events in the future. We create make-believe worlds in our heads to prepare ourselves for complex problems. What more pressing social problem is there than the raising of a baby who is entirely dependent on its parents for the first years of life? The story of a parent who is herself still dependent on her parents is something our minds can't let go of. After all, if our human ancestors weren't wired to pay attention to the care of young children, particularly children in need, we wouldn't be where we are today as a species.[6]

This brings us to our perceptions around teen pregnancy rates. Teen pregnancy across the thirty-eight countries we studied is rare, with about 2 per cent of girls between fifteen and nineteen giving birth in any given year. On average, however, people estimated that 23 per cent of teenage girls were having babies each year. Think about that. In a class of thirty girls, that would mean seven or eight babies in each class, each year. The reality is one birth for every two classes of thirty girls.

Of course, in some of the countries covered, many girls will have left school by the upper end of this age range. But in these countries with lower levels of schooling, the guesses were even wilder. Brazil was the furthest out. It's true that teenage births are relatively common in Brazil, with around 6 per cent of teenagers giving birth each year, but the guess was 48 per cent. Even in rich Western countries, where the large majority will still be in school, the guesses were miles out. For example, the Americans guessed 24 per cent, when the actual figure is 2 per cent.

No country was particularly good at estimating this, even those with virtually no issue with teenage pregnancy: for example, the actual rate of teenage births is 0.6 per cent in Germany, but the average guess was 16 per cent. The German people thought that one in six girls get pregnant each year, rather than the reality of one in 166 girls.

These are averages that hide even more extreme answers. In the UK, for example, one in ten people thought that at least 40 per cent of teenage girls in the UK give birth each year.

So what's going on here? We're storytelling animals who remember vivid anecdotes far more readily than boring statistics, and some stories are more attractive to the human brain than others. Of course, the fact that we like a story doesn't give the media free rein to feed our delusions: they have a responsibility to reflect reality, arguably particularly where our direct experience is more limited and therefore the media's impact is greater. In the past,

Q. What percentage of women and girls aged 15–19 in your country do you think give birth each year?

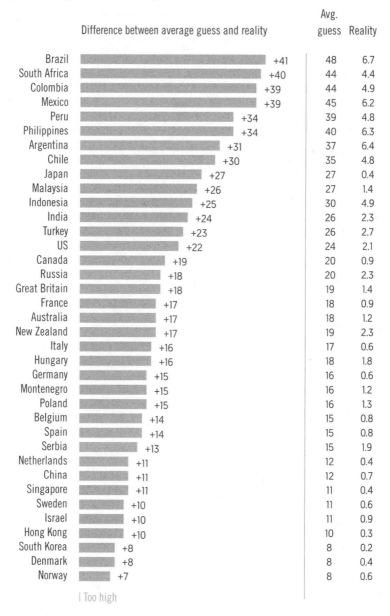

	Difference between average guess and reality	Avg. guess	Reality
Brazil	+41	48	6.7
South Africa	+40	44	4.4
Colombia	+39	44	4.9
Mexico	+39	45	6.2
Peru	+34	39	4.8
Philippines	+34	40	6.3
Argentina	+31	37	6.4
Chile	+30	35	4.8
Japan	+27	27	0.4
Malaysia	+26	27	1.4
Indonesia	+25	30	4.9
India	+24	26	2.3
Turkey	+23	26	2.7
US	+22	24	2.1
Canada	+19	20	0.9
Russia	+18	20	2.3
Great Britain	+18	19	1.4
France	+17	18	0.9
Australia	+17	18	1.2
New Zealand	+17	19	2.3
Italy	+16	17	0.6
Hungary	+16	18	1.8
Germany	+15	16	0.6
Montenegro	+15	16	1.2
Poland	+15	16	1.3
Belgium	+14	15	0.8
Spain	+14	15	0.8
Serbia	+13	15	1.9
Netherlands	+11	12	0.4
China	+11	12	0.7
Singapore	+11	11	0.4
Sweden	+10	11	0.6
Israel	+10	11	0.9
Hong Kong	+10	10	0.3
South Korea	+8	8	0.2
Denmark	+8	8	0.4
Norway	+7	8	0.6

I Too high

Figure 10. People in all countries overestimated teenage births.

academics suggested that the media 'set the agenda' for society; they couldn't tell us *what* to think, but they set the focus and tone.[7] Perhaps they did in the days when everyone sat down at 6 p.m. to watch the news. Now, the media's influence is discussed much more in the form of 'consonance' and 'dependency'.[8]

If we are exposed to a story that chimes with our experience, it is consonant—the media reinforces what we believe. On the flip side, if we are frequently exposed to the same, or a very similar, story through the media, we're more likely to notice the information in the world around us that confirms the stories we've heard and seen. Media consonance is a form of 'confirmation bias' (where we are drawn to and focus on information that reinforces our pre-existing beliefs).

Where we are more dependent on the media for information—that is, where our personal experience is scant—what the media says on the subject has a greater influence on our perceptions. Few of us know a lot of girls between the ages of fifteen and nineteen. Still fewer of us know a girl of that age who has given birth to a child. How could we when the actual rate of teen pregnancy is around two in one hundred? Our personal experience of pregnant teens is low, so we have no evidence to contradict the media's focus on it, which makes teen pregnancy seem like a frequent occurrence.

Further, the media's morality plays of pregnant teens hold our attention. These are ancient issues of good and bad behaviour, all of which engage the emotional parts of our brains, worming their way into our memory, where they are difficult to dislodge. The oversized characters stick—much more so than some dry statistic—and they occupy our minds long after they are relevant.

These sticky negative mental images don't even have to be about fellow humans. A *Denver Post* journalist reviewed all of the newspaper's headlines over a five-year period, and, of the twenty dog-attack stories the newspaper had covered, nine mentioned the breed of dog, and eight of those mentioned were pit bulls. This is despite pit bulls accounting for just 8 per cent of reported dog bites in Colorado (with the supposed 'good boy' Labrador actually the biggest biter). The American Society for the Prevention of Cruelty to Animals tells how animal control officers reporting dog bites to the media are told there is no interest unless it's a pit bull.[9] There is one grain of comfort for poor pit bulls (who actually have a very friendly 'temperament score'): our mental images do shift over time, and the trail of canine villains will likely move on, as it has in the past from bloodhounds and then Dobermans.[10]

In general, our perception of the world is often behind the curve of reality. If you trawl for articles on teen pregnancy, you'll find that most of the alarmist articles in places like Britain and the United States are quite old—they date from a decade or more ago—and you're likely to find quite a few pieces on how the rate has declined in recent years. In both the United States and Britain, for instance, the rate has fallen, and among some groups it has fallen pretty precipitously, as Figure 11 shows.[11] Unfortunately for the reputation of teen girls everywhere, there are no vivid anecdotes that can bring these boring trend lines to life; I feel confident guaranteeing that you will never see this headline: 'Yet another teenager hasn't given birth and is just getting on with stuff'.

Chip and Dan Heath, authors of *Made to Stick: Why Some Ideas Take Hold and Others Come Unstuck*, point to six success factors that sticky ideas have: they're simple, unexpected, concrete, credible, emotional, and tell a story.[12] Teen pregnancy anecdotes have most of these in spades.

We can also be very resistant to changing our opinions once they've stuck. This has been a recognized human trait for centuries, probably long before Francis Bacon summed it up so neatly in 1620:

> The human understanding when it has once adopted an opinion draws all things else to support and agree with it. And though there be a greater number and weight of instances to be found

Birth rate per 1000 females aged 15–19

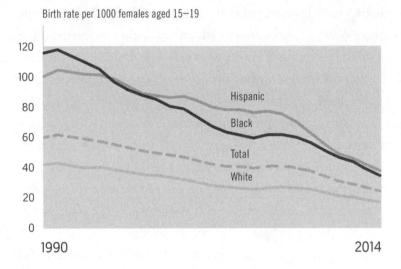

Figure 11. Trends in birth rates per 1,000 females aged 15 to 19, by ethnicity, in the United States.

on the other side, yet these it either neglects or despises, or else by some distraction sets aside and rejects.[13]

Of course, Bacon wasn't thinking of teenage pregnancy when he wrote this (which probably wasn't much of a talking point in his day), but rather political positions, but the principle is the same.

Our strong attachment to an idea, once formed, has been the subject of much study since the mid-twentieth century. The field was spurred by the seminal work of social psychologist Leon Festinger, who developed the theory of 'cognitive dissonance' (the feeling of discomfort experienced by someone who has inconsistent or challenged thoughts, beliefs, or values).[14] In the fifties, Festinger studied an apocalyptic cult in Oak Park, Illinois, whose prophecies did not come to pass: on the appointed Day of Judgement, when the true believers were to be carried off to their salvation by an alien spaceship, nothing happened.

This created a profound cognitive dissonance among the cult's followers, who had invested a huge amount of emotional energy in creating a worldview completely out of step with the rest of society. But many of the cultists didn't collapse in despair at the exposure of their beliefs as nonsense; instead they searched for a misunderstanding in their interpretation of the prophecy.

First, they accepted that they hadn't got the time quite right, then that they hadn't prepared adequately for the aliens' arrival. Finally, when it was clear that the spaceship was not showing itself, they explained away the failed prophecy: the aliens had arrived, and indeed one had been seen out on the street, but there were too many nonbelievers around, and they had not 'felt welcome'.[15] When they were asked about their plan to leave earth with the aliens, the cult's followers stoically claimed that they'd never had such a plan (though they 'were willing', if such an offer happened to come their way).[16]

Once we've made a decision about an idea—be it deliverance by flying saucer or the rate of teen pregnancies—we become attached to it, and, according to Festinger's analysis, it causes us psychological pain to give it up. We seek out information that confirms the rightness of our conviction—even if it requires us to twist our grey matter into knots.

My personal favourite from Festinger's many brilliant examples of cognitive dissonance deals with people's beliefs about the link between smoking and lung cancer. He was writing at the very birth of research on the causes of cancer. It was a unique window of time during which it was possible to test whether groups of smokers and nonsmokers would accept or reject new information that had been uncovered about a link. Festinger saw the effects you'd expect from anyone suffering cognitive dissonance: heavy smokers—those who had the most to lose from the new research being right—were the most resistant to believing that a link had been proven; only 7 per cent accepted the validity of the new research. Twice as many moderate smokers accepted the link, at 16 per cent. Nonsmokers were much more willing than smokers to believe the link had been proven, but as a mark of just how far social norms have swung since then, only 29 per cent of them believed the link had been proven, despite having nothing to lose.

We've also come a long way in refining Festinger's ideas. Academics now talk more about our 'directionally motivated reasoning', which leads us to seek out information that reinforces our preferences ('confirmation bias'), counter-argue information that contradicts our preferences ('disconfirmation bias'), and view pro-attitudinal information as more convincing than counter-attitudinal information.[17] Rolf Dobelli calls this group of effects the 'mother of all misconceptions and father of all fallacies'.[18] He tells a story about Charles Darwin, who was well aware of the need to fight these biases, to counter the brain's natural tendency to actively forget disconfirming evidence. Whenever Darwin saw observations that didn't fit with his theory, he noted them down immediately—and the more correct he thought his theory was, the more actively he sought contradictions.

However, none of us are Charles Darwin, and I'm guessing few of us are obsessively building a completely new explanation for the nature of life. For the most part, we'll get only so far trying to correct normal people's delusions solely with more facts, because doing so misdiagnoses a chunk of the underlying condition, which is more emotional, more tied up with our sense of identity. Telling people that they're wrong may simply make them more rigid in their convictions, and look for any bit of information that will help support and maintain their view of the world. If we want to shift someone's opinion, we need to provide vivid stories alongside facts. That's easy to say and very difficult to do.

But there are examples. The communications campaign for *This Girl Can*, run by Sport England in the UK, presented a much more positive, but still realistic and vivid picture of female behaviour than that seen in anecdotes of teenage pregnancy. Its aim was to encourage physical activity among women and girls, which is a serious challenge: Sport England estimated that there were 2 million fewer women than men taking part in sport or exercise. This was not because of lack of interest—based on their estimates, the equivalent of 13 million women said they would like to do more. But the campaign didn't use stats and figures about the scale of the issue or the benefits of exercising. It focused on vignettes of real women and girls taking part in physical activity—not the airbrushed, impossible-to-achieve images from many sportswear advertising campaigns, but the reality. Many of the principles they based their campaign on chime perfectly with the themes we've already seen in this book. One of their key tenets is, 'Seeing is believing. Making sport the "norm" for women relies on local women of all ages, sizes and faiths not only becoming active but celebrating it and encouraging others to join in'. And another: 'Use positivity and encouragement to drive action—stimulating action through fear of consequences will have little traction. Don't let women beat themselves up about what they do or don't have'.[19]

And the campaign has stuck. It has won multiple awards, but more important, the evidence of impact on behaviour is clear: 2.9 million women aged between eighteen and sixty say they have done more exercise as a result of the campaign. The job is far from done, with the sports gender gap still very much in place, but the progress achieved by a sensitive campaign based on reality and working with—rather than against—our patterns of thinking is still remarkable.

A MORAL COMPASS

We started our studies on delusions by asking people only about objective social realities—things we could get reliable measures of, like what percentage of people are overweight or obese, or how many teenage girls have a baby each year. Sex is not just about what we think others are doing. It's also about what we think everyone else thinks is normal. So at IPSOS, we set out to understand what people think other people think about social issues—that is, people's perceptions of others' perceptions.

There aren't many studies of our perception of perceptions. That's understandable, because it's a messy subject: we cannot take a set of scales or a tape to objectively measure our level of tolerance, for example. But that doesn't make it any less important to try to understand whether we have entirely the wrong view of what other people think.

The importance of understanding what other people think the norm is is not merely an academic pursuit. Social norms determine the acceptability of behaviour in all sorts of spheres of life, including legal frameworks. For example, the Roth test was a legal standard under which material was deemed to be obscene (or not) in the United States, after *Roth v. United States*, a Supreme Court decision in 1957.[20] It's well known because of the slippery definition—something is considered obscene if 'the average person, applying contemporary community standards' would disapprove of the content. It remains a part of American law that knowing what's acceptable and what's unacceptable to 'the community' (i.e., to other people) determines whether something is legal or not.

However, if we think everyone thinks one way—whether we're correct or not—our perception of the dominant train of thought is likely to affect our own thinking. This is related to a concept called 'pluralistic ignorance', where having the wrong idea about what others think (or do) can affect how we think and act ourselves (even where we've got it completely wrong!). In some cases, our private view may actually be more common than we realise—but we have no way of knowing it, as everybody around us is also self-editing in order to fit in with what they think is the prevailing attitude.

The power of pluralistic ignorance can be seen in many everyday interactions. Say you've just sat through a very difficult lecture by your suave psych professor, or—if your college days are a distant memory—a tediously technical presentation on the financial performance of your company. You were paying close attention, but you didn't have a clue what many of the terms meant or what the point was. The presenter asked if anyone had any questions. Silence. You knew you were completely lost, but you didn't say anything.

The tragedy is that everyone else was in the same boat, but you just didn't realise it. You assumed other people had followed along without any difficulty, that you were the only one who was bewildered. So everybody trooped out, none the wiser and just a little sadder about themselves and their lives.

Such misunderstandings can have a real impact on us. The classic proof comes from a series of experiments on the drinking culture at Princeton University, New Jersey. Students frequently drank at parties on campus, and the behaviour was widely accepted (despite the fact that the legal drinking age is twenty-one, and so most students weren't old enough to drink under the law). The president of Princeton wanted to send a signal to students and banned kegs of beer from parties—not alcohol (that would have been a step too far), just kegs. He argued that 'the keg has become a symbol of the free and easy availability of alcohol'.[21] The new rule provided a wonderful natural experiment for researchers, who interviewed students about their own and other students' views of the ban and drinking more generally. No matter whom or how they asked, the students thought others loved the school's drinking culture *far more than they themselves did*. So each weekend, when the parties rolled around, everybody got drunk because they thought everyone else wanted to and were therefore scared to reveal their real preferences. Students either conformed to what they incorrectly understood to be the social norm, despite their own preferences being closer to the truth, or they felt alienated from their peers.

Pluralistic ignorance appeared to come into play when we asked people about the acceptability of homosexuality in their country. To be clear, we weren't asking people to estimate the prevalence of homosexuality in their country, and then comparing it with the actual proportion of people who identified as gay; instead we asked them what percentage of people would say in a survey that homosexuality was *morally unacceptable*, and then we compared that number with the percentage of people who actually said (in representative surveys conducted by the Pew Research Center) that they thought homosexuality was unacceptable.

After you've had your own guess for your country, take a minute to marvel at the vast range of responses in the Pew studies from country to country. Only 5 per cent of people in Denmark and Norway said that homosexuality was unacceptable, but 93 per cent thought so in Indonesia and 88 per cent in Malaysia. Between these extremes you'll find the United States, where about four in ten said they found homosexuality unacceptable, and the UK, where, as is so often the case, citizens took a fairly 'mid-Atlantic' stance, falling between the Americans and the majority of Europeans, with 17 per cent saying homosexuality was unacceptable.

When we asked people whether their fellow citizens believed homosexuality was acceptable or unacceptable, the average guess was almost universally wrong. One striking contrast can be seen in the responses in the Netherlands, where only 5 per cent of people said homosexuality was morally unacceptable but people thought the figure would be 36 per cent. The same sort of trend, if less extreme, was found throughout Western Europe and Latin America. In only one area of the globe that we surveyed—Asia—were people less accepting of homosexuality than they thought their fellow citizens would be.

The dominant pattern was for people to overestimate other people's prejudices—they thought the view they held in private was much rarer than it actually was, because the social norm had been, for so long, that homosexuality was morally unacceptable.

Q. When asked in a survey, what percentage of people do you think said they personally believe that homosexuality is morally unacceptable?

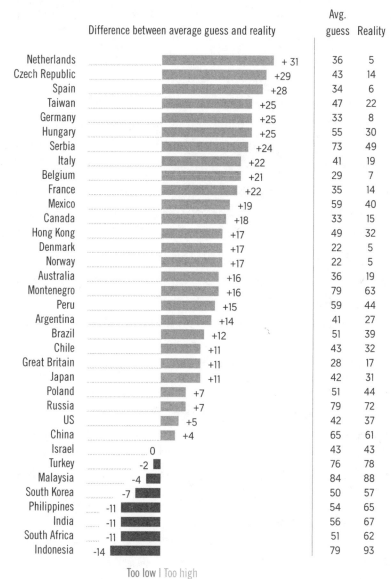

	Difference between average guess and reality	Avg. guess	Reality
Netherlands	+ 31	36	5
Czech Republic	+29	43	14
Spain	+28	34	6
Taiwan	+25	47	22
Germany	+25	33	8
Hungary	+25	55	30
Serbia	+24	73	49
Italy	+22	41	19
Belgium	+21	29	7
France	+22	35	14
Mexico	+19	59	40
Canada	+18	33	15
Hong Kong	+17	49	32
Denmark	+17	22	5
Norway	+17	22	5
Australia	+16	36	19
Montenegro	+16	79	63
Peru	+15	59	44
Argentina	+14	41	27
Brazil	+12	51	39
Chile	+11	43	32
Great Britain	+11	28	17
Japan	+11	42	31
Poland	+7	51	44
Russia	+7	79	72
US	+5	42	37
China	+4	65	61
Israel	0	43	43
Turkey	-2	76	78
Malaysia	-4	84	88
South Korea	-7	50	57
Philippines	-11	54	65
India	-11	56	67
South Africa	-11	51	62
Indonesia	-14	79	93

Too low | Too high

Figure 12. People were often very wrong on how acceptable their fellow citizens find homosexuality.

They assumed that a lot of people had not moved on from this norm, unlike themselves.

As with happiness in the previous chapter, this might partly be a function of our tendency to think we're better than average—including in being more tolerant of others. However, the gap between our own perceptions and our perceptions of others' perceptions seems more likely to be determined by how we construct our 'comparison set'—those we have in mind when we answer the question. As usual, what will come to mind is what's 'most available'—stereotypes of national character that will stick with us long after they're outdated.

Of course, in this focus on the difference between real and imagined perceptions, we shouldn't lose sight of the fact that homosexuality remains morally unacceptable to 37 per cent of people across these countries. Although this is partly driven by very high levels of concern in a small number of countries, in most countries there are still significant minorities who object.

This is amplified by the hidden power of pluralistic ignorance. Social norms can linger long after their sell-by date, partly because we think some beliefs and behaviours are much more common than they really are. We should have more courage in our own convictions and guard against stereotyping our fellow citizens.

———

This chapter has focused on things we don't talk about much, like sex and our views of homosexuality, and things in which we have little direct experience, like teenage pregnancy. This lack of discussion of sex and sexuality creates the ideal conditions for delusions to take hold, where we think the worst and exaggerate the issue. We are drawn to extreme examples, and that's more powerful when we have little to counter it in our own experience.

Of course, as with all delusions, these examples are not created solely in our heads; they are a reflection of what we're told, as part of our system of delusion. For example, men's particularly massive misperceptions about the sex lives of young women are likely due to a twisted mental image drawn from the representation of women in the media, entertainment, advertising, and myriad other cultural cues, combined with men's own insecurities and biases, thinking that women are having 'all the sex'.

Talking more about the reality of sex and sexuality, then, is a key approach to reduce our misperceptions—our silence allows clichés and stereotypes to breed delusion. It's been said many times before, but we really do need to talk about sex.

CHAPTER 3

ON THE MONEY?

Our finances are complex: they involve trade-offs between the present and the future; they often entail calculating risk, which we're very bad at; the decisions can be emotional because they are tied up with significant life choices; and there is little chance to learn, as they often involve rare events like picking a pension plan. There are so many bias and heuristic traps we can fall into. They are, in essence, a perfect study in human delusion.

In addition, we are wildly overconfident in our financial prowess. In a UK study, 64 per cent of participants gave themselves a score of 5 to 7 out of 7 on their understanding of financial decisions.[1]

We do seem to be pretty good at some simple things—for example, understanding discounts. We told people in one study that they had two options for the same television in two stores, with an original price of £500: one store is offering 10 per cent off, the other, £100 off. Which do you go for? Admittedly this is very simple—and 91 per cent correctly chose the £100 off (although note that 9 per cent didn't, which again suggests around 10 per cent of us just don't understand percentages).

Even when we make the maths quite a bit trickier, we still do alright: we asked the same people about the same £500 television—but this time offered them 15 per cent or £80 off. A few more people struggled, but still 85 per cent (correctly) chose the £80 off.[2]

More than any of the other subjects we explore in this book, good decisions on personal finance often just absolutely require an understanding of the facts—we cannot intuit how much we need in a pension pot—but that's not to say there are no emotions or biases in our financial decisions; quite the opposite.

Indeed, the financial services industry was one of the first to embrace behavioural economics, and the centrepiece interventions described in key books like *Nudge* by Richard Thaler and Cass Sunstein were about how to help us save more.[3] The potential to help people come to better financial decisions if they have a better understanding of their biases and heuristics—and work with these—is huge.

We have seen that most of us can be trusted to buy a telly, but on some of the biggest financial decisions in our life, we're often absolutely clueless. Some of the data that follows is from the United States and UK only—because the exact financial context and differences in regulation make it very difficult to compare like with like internationally. But we can be sure it's not just the dumb Yanks and Brits who make these mistakes; it will be the same in your country.

THE BANK OF MUM AND DAD

Deciding to have children is one of the single most expensive choices you will make in your life, but hardly any of us will have approached it with a spreadsheet. It is an emotional calculation above all else, not driven by the cost (and given falling fertility rates in many countries, it's a good thing we don't add it up). But we would be well served to force ourselves to do a bit more thinking, if not to shape our decisions, then to prepare for the consequences.

What would you guess if you were asked how much it costs to raise a child from birth to adulthood in Britain and the United States? If you're anything like the general public, you'll be way off. The actual average cost is £229,000 in the UK and $235,000 in the United States. Before we look at the guesses, readers in the UK will immediately be vexed by this, with its echoes of 'Rip-off Britain', and how Brits always seem to be charged more than Americans for the same stuff: not only can you pick up iPhones in the United States for the same dollar amount as you pay in pounds, it seems you can do the same with kids.

There will undoubtedly be some truth in this, but there are other explanations too—not least that the data is based on a different definition of adulthood. The US figure, calculated by the US Department of Agriculture (I've no idea why), only goes up to seventeen years old, whereas the UK version (calculated by an insurance company) goes all the way to twenty-one (which we specified in the surveys).

In any case, our interest is in how the guesses compare with these realities—and both countries went way too low. In the UK, the guess from the average person was £100,000, whereas in the United States it was $150,000. So in the UK the guess was well under half the actual cost, whereas the United States did only a bit better, at around 60 per cent. Within this, many were very low indeed: around a quarter of Americans and a third of Brits thought that it cost less than $50,000 or £50,000 to raise a child—barely enough to cover four years of the average child's life.

No wonder so many parents—and I include myself here—are surprised at how poor they are, scratching their heads at where their money could have gone every month.

The main issue is that we don't think about the whole cost of child-rearing. The studies that the actual estimates come from list out the items—and there are obvious things like childcare, food, and education (however, note that the figures do *not* include private education, just the associated costs around a state education). But there is also furniture. Sure, I understood that I'd need to buy cots for my two daughters. But then there was the bunkbed. Then the separate single beds when they couldn't stand sleeping in the same room together (the younger one 'snores like you, Daddy'). When they reach their later teenage years, there will no doubt be the double beds, for reasons that I really don't want to think about right now. That's already £3,400 on these and other bits of furniture.

Then there are holidays. Every parent will know the deep sense of injustice at having to pay for an aeroplane seat for someone who won't stay sitting in it beyond a screaming takeoff as you try to melt into your own seat in embarrassment. But that adds up to £16,000 on average.[4] In the United States the report highlights the cost of transportation. Ferrying your little ones around will cost you $35,000. Even the 'miscellaneous expenses'—everything from toothbrushes and haircuts, to technology and magazines—add another $17,000.

Of course, this is a very difficult and unfamiliar calculation—it's tough to do off the top of your head. Adding up the total cost of children over twenty-one or seventeen years is a very difficult 'System 2' (our slower, more analytical basis for decision-making) challenge, as Kahneman would characterize it. In surveys such as this, there is little time or incentive to take it very seriously.

However, there is no sign that we give it much more consideration in real life, or even learn from our experience. In an earlier study we conducted in the UK only, parents were actually *worse* than the average respondent, guessing 20 per cent less.[5]

One of our main financial biases is our tendency to focus on the short term and discount the impact of our decisions on the future. Shifting that is one of the keys to better financial decisions. Taking a longer view on having children is increasingly important, as the cost is now much more likely to extend way beyond their 'child' years, with many more in the latest generation of young people ending up reliant on their parents well into adulthood.

STUCK IN THE NEST

The struggle for independence facing many in this current generation of young people is an issue very close to my heart, as another of my main areas of study is generational differences, and in particular how this generation of young adults, who have (mainly disparagingly) been branded as 'millennials', has been financially screwed in much of the Western world.

Study after study shows how wages have stagnated for the young in particular, that their debt levels have increased, wealth has transferred to older generations, and youth employment has become more precarious. Sure, they've benefited from an explosion of technological and communications possibilities, but Snapchat and Netflix are poor compensation for the real economic woes they face, and the knock-on effects that creates for so many aspects of their lives.

That includes being able to leave home. So what percentage of young adults aged twenty-five to thirty-four in your country do you think still live at home with their parents? Your answer will probably depend a lot on where you live—as the actual answers show an enormous range of living arrangements around the world. In Norway and Sweden, only 4 per cent of these young adults are still at home, whereas in Italy it's 49 per cent. This reflects hugely different social norms, driven by varying cultures and economics, and yet every country where we asked this question overestimated how many young people still live at home, and some significantly so. Britain was the furthest from reality, with a guess of 43 per cent, when the reality is 14 per cent.

Q. Out of every 100 young adults aged 25–34, about how many do you think live with their parents?

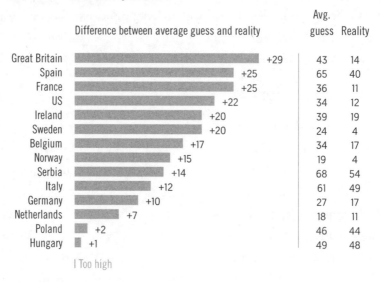

	Difference between average guess and reality	Avg. guess	Reality
Great Britain	+29	43	14
Spain	+25	65	40
France	+25	36	11
US	+22	34	12
Ireland	+20	39	19
Sweden	+20	24	4
Belgium	+17	34	17
Norway	+15	19	4
Serbia	+14	68	54
Italy	+12	61	49
Germany	+10	27	17
Netherlands	+7	18	11
Poland	+2	46	44
Hungary	+1	49	48

| Too high

Figure 13. People in all countries overestimated the proportion of 25- to 34-year-olds living with their parents.

Why are our guesses so consistently wrong? It is likely to be at least partly an example of emotional innumeracy. The mechanism behind this effect is that when we're answering questions like this, we have two different goals, whether we're completely aware of that or not. First, we have an *accuracy* goal—we want to get the right answer. But we also have *directional* goals, where we want an answer that conforms to our worldview. So cause and effect run in both directions: we overestimate what we worry about as much as worrying about what we overestimate. There is some evidence that both of these effects exist: researchers have found that we get more accurate on some questions if we're offered an incentive if we get close. This emphasizes the accuracy goal, rebalancing our calculation.[6]

We know that young people being unable to leave home is a serious issue—we have seen coverage of out-of-control house prices, heavy debt burdens from education, and how the 'gig economy' (a labour market dominated by precarious, temporary, or freelance work, rather than permanent jobs) disproportionately affects the young. Even my opening paragraphs may have led you to go high in your estimate. All of the points I outlined are absolutely true in a number of countries, but they lead to an emotional reaction and an overestimation of the scale of the issue—our concern results in exaggeration.

OUR GOLDEN YEARS?

Good news! If you've got through the huge costs of raising your children, and you've finally shipped them out (probably in their late twenties), you can comfort yourself that you're going to live longer in retirement than you expect. For example, in Britain, respondents guessed that someone turning sixty-five would live another nineteen years on average—when actually they'll live for twenty-three more years. This highlights an interesting aspect to how life expectancy works, how we pick up the easily available but wrong information, and how that can mess with our calculations.

Most people will have in mind that the average life expectancy in the UK is somewhere around the early eighties. In fact, we asked this on a different survey across a range of countries, and people were mostly pretty good at estimating life expectancies at birth. In Britain, the actual life expectancy for a child born in 2014 is eighty years—and the guess was eighty-three. It's not just the Brits who know this; most people in other countries do too, with, for example, the Australians spot on with their average guess of eighty-two years. It's only the South Koreans who significantly overestimate their life expectancy, thinking it's eighty-nine years on average, when it's eighty, and only Hungarians who are too pessimistic, thinking they'll only live to sixty-eight on average, when it's seventy-five.

Of course, we are talking here about life expectancy *at birth*. The lucky ones among us who make it to sixty-five will live longer, on average, because none will have died before: the 'at birth' life expectancy figure is dragged down because of earlier deaths. This means that if you've made it to your retirement years in Britain, you can, on average, expect to make it to your eighty-eighth birthday.

But now for the bad news. This means we need to build up even more retirement savings or income to last us—assuming we can't claw back the £229,000 each of our kids unexpectedly cost us to raise, by moving back in with them.

When asked how much someone in Britain would need to have in a private pension savings pot to get a total income of around £25,000 per year after they stopped working at age sixty-five, respondents were woefully wrong. The various responses given in the survey were worrying and suggested that people really don't have a clue—particularly the three in ten people who thought it was £50,000 or less!

What would your guess be (remember to include the state pension, which would make up around £6,000 to £7,000 of that pension pot)? I hope it was better than the UK national average guess, which was just £124,000. In reality, at the time we asked our respondents, back in 2015, they would actually have needed around £315,000, and that is with the most generous assumptions from a pension calculator, to give the lowest required pension pot. Of course, because of falling yields on pension fund investments and increasing life expectancy, this figure is shifting constantly: if I try the same calculation now, it's already more like £350,000. By the time you read this book, it will probably have gone up again.

Only those who were already *in* retirement were significantly closer to reality, thinking you need £250,000. Even the fifty- to sixty-four-year-old age group, who should have been taking their retirement planning very seriously, thought they would only need £150,000, not massively better informed than the overall average.

This is a big worry for many countries. Governments across the world see the 'pre-retirement' group in their fifties as crucial— that's when you can effect at least some change and improve your life substantially, and reduce the burden on the state. But despite all efforts to engage them, people are just not getting the message. This truly is a global 'time bomb': the combined pension savings gap for just eight countries around the world—the United States, the UK, Japan, the Netherlands, Canada, Australia, India, and China—will be around $400 *trillion* by 2050, which is five times the size of the current global economy.[7]

What explains the considerable underestimations? There will be biases and faulty shortcuts we take, but, frankly, the cost of a pension is a very tough thing to just work out on the spot—we need to go and check it.

Still, there is hope in careful planning. As mentioned earlier, personal finance is one of the areas where some of the greatest good has been done. It has been a particular focus for Richard Thaler, the Nobel Prize winner for economics, and a number of his long-time collaborators, including Cass Sunstein and Shlomo Benartzi. Between them they've had a huge impact on US retirement saving, through their 'Save More Tomorrow' plan.

Thaler and his colleagues studied the biases in our attitudes and behaviours on saving over many years, and concluded that there were two main behavioural drivers: a lack of willpower and inertia.[8] First, that lack of willpower creates what they call 'present bias', which is our tendency to favour more immediate gratification over long-term rewards. They describe a study from the late nineties in which people were asked to choose between two snacks: a healthy piece of fruit or less virtuous chocolate. When people were asked to choose which snack they wanted for the following week, three-quarters chose the fruit. But when they were asked which snack they wanted right now, the same proportion chose the chocolate. The same sort of short-term thinking drives many of our poor financial decisions.

Added to this is our tendency to inertia, to stick with the status quo, particularly when changing seems difficult or complicated. They outline an example from the UK where researchers looked at enrolment rates in twenty-five pension plans that didn't require employees to pay in *anything*—basically free money. Even in these (mostly long-gone) generous conditions, only half of employees took the handout!

The 'Save More Tomorrow' programme tackles both of these barriers head-on, first by auto-enrolling people into workplace saving plans to combat inertia. People are obviously completely free to opt back out, but, human nature being what it is, 90 per cent stay on the plan, with their inertia now working for them rather than against them. An auto-escalator then ups the contributions, not immediately but over time (the tomorrow bit). This shifted the reluctant hugely: when asked whether they would up their contributions *now* by five percentage points, most said no (we need the chocolate now). But when asked whether they'd commit to saving more *in the future*, 78 per cent said yes.

The impact of 'Save More Tomorrow' has been substantial. Before the programme, the average saving rate for workers in the sample was 3.5 per cent, but after four years this had increased nearly four-fold to 13.6 per cent. And the approach is now enshrined in US government guidance, helping around 15 million Americans, with similar approaches rippling out across the world.

These programmes are incredibly powerful and offer practical help for people, but our massive misperceptions suggest that we should also raise awareness of the facts. There are still many for whom auto-enrolment is not available—for example, the self-employed or contract workers. More generally, different approaches work for different people, and for some a more conscious approach would help.

This is particularly the case as people appear to have a false sense of security in thinking it's the norm to not have enough money to retire on. We have seen that our understanding of social norms is powerful, because we imitate the majority or follow the herd. And there are signs of that with pension saving.

In a different study across six countries, we asked people whether they felt they were under-saving for their retirement and to estimate how many other people they thought were too.[9] Their guess for other people was 65 per cent, very close to how many admitted themselves that they were under-saving, at 60 per cent. So we think it's a substantial majority who are under-saving, and we're happy to admit to it ourselves. This was almost identical in every country in the study: in the United States, Britain, France, Germany, Canada, and Australia, people said that around two-thirds were under-saving, and that was similar to themselves.

Now, what under-saving means is subjective, so whether they're right or not is difficult to measure. It depends on whether we want to go to bingo once a week or scuba dive in the Maldives for a month every year. But the UK government does have a definition based on income replacement rates—that is, how much of our final income we'll each be able to replace when we retire through our pension plans. It's complicated and dependent on how much you're earning when you retire, but the principle is you need a decent chunk of what you were earning as a pension, but this can be a lower proportion if you were on a particularly high salary in your final job.

According to the UK measure, 43 per cent of people are under-saving for their retirement. This is a huge societal problem, but it is *not* the norm. Even in the United States, different estimates suggest it's just over half, still well below the guess by Americans. Of course, what the government or researchers think is acceptable and what we think is acceptable could be very different (the Department for Work & Pensions in the UK won't be thinking of the Maldives, for example). It's worth bearing in mind two points here.

First, we think under-saving is 'normal'—we think two-thirds of people are doing it. This is a risk—as we've already seen, we have a strong tendency to follow the herd.

Second, we place ourselves very close to the norm—there is no 'shame gap' with pensions; this isn't a problem we only put on other people and deny applies to us. We're not reluctant to admit we're not preparing properly for our own old age. This is very different from what we saw with sugar consumption or other shameful behaviours we asked about, like tax avoidance. That's dangerous on an issue like pension savings, when there is a rude awakening waiting for many of us.

Because of this misperception of the norm, I'd argue that a bit of knowledge of the facts could help, alongside using the power of our unconscious biases. The aim needs to be to find a short, memorable way to make people aware—the communication equivalent of eating 'five a day'. The complexity of individual situations on pension needs makes that harder, but it's such an important issue that we could do more. We've seen that there is a big gap between knowing what we should do and actually doing it (I'm lucky if I average three bits of fruit or veg a day), but it's clear that we have a better chance if at least some people act as if they're more aware of the issue.

It's not as if we are utterly incapable of remembering any financial information. We've been focusing on what people get wrong, but there is one financial statistic that people consistently get right across countries, that has made it into our consciousness. And that is house prices. On average, people are incredibly accurate about the value of property around the world, because it is caught up with their sense of wealth and worth, and is discussed regularly in the media in many countries. It would be such a great thing if people were equally aware of what they had and what they needed to save for retirement, as that will become just as important an asset for them.

If you do only *one* thing as a result of reading this book, fight your inertia, look up a pension calculator, and check your pot!

UNEQUAL MEASURES

Of course, that assumes you're like me and need to worry about pension pots. But you could be one of the world's super-wealthy, in which case you'll have someone else looking after that for you— and you probably don't have to worry much anyway, because you're only getting richer.

As of 2017, the top 1 per cent wealthiest people in the world own more than the rest of the population put together. This is the first time we've seen this, at least since the Industrial Revolution and reliable wealth measurement, and it continues the recent trend of an incredible concentration of global wealth.[10]

At the other end of the wealth pyramid, those who have less than $10,000 in net wealth make up 73 per cent of the global population, but own only 2.4 per cent of global wealth. Among them are 9 per cent of the global population who are actually 'net debtors' (they owe more than they own). No wonder income and wealth inequality have become such a focus in recent years and studied in a stream of books, from *The Spirit Level* to *Capital* and even discussed at that bastion of the elite, Davos.

Some of you reading this may be lucky enough to be in the top 1 per cent of wealthiest people globally, which has a cut-off at around $744,000 of net assets. The chances of that will depend a lot on exactly where you're from. For example, 7 per cent of the world's top 1 per cent live in the UK and 5 per cent in Germany— but this is utterly dwarfed by the 37 per cent who live in the United States. You can tell a bit about the super-concentration of wealth in Russia (which we'll see in a second) that, despite the size of its economy, only 0.2 per cent of the world's wealthiest people are based there.

You may be puzzling about the threshold for the top 1 per cent. Sure, three-quarters of a million dollars is a lot, but it doesn't necessarily make you feel like you're the global elite, with a private jet and a golden elevator, someone that the '99 per cent' would hate. Of course, that's because, on a global scale, there are very many people living with very little or no wealth at all.

You may have seen figures for qualification to the top 1 per cent in your own country—and if it's a more developed country, it will be a lot higher. In the United States it's over $7,000,000[11]; in Switzerland the figure is over $5,000,000[12]; and in the UK it stands at around $4,000,000.[13] Across Europe as a whole, it's $1,500,000.[14] (I'm guessing a lot of you have dropped out of this 1 per cent!)

We asked people in our study about the wealth of the top 1 per cent in their individual countries. Because of the global skew in wealth, the proportions of total national wealth the top 1 per cent own in each individual country is (mostly) a lot lower than 50 per cent, as we'll see. But that's giving you a clue—before you look, what percentage of total household wealth do you think the wealthiest 1 per cent in your country own? The actuals and guesses are shown in Figure 14. The general picture was that people were way off in most countries.

Britain and France were the worst at guessing. The actual proportion of wealth owned by the top 1 per cent in both is the same, at 23 per cent. But Brits thought the top 1 per cent owned 59 per cent of wealth, whereas the French thought it was 56 per cent.

People in some countries did underestimate this concentration, with Russians the most likely to. The average guess there was 53 per cent, which is actually not that different from the guess in the UK and France—but the top 1 per cent in Russia actually own an

Q. What proportion of the total household wealth do you think the wealthiest 1% own?

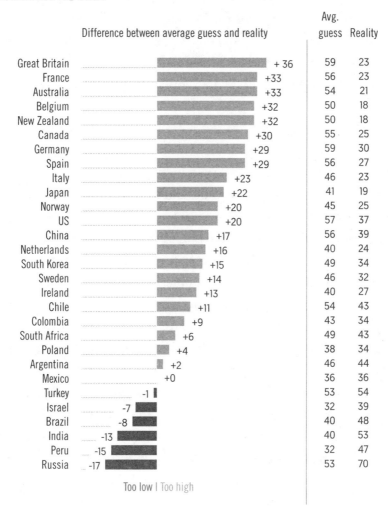

	Difference between average guess and reality	Avg. guess	Reality
Great Britain	+ 36	59	23
France	+33	56	23
Australia	+33	54	21
Belgium	+32	50	18
New Zealand	+32	50	18
Canada	+30	55	25
Germany	+29	59	30
Spain	+29	56	27
Italy	+23	46	23
Japan	+22	41	19
Norway	+20	45	25
US	+20	57	37
China	+17	56	39
Netherlands	+16	40	24
South Korea	+15	49	34
Sweden	+14	46	32
Ireland	+13	40	27
Chile	+11	54	43
Colombia	+9	43	34
South Africa	+6	49	43
Poland	+4	38	34
Argentina	+2	46	44
Mexico	+0	36	36
Turkey	-1	53	54
Israel	-7	32	39
Brazil	-8	40	48
India	-13	40	53
Peru	-15	32	47
Russia	-17	53	70

Too low | Too high

Figure 14. People generally overestimated the total household wealth owned by the wealthiest 1 per cent in their country.

extraordinary 70 per cent of the country's wealth, three times the level of wealth concentration in the UK and France.

The United States also stands out as one of the most unequal countries on wealth distribution from the developed nations in the study, with the top 1 per cent owning 37 per cent of the country's wealth, but with the guess again similar to France and the UK, at 57 per cent.

What explains our overestimation? It may well be the case that some people have vaguely heard of the global figure—and lots of the averages do cluster around 50 per cent. As with other questions, we may be answering a different question to the one we're actually being asked. However, it won't just be our vague recollections of stories on global wealth that mean we mostly over-estimate. It seems highly likely that it will be at least partly an-other example of 'emotional innumeracy': we know inequality is a big and growing issue, and we hear regular, vivid anecdotes of excess coupled with stories of lack of resources for many, so our guesses become exaggerated. We're partly sending a message that this is a big and worrying issue, and this can have real political effects. A study by Russian and US academics showed that feel-ings of tension between social classes and calls for governments to redistribute wealth more equitably were only slightly related to actual inequality—but the relationship with perceived inequality was around three times larger.[15] This should not be surprising to us: our view of reality is as much shaped by our concerns as the other way round.

We can see the importance of recognizing and understanding that there is an emotional element to our understanding of this re-ality when we look at a follow-up question: what people think the top 1 per cent *should* own. This seemed a worthwhile thing to ask—it's an issue that is relevant to redistribution efforts by government, and there is no obviously correct answer. People will have different views on the appropriate level of equality we should be aiming for, and the average views *did* vary across countries: the lowest proportion suggested was 14 per cent, in Israel, and the highest was 33 per cent, in Brazil, with the average across all thirty-three countries at 22 per cent. On the whole, therefore, people are not calling for complete equality of wealth.

Which country do you think had the most people calling for wealth parity? It was actually Britain, with 19 per cent of Brits saying the top 1 per cent should only have 1 per cent, followed closely by Russia, where 18 per cent said they should only have 1 per cent. That's an interesting mix, with Russia maybe more predictable than Britain, given its communist past. The United States, perhaps not surprisingly, given the national focus on being the 'land of opportunity' where individual effort should get its just reward, was not as keen on wealth parity; only 9 per cent said that the 1 per cent should have 1 per cent. But they weren't the least focused on this as an outcome—that was in aspirational India and China, where only 3 per cent wanted wealth parity.

If we go back to the averages of what we say inequality should be and compare that with our guesses of what it actually is, something immediately jumps out—that, on the surface, people seem pretty comfortable with the current state of wealth inequality in many countries. For example, the French said the top 1 per cent *should* own 27 per cent, when actually they currently own 'only' 23 per cent. A simplistic reading of this is that the French—a country that has '*égalité*' as part of its national strapline—are actually saying give the wealthiest a bit *more*. Of course, that's the completely wrong interpretation. We know from our question on how people currently see the 'reality' that the French, on average, think the top 1 per cent currently own 56 per cent of the country's wealth. So what they're actually saying is wealth concentration among this top 1 per cent should be about half that.

There are two points to take from this. First, people don't think precisely but ordinally when answering these types of estimation questions—their view is just of what 'the rich' do and should have. Second, their answers are basically saying that they recognize the rich currently have 'a lot' and that they should have less—in fact, about half of what they currently have.[16]

This is one of the vital benefits of questions on delusions: we need to know what people think the current situation is before we ask them what they think it should be. Or, the other way round: not knowing how wrong we are about realities can lead us to very wrong conclusions about what we should do.

———

There are a lot of lessons for our own financial thinking in this chapter, building on *how* we think. There has been great progress, drawing from behavioural science, in defaulting us into better options and using our biases in thinking for our own good. But they won't be the answer to everything, because it's practically and ethically impossible to use similar approaches for all aspects of everyone's financial lives. We need a range of actions, including helping us engage 'System 2', our slower, more analytical basis for decision-making.

This is reflected in the concept of 'financial capability', which governments around the world have adopted to shape support for their citizens, and which takes a more systemic view of why we go wrong. It identifies three key factors we need in order to make better decisions.

First, we need some raw *knowledge and skill*—we just need to know some stuff like the size of pension pot we need and how to cope with the sort of calculations required for financial management. *Attitudes and motivation* are important too: governments have recognized that our biases, heuristics, and general views about money are vital. We also need the *opportunity*. The context matters; it's not just about our abilities and motivation—we need access to financial advice and to be able to give enough time to the decisions. This is easier said than done, as the biases influencing our financial decisions are strong, and no level of capability or motivation can magically create more money for those who are barely getting by. But for many of us, having these building blocks more clearly in mind when thinking about our own finances can help. One study showed that increasing our financial capability actually had relatively little impact on people's finances, but it did significantly improve their psychological well-being, because they felt more in control and resilient to shocks.[17]

It is not all about dispassionate, rational calculations, and we shouldn't ignore our emotional reactions. For example, for governments, our delusions are a real clue to our concern about two growing phenomena: wealth concentration at the top and the (partially related) pressure being felt by our young people, and the consequences that has for how they live. Our delusions are often a more direct, less conscious or mediated clue to our deep concerns than simple opinion polls. The signs are clearly there in our misperceptions that these are two very emotive issues for many people in many countries, and we should not be surprised by a growing pressure to intervene on both.

CHAPTER 4

INSIDE AND OUT: IMMIGRATION AND RELIGION

Immigration and religion are two of the most divisive issues in the world today. Emotions are high, and our delusions, not just about the scale but the nature of immigrant and minority religious populations, are frightening.

Numerous studies, including our own, show immigration concerns were one of the key drivers of the Leave vote in Britain's EU Referendum, and it remains a key political issue across much of Europe, with concern high and rising in nearly all countries. While the extreme right has not had the electoral success that many feared following Brexit, disquiet about immigration, religion, and integration has helped shape the political debate in every recent European election, from the French presidential election in 2017 to the Italian general election in 2018. Just about every country in Europe has at least one high-profile, extreme political party that has immigration and broader cultural concerns at the heart of its offer, from AfD in Germany to PVV in the Netherlands. Our analysis of Donald Trump's success in the United States showed how 'nativism'—the sense that your own people, those born in the country, should come first—drove the president's support more than any other single factor.

Within these themes, there has also been a focus on religion, and particularly Muslim populations, with discussion of Islam linked to very emotive debates on terrorism and a sense of cultural threat, across European countries and the United States. People are split down the middle on religion more generally: exactly half the global public in our surveys believe that religion does more harm than good.

Ignorance and misperceptions abound between those inside and outside each of these identity groups. A lot of our fear is driven not just by the unknown, but by an apparent misunderstanding of the facts. But, of course, it's not as simple as that.

IMAGINED IMMIGRATION

Asking people to estimate the proportion of immigrants among their country's population is one of the most asked and analyzed variations of delusion questions. The repeated pattern across all these studies is that people report percentages that are way above the actual proportions. This is true throughout Europe and in the United States—but the top of the league chart in our latest study was occupied by the citizens of Argentina, Brazil, and South Africa, who hugely overestimated the number of immigrants. (Only the people of Israel and Saudi Arabia underestimated the number of immigrants in their country.)

People in the United States guessed that 33 per cent of their population were immigrants, when it's actually 14 per cent. France and Germany had identical figures to each other in both their

Q. What is the proportion of immigrants among your country's population?

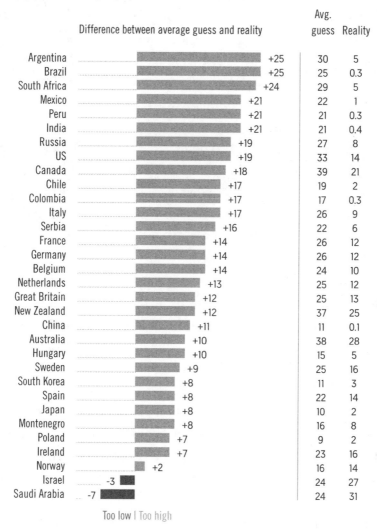

	Difference between average guess and reality	Avg. guess	Reality
Argentina	+25	30	5
Brazil	+25	25	0.3
South Africa	+24	29	5
Mexico	+21	22	1
Peru	+21	21	0.3
India	+21	21	0.4
Russia	+19	27	8
US	+19	33	14
Canada	+18	39	21
Chile	+17	19	2
Colombia	+17	17	0.3
Italy	+17	26	9
Serbia	+16	22	6
France	+14	26	12
Germany	+14	26	12
Belgium	+14	24	10
Netherlands	+13	25	12
Great Britain	+12	25	13
New Zealand	+12	37	25
China	+11	11	0.1
Australia	+10	38	28
Hungary	+10	15	5
Sweden	+9	25	16
South Korea	+8	11	3
Spain	+8	22	14
Japan	+8	10	2
Montenegro	+8	16	8
Poland	+7	9	2
Ireland	+7	23	16
Norway	+2	16	14
Israel	-3	24	27
Saudi Arabia	-7	24	31

Too low | Too high

Figure 15. People generally overestimated the level of immigration in their country.

guess and the actual level—they thought it was 26 per cent, when it's actually only 12 per cent.

Why are most countries so consistently high in their estimates? Across academic and other studies,[1] the most frequently posited explanations are ones that are already very familiar to us: that our answers are based on an emotional reaction reflecting our concern, and that this is also partly driven by biased media coverage and political discussion.

We remember vivid anecdotes far more readily than boring statistics. And some stories are more attractive to the human brain than others, particularly those that play on our sensitivity to threats or danger—and that is often how discussions of immigration are framed in the media and politics. Our delusions about immigration are systemic, not due solely to media or political misdirection on the one hand or our own wrong thinking on the other, but a result of these two groups of effects interacting.

Our delusions are important because they are related to our wider views of immigration and our political preferences: those who overestimate the scale of immigration tend to have more negative views of its impact, and there is a clear association between which political party you support and your guess on immigrants' share of the population. In the UK, supporters of UKIP, a party that builds much of its message around stronger immigration control, estimate immigration at around 25 per cent, whereas at the other end of the scale, supporters of more pro-immigration parties (like the Liberal Democrats and the Scottish National Party [SNP]) are much closer to reality, at 16 per cent. This pattern is repeated across all other countries, with supporters of expressly anti-immigration parties, from Front Nationale in France to the Northern League in Italy, always overestimating immigration. International studies across multiple countries also show that support for immigration restriction is higher among people who overestimate immigrant numbers.[2]

Misperceptions on immigration go way beyond simple estimates of how many immigrants there are. Our mental image of
the typical 'immigrant' is also very wrong. When we asked in the
UK what comes to mind when thinking of an 'immigrant', there
were many more mentions of 'refugees' and 'asylum seekers' than
reflected in the actual makeup of the immigrant population. At
the time, refugees and asylum seekers made up around 10 per cent
of the immigrant population in the UK, but when we asked people
what group comes to mind (not even getting them to estimate a
number), the share of mentions for refugees and asylum seekers
was a third. They were the most mentioned type of immigrant,
more than those who came for work, study, or family reasons—
despite refugees being the smallest of those four immigrant groups.

These are the vivid images and emotional stories that people
remember—they swamp our mental image of the much bigger but
less attention-grabbing groups. Scott Blinder at the University of
Oxford calls this sort of effect our 'imagined immigration'.[3]

This brings us to a further, currently disputed, aspect of our
delusions—what happens when you tell people the true values (for
example, the actual share of the total population who are immigrants)? Does this shift our estimates or our policy preferences?
In the dozens of focus groups we've run on immigration attitudes
across many countries, and also in larger-scale surveys, people defend their estimates. We asked people in fourteen countries to estimate the percentage of immigrants, and then asked a follow-up
question to those who guessed at least ten percentage points more
than the actual figure in their country. Let's take Italy as an example. Immigrants actually make up 9 per cent of the Italian population, so we said to all those who guessed 19 per cent or more, 'Your
national statistics service says that immigration is actually only
9 per cent, but you say it is much more—why do you think that?'

Even after people were shown that the numbers were much
lower than they had guessed, they *insisted* that their estimate was

accurate. When we asked them why they thought their numbers were more accurate than the government's statistics, the top two answers given were that the government's figures were wrong because they don't include illegal immigration—or 'I just don't believe you'.

People come into the country illegally so aren't counted	47%
I still think the proportion is much higher	45%
What I see in my local area	37%
What I see when I visit other towns/cities	30%
I was just guessing	26%
Information seen on TV	11%
The experiences of friends and family	11%
Information seen in newspapers	8%
Other (specify)	3%
Don't know	3%
I misunderstood the question	2%

Figure 16. People still thought that their (incorrect) estimates of immigration were right, even when given the correct figures. We asked them why. The above statements outline the main reasons given. The percentages indicate the proportion of respondents who gave each response.

People are hopelessly wrong that illegal immigration could get them anywhere near their guesses. For example, even the most generous estimates of illegal immigration in the UK (from a group campaigning for greater immigration control) would add less than one percentage point to immigrants' population share.[4]

There is a long tradition of attempting to test whether the truth changes people's perceptions, both in academic and campaigning work, but the results remain mixed and inconclusive. Some studies show no impact at all on perceptions when people are told the correct figures, whereas other studies show some impact on certain beliefs but not others.[5] And some show more marked changes. In one more hopeful, recent example from a study in thirteen countries, the researchers split the group of respondents in two.[6] They told half some facts about actual immigration levels, and said nothing to the other half. Those armed with the correct information were less likely to say there were too many immigrants. However, on the other hand, they did not change their policy preferences: they were not more likely to support facilitating legal immigration. When the researchers went back to the same group four weeks later, the information had stuck for most—although so had the policy preferences. This fits with long-identified theories that facts struggle to cut through our partisan beliefs, or our 'perceptual screen' as Angus Campbell and colleagues called it in their classic book, *The American Voter*, in 1960.[7]

More generally, the evidence from reviews across more varied policy areas shows that typically about one in four studies identifies a significant impact on our beliefs from actually being told the truth.[8] This is a vital conclusion and a point to emphasize: people generally do not shift their views easily, but some *do* shift in some circumstances, and facts can still help to achieve that. The key point is that facts still matter, but they are not always completely effectual in shifting views and are far from the full story in themselves.

Another very live debate concerning using facts to 'convince' people is whether providing people with the correct facts can actually result in 'backfire effects'. Some studies have suggested that correcting delusions actually results in people more strongly asserting an incorrect belief that fits with their ideological view. When presented with factual information about the absence of weapons of mass destruction in Iraq, some people became more convinced that such weapons had actually been found. This has been measured on other issues ranging from whether vaccines are safe for children to man-made climate change.[9] In each case providing evidence for the true position entrenched the delusions among many of those predisposed to the opposite view.

However, important new research has questioned whether this 'backfire' risk is as great as we might think. Thomas Wood from The Ohio State University and Ethan Porter from George Washington University looked across thirty-six different issues in a series of experiments and couldn't find any decent evidence of people actually reacting to the correct factual information by becoming more sure of their error.[10] This is not at all to say that people weren't still more likely to believe facts that fitted with their worldview—they clearly were. In fact, the study demonstrates very significant partisanship in beliefs about everything from changes in abortion rates to criminality among immigrants. It's just that people did not actively backfire against the correct information: it did not make it worse.

This is both encouraging and believable from what we've seen on how people think. Just as we shouldn't try to change people's minds by bludgeoning them with data that says they are wrong, we shouldn't be afraid to use facts. We need to engage people with stories and explanations, but facts should be a part of that mix.

Of course, we also need to avoid simplistic interpretations of what people think of such a massive and varied group as 'immigrants': there is much more nuance and contradiction in public opinion than is sometimes conveyed. We can see that in the remarkable fact that many of the same respondents in the same survey will agree with the statements 'immigrants take jobs from the native population' *and* 'immigrants create jobs through setting up businesses'. Try it yourself—ask yourself both questions, and there is a decent chance that some of you will agree with both, because the way the questions are framed prompts different mental images, even though they are ostensibly asking about the same population.

Both *are* true to at least some degree and in specific instances. There is a fairly one-sided debate about whether, in aggregate, immigrants do take jobs away from native populations, with nearly all economists disagreeing—the view that there is a 'lump of labour' is indeed a fallacy. There is no zero-sum game of employment— the theory that one person's gain is another person's loss. Immigration overall usually creates jobs, and if an immigrant takes a job, it's not straightforwardly the case that one less job is available in a nation. However, there is evidence of displacement of workers in certain sectors (notably in lower skilled industries)—*some* individuals can legitimately feel their jobs have been taken away.[11] This is one of the key issues with economic arguments around the benefits of immigration, and why they leave people cold. It is true that at a national (macro) level, immigration adds more to the economy than it takes out. But people don't see the national impact—the increased tax take or consumer spending. People live in their local (micro) communities, where they see individual job competition and more people waiting in their doctor's office or ahead of them in the public housing queue.

Of course, the media and political discussions do clearly have a role to play in building these negative images. It is very wrong, though, to classify immigration concern as entirely a media effect, as our historical data for the UK shows.

Immigration concern was very low throughout the eighties and nineties. But then net migration to the UK increased significantly in the late nineties, with the expansion of the European Union. As Figure 17 shows, there is a clear sequence to the events. First, the migration numbers go up. The media don't notice for a while, so there is a lag before mentions of immigration in news stories increase. Then the public's level of concern goes up. Media coverage was a transmission mechanism for a reality that was already happening.[12]

If the media is not the sole creator of immigration concern, people's choice of media source is definitely a brilliant predictor of how concerned they will be. As Figure 18 shows, in the UK

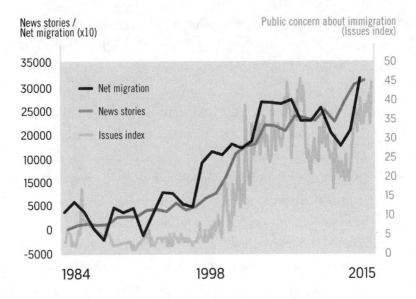

Figure 17. The relationship between public concern about immigration, net migration, and media coverage of the issue: immigration numbers rise before the media and then the public notice.

around 55 per cent of *Daily Mail* (a right-leaning newspaper) readers thought that immigration was one of the top issues facing Britain in 2014, compared with only 15 per cent of more liberal *Guardian* readers. It is one of the most differentiating factors we can find—although of course that doesn't mean your newspaper reading causes your views, as people choose media that reflect what they already think. It's impossible to fully unpick cause and effect, but it seems reasonable to assume there are elements of both.

One of the drivers of concern about immigration, sometimes stoked by sections of the media, is the perception that immigrants commit more crime than other groups. However, the actual evidence is complicated and mixed.

IMMIGRANT PRISONERS

A UK review found no relationship between violent crime and immigration, a weak relationship between asylum seeker populations

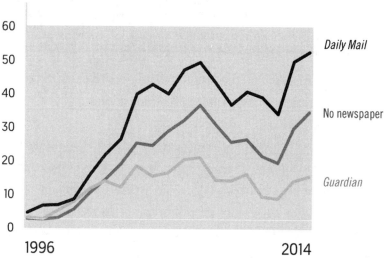

Figure 18. Attitudes to immigration were starkly different depending on respondents' preferred choice of media.

and increases in property crime, but a decline in property crime related to wider immigration.[13] Research in Italy found there is no overall impact of immigrants on either violent crime or property crime, whereas a US study has shown that there is no evidence of a causal link between immigrants and violent crime, but suggests that there is a significant link with property crime.[14] You can understand why it would be complex, as crime rates are highly related to other factors, particularly poverty, and given immigrants tend to be poorer, cause and effect become difficult to unpick. Crime rates also shift constantly because of other factors, from economic conditions to technological advances. Most reviews conclude that there is a weak relationship, and, if anything, crime reduces with increased immigration. There is also fairly clear-cut evidence in a number of countries, including the United States, that immigrants themselves are less likely to commit crimes.

However, the perception among many is certainly that criminal behaviour is more prevalent among immigrants. When we ask people why they want immigration reduced, crime doesn't come out as a top issue, but it is often prominent in the reasons that are given. The link to terrorist threat is particularly strong among a proportion of the public: global polling shows that six in ten believe that terrorists are pretending to be refugees to enter the country, which increases to seven in ten in France, and eight in ten in Germany and Italy.

So is this delusion reflected in overestimating the proportion of immigrants who are prisoners? Yes, it is. Nearly every country thinks that immigrants make up a far greater proportion of the prison population than they actually do: across the thirty-seven countries we asked this question, the average guess was that three in ten prisoners are immigrants, when the actual figure is half that, at 15 per cent.

The most wrong were the people of the Netherlands, who guessed that half of the prison population was immigrants, when the actual proportion was one in five. There may be a very particular and unusual pattern that explains some of this delusion. Such is the success of the criminal justice system in the Netherlands that they actually have excess capacity in their prison system, which is a very unusual thought for someone like me, sitting in Britain, where prison overcrowding is a significant concern. The Netherlands has been closing prison facilities, but it has also imported prisoners from Norway. This has made it into national discussion in the Netherlands and may be part of the reason for the overestimation—which is less about immigrant fear and more about penal system success.

Many other countries that certainly don't have the capacity for a thriving business in prisoner importation were also a long way off—for example, South Africa, France, and the United States. It's probably no coincidence, either, that these countries are often near the top of tables of concern about immigration, or overestimation of immigrant populations as a whole.

As with many other questions, it's worth reflecting on the incredible range of realities in different countries around the world. Take three examples, with similar immigrant populations: Belgium has an actual immigrant population of 10 per cent, the UK's is 13 per cent, and in the United States it is 14 per cent. But immigrants' share of the prison population in each is very different. In Belgium, the immigrant share of the prison population is much higher than their share of the population, at 45 per cent. In the UK it's about on a par at 12 per cent, and in the United States it's way below at 5 per cent.

So immigrants make up nine times as much of the prison population in Belgium as in the United States, despite making up slightly less of the overall population. The reasons for this huge variation will be a complex web of historical, cultural, and economic factors, reflecting the diverse nature of immigration to these two countries. Belgian prisons have become a focus of particular concern about Islamic radicalisation, with 35 per cent of the prison population being Muslim, whereas Muslims make up just 6 per cent of the population. The US prison population, on the other hand, is dominated by native-born African Americans: around 40 per cent of US prisoners are black, despite making up only 13 per cent of the adult population.

Our main concern is why most countries tend to significantly overestimate the proportion of prisoners who are immigrants, at least in these raw estimations. We can see why media and political rhetoric may play a role in this, particularly because crime and immigration hit a lot of emotional nerves individually, and even more so when combined. Take, for example, this headline from the UK's *Daily Mail* in 2012:

'Immigrant Crimewave' Warning: Foreign Nationals Were Accused of a QUARTER of All Crimes in London.[15]

This is not 'fake news'; the figures are correct and taken from Metropolitan Police statistics on the nationality of those who were 'proceeded against', either charged and taken to court, fined, or cautioned. This eye-catching headline is followed, within a couple of sentences, by a case study outline of one particularly terrible crime committed by immigrants. However, nowhere in the article is there any mention of the fact that foreign nationals make up around 40 per cent of London's population and so are significantly underrepresented in these crime statistics!

ISLAMIC STATES OF MIND

'Out of every 100 people in your country, about how many are Muslim?' By now, having seen the patterns in previous data, you've probably trained yourself to go low on these types of questions. But the public didn't. Again, nearly every country massively overestimated what proportion of their population is Muslim. Only majority Muslim countries like Indonesia and Turkey went too low.

And there were some truly wild guesses. France stands out, with the average guess that 31 per cent of all French people are Muslims, against an actual figure of 7.5 per cent. This figure is based on a Pew Research Center estimate rather than an official census or government statistics figure, as you're not allowed to ask about religion in France in official measures. This may provide part of the explanation for the perception gap in France: not that the actual figure is wrong, but that the lack of discussion of the scale of religious populations may contribute to uncertainty and delusions.

In addition to this static view of Muslim populations, we wanted to get a sense of how people thought their population share was changing, because much of the rhetoric is around the speed of growth, a sense that countries are undergoing 'Islamification', partly through the sheer weight of increasing numbers.

Q. Out of every 100 people in your country, about how many are Muslim?

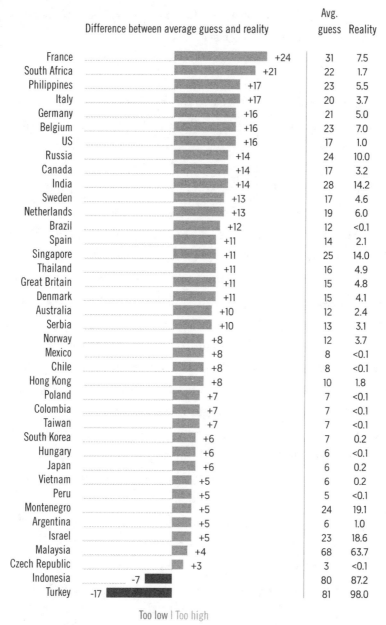

	Difference between average guess and reality	Avg. guess	Reality
France	+24	31	7.5
South Africa	+21	22	1.7
Philippines	+17	23	5.5
Italy	+17	20	3.7
Germany	+16	21	5.0
Belgium	+16	23	7.0
US	+16	17	1.0
Russia	+14	24	10.0
Canada	+14	17	3.2
India	+14	28	14.2
Sweden	+13	17	4.6
Netherlands	+13	19	6.0
Brazil	+12	12	<0.1
Spain	+11	14	2.1
Singapore	+11	25	14.0
Thailand	+11	16	4.9
Great Britain	+11	15	4.8
Denmark	+11	15	4.1
Australia	+10	12	2.4
Serbia	+10	13	3.1
Norway	+8	12	3.7
Mexico	+8	8	<0.1
Chile	+8	8	<0.1
Hong Kong	+8	10	1.8
Poland	+7	7	<0.1
Colombia	+7	7	<0.1
Taiwan	+7	7	<0.1
South Korea	+6	7	0.2
Hungary	+6	6	<0.1
Japan	+6	6	0.2
Vietnam	+5	6	0.2
Peru	+5	5	<0.1
Montenegro	+5	24	19.1
Argentina	+5	6	1.0
Israel	+5	23	18.6
Malaysia	+4	68	63.7
Czech Republic	+3	3	<0.1
Indonesia	-7	80	87.2
Turkey	-17	81	98.0

Too low | Too high

Figure 19. People in nearly all countries overestimated their Muslim population.

So we went a step further and asked people to project forward to 2020 and tell us what they thought the Muslim population would be then. It's important to say that 2020 was only four years away when we asked this question in 2016—we weren't asking for some distant future forecasting. But you wouldn't think that from the scale of change people were expecting.

Taking France again as the most extreme example, the actual projection from Pew is that the Muslim population will go from 7.5 per cent to 8.3 per cent: a pretty speedy growth in the world of population change (it's a growth rate of 11 per cent and would mean around an extra 500,000 Muslims in just four years). But the French public thought that the proportion would move from 31 per cent to 40 per cent. On average, they thought that by 2020 four in every ten French people would be Muslim. That's the equivalent of saying every adult male in France would be Muslim, and is equivalent to a growth rate of 29 per cent, nearly three times the actual projected rate.

While the French stood out, they were far from alone. Italy, Germany, Belgium, and the United States were all expecting growth rates way in excess of realistic estimates. Indeed, nearly all countries overestimated once again.

Of course, we need to recognize this is not an independent question. We had already asked our respondents immediately before what they thought the current Muslim population was, and in some ways they'd already given themselves an 'anchor'.

According to research by psychologists Kahneman and Tversky, we are influenced by previously provided information, and this can have a powerful impact on us, even when that information is irrelevant. This was shown in a famous experiment in which they asked people to estimate the percentage of African countries in the UN.[16] Before people gave their guess, a starting value between zero and one hundred was picked out by spinning a 'wheel of fortune' in their presence, with the wheel rigged

Q. What percentage of the population in your country will be Muslim in four years' time?

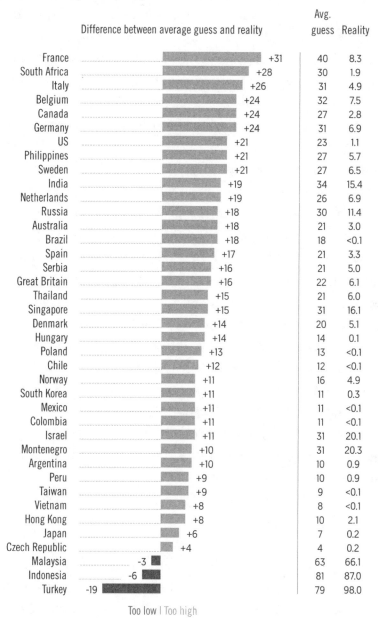

	Difference between average guess and reality	Avg. guess	Reality
France	+31	40	8.3
South Africa	+28	30	1.9
Italy	+26	31	4.9
Belgium	+24	32	7.5
Canada	+24	27	2.8
Germany	+24	31	6.9
US	+21	23	1.1
Philippines	+21	27	5.7
Sweden	+21	27	6.5
India	+19	34	15.4
Netherlands	+19	26	6.9
Russia	+18	30	11.4
Australia	+18	21	3.0
Brazil	+18	18	<0.1
Spain	+17	21	3.3
Serbia	+16	21	5.0
Great Britain	+16	22	6.1
Thailand	+15	21	6.0
Singapore	+15	31	16.1
Denmark	+14	20	5.1
Hungary	+14	14	0.1
Poland	+13	13	<0.1
Chile	+12	12	<0.1
Norway	+11	16	4.9
South Korea	+11	11	0.3
Mexico	+11	11	<0.1
Colombia	+11	11	<0.1
Israel	+11	31	20.1
Montenegro	+10	31	20.3
Argentina	+10	10	0.9
Peru	+9	10	0.9
Taiwan	+9	9	<0.1
Vietnam	+8	8	<0.1
Hong Kong	+8	10	2.1
Japan	+6	7	0.2
Czech Republic	+4	4	0.2
Malaysia	-3	63	66.1
Indonesia	-6	81	87.0
Turkey	-19	79	98.0

Too low | Too high

Figure 20. People in nearly every country thought their Muslim population would grow much more than projected.

to land only on either ten or sixty-five. Subjects were then asked to indicate whether they thought that value was too high or too low, and reach their estimate by moving upwards or downwards. There was a marked effect on estimates depending on what the completely arbitrary starting point was. When the wheel stopped on ten, the median estimate from participants was 25 per cent, and when it stopped on sixty-five, the median estimate was 45 per cent. Even providing a reward for accuracy did not reduce this anchoring effect.

Dan Ariely, a professor of psychology and behavioural economics at Duke University, along with colleagues George Loewenstein and Drazen Prelec, outlined the similar impact of what they called 'arbitrary coherence', by showing that the amount students were willing to pay for a range of items—from bottles of wine to cordless keyboards and boxes of chocolates—was influenced by the last two digits of their social security numbers, once the students had been told to write those down, ahead of a classroom-based auction. Those with high digits paid more, and those with lower digits paid less. If two completely random digits affect what we're willing to pay for wine, it's no wonder that we're firmly anchored to our own guesses.[17]

Of course, with our question on future Muslim populations, we still need a cue in which direction to make our adjustment from our baseline. This may be affected by our personal experience of noticing more Muslims in our country—Muslim populations *are* actually growing in many countries, just not by as much as we think.

As with immigration more broadly, media coverage also plays a role, both in terms of the scale and slant of what we're shown. In particular, what we see in the media on Muslim populations in the West is massively weighted towards negative coverage, with academic studies in both the UK and United States showing that 80 per cent to 90 per cent of coverage had a negative slant or tone.[18]

There is very little coverage of regular Muslim lives and their positive impact on local communities and countries. This is not at all surprising once we recognise the importance of the feedback loops between how we think and what we're told. We get the vivid anecdotes we want, and negative information draws and holds our attention more than positive information. This is a result of our evolutionary past, when negative information was often more urgent, even life-threatening, so we had to act on it: if we were warned by our fellow cavepeople about a lurking sabre-toothed tiger, we had to listen (and those who didn't got edited out of the gene pool).

Our brains handle negative information differently and store it more readily and accessibly. Losing money, being abandoned by friends, and receiving criticism all have a greater emotional impact on us than winning money, making friends, or receiving praise. This stems from the very basics of our brain functioning. In one experiment, social neuroscientist John Cacioppo showed people pictures known to arouse positive feelings, like pizza or Ferraris, and also those that stir up negative feelings, like a mutilated face or a dead cat, and recorded electrical activity in the brain.[19] He found that the brain did indeed react more strongly to negative images. Further MRI studies by other academics have confirmed that negative images are processed with different intensity in different parts of the brain.[20]

As an aside, because our weighting of positive and negative information is unbalanced, we need more positive than negative signals in successful personal relationships: 50:50 doesn't work. Neither does utter positivity all the time—after the initial honeymoon period, that would drive most people insane. Indeed, researchers have shown that the perfect ratio needed for partners to be happy together is 5:1—five times as much positive feeling and interaction as negative (I need to up the number of date nights with my wife).[21]

We conducted our own simple demonstration of our over-weighting of the negative in a survey in the UK. We told people to imagine that they had a life-threatening illness (another one of our more cheerful studies) and that their doctor had told them they would need an operation to treat it. We then asked people how likely they would be to have the operation under two scenarios. This is where we split the sample in half. We told half that their very straight-talking doctor told them that 10 per cent of people who had the operation would be dead within five years. The other half of the sample were told that 90 per cent were still alive five years after the operation.[22]

These two statements are clearly statistically identical despite presenting the information in a different way: one focusing on the positive and one on the negative. Fifty-six per cent of the participants who were told '90 per cent would live' said they would be very likely to have the operation, but only 39 per cent of the participants who were told '10 per cent would die' would. The focus on death made some pause as they moved to 'don't know' rather than 'no'. This is exactly what you'd expect from the theories: our instinctive response is that we need to pay more attention when a clear threat is involved.

We can see from this how important exactly what we say to people is. Negative framing of the same reality can give rise to very different thought processes, that apply as much to how we see social realities or whole communities as to our own decisions. We have to be aware of any stereotyping we're doing ourselves, and how much we're relying on the more immediate, easier to recall negative information rather than a fair representation of the issue or decision.

ALL IN OUR HEADS?

There is another intriguing possible explanation for many of the apparent delusions we've seen so far, derived from the study of 'psychophysics'. I hadn't heard of psychophysics before we started surveying global delusions, and you may not have either. I'm ashamed to say my immediate mental image was of insane scientists running terrifying, subatomic experiments. Instead, psychophysics explores and measures our psychological reaction to physical stimuli—how we perceive things like light and heat.

Psychophysics originated in the research of Gustav Fechner in the 1800s, and over decades of research it has identified a number of fascinating, distinct patterns.[23] For example, according to one of the key laws of psychophysics, when we're looking at a dim light, holding a small weight, or listening to a faint sound, we can detect small increases. But when the light is bright, the weight heavy, or the sound loud, we need larger increases to notice a difference, in a constant, predictable way. A further psychophysics law shows that the relationship between our estimates and the reality depends on the type of stimulus we're exposed to: for example, we perceive increases in electric shocks much more readily, exaggerating the scale of change when compared with increases in brightness, again in a predictable way.

The pattern that's most relevant for us is that psychophysics suggests we tend to overestimate small values and underestimate large values, again in a predictable way. There is a lot of clever maths behind it, but it is (very) basically a reflection of our sensible approach to uncertainty, where we rescale our answers, hedging our bets towards the middle of the available options (50 per cent in the case of asking people about percentages of populations).

Psychophysics doesn't explain all of our errors, but if you accept that it gives a useful insight into our responses (which I do), we may 'actually' be more wrong about a different set of factors than we'd conclude from the raw figures.

For example, it suggests that some of the things we're actually most wrong about are those we've already covered: even accounting for our hedging, people around the world do often significantly underestimate obesity, and we *really* underestimate how happy people are.[24] But looking across countries as a whole, immigration is actually *not* overestimated, when we take account of our hedging tendencies.

It is still overestimated in some countries, with those at the top of the list way over. For example, in Brazil, the actual immigration level is just 0.3 per cent of the population, but the guess is 25 per cent. The psychophysics model takes account of our innate tendency to overestimate small things, but even it suggests that an unbiased estimate that strips that out would be around 9 per cent—so an average guess of a quarter of the population is still way out. The US guess of 33 per cent is more or less spot on what the model would predict from an actual value of 14 per cent. And in countries like Sweden, we would expect people to go even higher than they actually do, purely on how we estimate scale. Immigrants actually make up 16 per cent of the population in Sweden, the guess is 25 per cent, but the model suggests that people should hedge towards 34 per cent.

Psychophysics offers fascinating and extremely helpful explanations, and it is an important addition to our understanding of our delusions. But I don't think it invalidates other explanations (and neither do the psychophysics researchers), for a number of reasons. Most important, for me, as the researchers say, we do not know at this point whether our simple reported view is actually still the most salient one for how we discuss and decide on our view about immigration. Unlike estimating a temperature, our assessment of the scale of immigration is something that we discuss explicitly with people, and where it is possible to be told or know the 'right' answer. Our explicit sense of the scale of immigration also forms part of political debate and campaign pledges.

Our misperceptions about immigration and religion are arche-
types of our system of delusion, in this case largely driven by our
own deep-seated tribal identities interacting with a media and politics that too often look to exploit this division. It's futile to try to
separate these into cause and effect, not just because we don't have
the means to measure what came first, but because it misses the
point—that it is systemic.

Recognizing this is not the same as saying nothing can be
done—in fact, seeing it fully in this way increases our chances
of change. Simplistic media and politician bashing lets us off the
hook, but blaming it on innate, immovable cultural division is
wrong too. The reality is more contingent, with one feeding off
the other. This means it's more complex, and no simple algorithm
will solve it—but it doesn't mean it's unchangeable.

And real, actual facts do have a role in this. It used to be assumed in some political circles that you just needed to put the facts
out (for example, on immigration's net benefit to the economy) and
people would come round to a 'sensible' view as a result. This has
been rightly discredited, as the power of identity, ideology, and
partisanship have been brought to the fore.

The emphasis then shifted to focus less on the facts and more
on the narrative, connecting with people through stories and emotion. But we've now started to question attention-grabbing evidence that seemed to show that telling people the correct facts
could actually make them more likely to hold a *contrary* view of
reality.

We're approaching a more balanced position, where both story
and facts should be recognized as important to the beliefs that
people hold. This is a good thing, not just practically but also for
the type of society we want in the future. I'm with Aldous Huxley when he said, 'Facts do not cease to exist because they are
ignored'.[25]

Of course, we also need to be clear that 'facts' don't exist in a pristine vacuum—they are mostly complex, and always contingent on a selective view of the underlying reality. But admitting this doesn't mean that clear lies, distortions, and manipulation are unimportant or that we shouldn't act.

In the long run, we do no one any favours by tacitly accepting that it's fine for people to just ignore or distort reality.

CHAPTER 5

SAFE AND SECURE

'Facts speak louder than statistics'.

This quote by Geoffrey Streatfield, a UK judge, in 1950, perfectly illustrates the unchanging disconnect between our perceptions of crime and the actual statistics. This particular quote is related to calls to bring back recently abolished sentences of corporal punishment (that is, whipping people) in the UK, driven by a perceived increase in violent crime. The *Manchester Guardian* from March 1950 outlines the very live debate driven by a series of brutal assaults.[1] Judges were outraged that they couldn't give the criminals a dose of their own medicine, and Justice Streatfield said,

The degree of violence in these cases, whether against women or men, old or young, is more brutal and cruel now than it ever was. In such circumstances, it is no comfort to the wounded and terrified victims of the most brutal and savage assaults to be told that there are fewer crimes of this character than there used to be.[2]

The judge at least recognized that the crimes were in decline, but not everybody accepted that, and MPs (Members of Parliament) talked openly about an increase. The actual figures showed a significant fall in violent robberies in the months since corporal punishment had been repealed. The news piece concludes,

There is a section of opinion in this country which habitually turns to the cat-o'-nine-tails whenever there is a run of well reported crimes.[3]

Nothing changes! It's very easy to find the same link in just about any country around the world between lurid reporting of crime, deep distrust of any statistical claims that crime is falling, and calls for tougher action.

Crime was one of the first areas in which I looked at delusions, precisely because people were much more pessimistic and worried than seemed justified from the figures. This negative view was a particular focus for the UK government under Tony Blair, because it had invested hugely in justice, giving people a lot of what they wanted in increased police numbers and other funding. Crime rates had undoubtedly fallen, whichever way they were measured, but people were not noticing, and crime still often topped monthly measures of what most worried people. Blair set up a task force to look into this, headed by (now) Dame Louise Casey, and we conducted various studies with them to understand what would reassure people. Separately, we did our own work on misperceptions of crime, which tried to bring together all the evidence we had and explain why we're wrong and what we could do about it. It was such a key issue that the then Home Secretary came to launch our report.

You can probably now guess why it's such an area of delusion. It's a topic that attracts media interest and vivid anecdotes that stir fear. It also serves up plenty of negative information for us to overly focus on. All these factors are exacerbated by our built-in tendency to think that everything is getting worse.

MORE MURDER?

Murder has a particular emotional resonance for humans. It features in the Ten Commandments and the seven great sins in Islam. Indeed, in the Qur'an, taking one innocent life is equated to killing all of humanity. That's not to say social attitudes towards murder have remained constant over time—there have, in fact, been big shifts in how we see it, from private settling of scores in the Middle Ages to public crime subject to state intervention. Pieter Spierenburg, professor of historical criminology at Erasmus University in the Netherlands, outlines these changes in his book *A History of Murder*, and how they have gone hand in hand with precipitous falls in murder rates over the long term. For example, his estimates suggest there were forty-seven murders per 100,000 people in Amsterdam in the fifteenth century, which had fallen to less than two per 100,000 in more recent times.[4]

We asked people about their perception of these trends—but over a more manageable period! When we asked people across thirty countries whether the murder rate had increased, stayed about the same, or reduced in the last twenty years, there was a pretty clear-cut perception that the murder rate was increasing, or, at least, it was certainly not falling. Overall, around half (46 per cent) thought it had increased since 2000, only 7 per cent thought it had decreased, and 30 per cent thought it was about the same.

The actual trends were very different from these perceptions. In fact, in twenty-five of the thirty countries, the murder rate was actually lower, and often it was significantly down. It was actually only higher in three countries—Mexico, Peru, and Canada—and it was about the same in Brazil and Sweden.

South Africans were among the most sure that the murder rate was higher—85 per cent thought it was, when it was actually 29 per cent *lower*. But those sorts of declines were not unusual—most countries had double-digit falls. For example, over half in the United States thought their murder rate was higher, when it was lower, by 11 per cent. This echoes other studies in America, more generally on gun crime, where a 2013 Pew survey showed 56 per cent (wrongly) thought the rate had gone up over the period they asked about.[5]

No country was particularly good at identifying the real trend, although China did stand out as the only one where people were more likely to (correctly) say it was lower rather than higher— although even here, the majority said it was higher or the same, when, according to official figures, it was actually down a whopping 65 per cent.

Q. Do you think the murder rate in your country is higher, lower or about the same as it was in 2000?

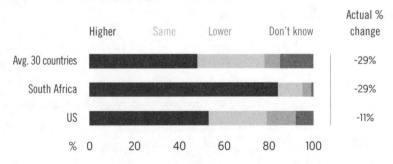

Figure 21. Only a small minority of people thought that the murder rate had declined in the last 20 years, despite that being true in most countries.

In some ways, we can forgive delusions on this question. Asking people to compare crime rates with twenty years ago—when recent incidents will be in their minds, and crime figures are generally compared year-on-year—is a difficult task. There are also numerous measures, and these are often discussed in quick succession in the media: perceptions will be affected by the mental links made between violent crime of particular types (for example, the growth in knife crime in the UK) and murder. Even with these caveats, the broad trend is for substantial declines in murder incidence in most countries, no matter how it is measured—but that is not the general impression people have.

Earlier in the book we saw how our answers to factual questions can actually be signalling our concerns. By saying that murders are increasing when they're actually falling, we're partly communicating our worries about these threats. According to psychologists Natacha Deroost and Mieke Beckwé at the Free University of Brussels, when we worry and ruminate about something, we lose some elements of cognitive control.[6] The threat becomes bigger and bigger in our brains.

However, in this case there is a further factor at play. Because we're asking people to make a *retrospective* comparison, weighing up the past with the present, each new event or series of crimes feels more pressing than in the past. The reason is that we're susceptible to a sense of 'rosy retrospection', a bias in which the past tends to be remembered as better than the present. The Romans referred to this phenomenon with the phrase '*memoria praeteritorum bonorum*', which roughly translates as 'the past is always well remembered'.

Terence Mitchell and colleagues from the University of Washington tested the extent of this effect in 1997, on the much happier subject of how we edit our memories of holidays.[7] In their study, three groups that were going on different holidays were interviewed before, during, and after their break. Most followed the pattern of initially positive anticipation, followed by mild disappointment (we've all been there). But, in general, most subjects reviewed the events more favourably the further in the past they were. Again, this is not a dumb fault in our brain—it could well be pretty smart. As Mitchell argues, it helps with our sense of well-being and self-esteem to remember things with a rosy glow that might not be completely accurate.

Many other experiments show similar effects in a range of contexts. For example, do you remember how well you did at school, specifically what grades you got? Maybe not as well as you think, if you're like a large chunk of the population: we're likely to believe we performed better than we actually did. In one study, participants were asked to recall their grades, but then the researchers went back to check them against school records. Three in ten people recalled their grades incorrectly, and this wasn't in a neutral, random way—far more grades were shifted up than down. 'A' grades were recalled accurately nine times out of ten, but 'D' grades were accurately remembered only three in ten times.[8]

Given the rarity of these most extreme of crimes (for example, there was only one murder per 100,000 people in Australia, Denmark, the UK, Italy, and Spain in 2015),[9] and therefore our very limited direct experience, our explanations should look in detail at the role of media and political discussions.

Journalists have always covered crimes extensively—'If it bleeds, it leads' is a frequently repeated cliché for a reason. The greater the intensity of the crime—the 'more gruesome' the murder—the more likely it will be splashed across the front page. Media studies experts Tony Harcup and Deirdre O'Neill found that one-third of media stories in British newspapers focused on something negative.[10] Of course, this isn't the only criterion determining what news organisations focus on, and many studies have attempted to identify what does define newsworthiness, or what academics often call 'news values'. A seminal Norwegian study by media researchers Johan Galtung and Mari Holmboe Ruge in the sixties identified twelve factors—things like how suddenly or unexpectedly an event occurs, whether it involves elites, whether it is consonant with expectations, and, of course, whether it is negative, with bad news more newsworthy than good.[11] Many researchers have tested and updated this since (to add factors like whether it involves celebrities), but negativity has remained a constant important feature. As highlighted in the previous chapter, this makes sense—we are generally wired to focus on the negative, because that is often vital, urgent information.

We also have a keen interest in gossip and, in particular, who is and who isn't upholding the moral standards of the group. This is hardwired into us through evolution. Our ancestors lived in small communities and so had to quickly understand who they could and could not rely on. In those conditions, an intense interest in the private behaviour and standards of conduct of others was actively helpful. Those who were particularly skilled at harnessing this social intelligence ended up being more successful than those who were not, passing on our human gossip genes.[12]

Our view of social trends is also affected by what we're told by the media and politicians. As with other aspects of media and political discourse, dramatic change and absolutes attract attention. The study of news values by Harcup and O'Neill suggests that headlines highlight how a particular subset of crime is spiking, and not that there is a gradual decline in crime overall. It simply makes for a better story to do so. Also, crime is a key political subject and often referred to with wild rhetoric by politicians and partisan newspapers to score points. This is not a coincidence, but a reflection of the systemic drivers of delusion I outlined in the Introduction. Politicians and journalists know that crime stories elicit strong reactions and therefore use them for their own ends, whether that's votes, circulation, viewing figures, or clicks. We in turn lap them up, ensuring we get more of the same in the future.

In the United States, Donald Trump provides several examples of how crime can be politicized. In 2017, he tweeted an intervention on UK crime rates:

> Just out report: 'United Kingdom crime rises 13% annually amid spread of Radical Islamic terror.' Not good, we must keep America safe![13]

These were the correct published figures, and while the rise was partly attributed to the creation of new crime recording categories and greater accuracy, there was an underlying, like-for-like rise. However, there was no discernible connection to 'Radical Islamic terror'. Fraser Nelson, editor of the *Spectator* magazine, responded:

> 'Amid' is a word beloved by fake news websites, to conflate correlation and causation. UK crime is also up 'amid' spread of fidget spinners.[14]

A second example from the same source does involve misrepresentation of the figures, this time in the United States. President Trump said in an address to the National Sheriffs' Association (NSA) at the White House in February 2017,

> The murder rate in our country is the highest it's been in 47 years, right? Did you know that? Forty-seven years . . . the press doesn't tell it like it is. It wasn't to their advantage to say that.[15]

There was a reason the press didn't say that—because it wasn't true. It is true that the murder rate in *cities* in America had recently seen its *biggest increase* in forty-five years—as President Trump had previously pointed out. However, leaving aside that the correct statistics only refer to cities, the type of change in his more correct statement is clearly very different from his talk to the NSA. The actual statistic is for a year-on-year increase, in the context of murder rates that had fallen consistently over many years. Reported murders peaked at around 24,500 in the United States in 1993, and had declined steeply to around 14,000 by 2014.

President Trump's repeated use of this wrong presentation of the data is also important because we know that the mere repetition of a false statement increases its likelihood to be believed. Social psychologists call this the 'illusory truth effect'. As we've seen, people tend to believe things that are in line with their existing understanding of the world. They're also more likely to believe information that just feels more familiar. When we hear something for the second or third time, our brains respond faster to it, and we attribute this 'fluency' as a sign that it is true. Studies with college students have found that they are more likely to be confident that false trivia statements—for example, that basketball was included as an Olympic sport in 1925—are true when they are presented with it a second time, after a gap of a couple of weeks.[16]

This bias has toxic effects on political campaigning, where false claims are used repeatedly, because that sheer repetition means it will stick with some. This does not mean that any nonsense, if repeated, will be believed by everyone. But as we'll see when we come back to some statements around Brexit and the rarer examples of truly 'fake news', some repeated falsehoods are remarkably sticky.

MORE TERROR?

If there is one crime more terrifying than murder, it is terrorism. This is literally what it is designed to do, to draw the maximum attention and stoke fear to further some wider objective. It occurs at random and in day-to-day situations, where we can all easily imagine ourselves—at a pop concert, on an aeroplane, in a restaurant, or at a place of worship. The fear engendered by horrifying events causes us to lose all sense of proportion, exaggerating the risks, not just in general but to ourselves individually. Jennifer Lerner from Harvard University outlines research that showed, in the immediate aftermath of the 9/11 attacks, Americans thought there was a 20 per cent probability that they themselves would be the victim of a terrorist attack within the next twelve months, when, of course, the odds were nothing near that.[17]

As with the murder question, we asked people how they thought terrorism was changing; whether the number of deaths associated with terrorist attacks was increasing or decreasing, comparing the fifteen years before September 11, 2001, with the fifteen years after. We picked September 11 as a clear marker in time, and to remove the impact on the US figures of that terrible attack. Taking two quite lengthy periods of recent history also helps to smooth out the impact of what are, by their nature, one-off events. Excluding the year of the study (2017) meant that if any tragic event happened close to our interviewing, this should not affect our estimates (although we should recognize that people don't always answer the question they're asked, and fresh events inevitably cloud our judgement). The 2017 data was not available at the time of writing, but even though there were some very high-profile tragic attacks during the year, this would not have changed the overall trend, which shows a very significant fall between these two periods.

It takes time to get this data because it's complex to count terrorist-related deaths—the information needs to be pieced together from multiple sources, and inevitably there is an element of judgement involved. However, we are extremely fortunate that researchers at the University of Maryland have maintained a Global Terrorism Database (GTD) that runs all the way back to 1970. This database is drawn entirely from publicly available information, including news archives, existing data sets, books, journal articles, and legal documents. The researchers attempt to corroborate each piece of information from multiple sources, but they (correctly) do not make any claims for its absolute accuracy beyond that. It is an incredible resource, counting not just the number of deaths (of victims and terrorists themselves), but up to 120 other pieces of information, including everything from the tactics and weapons used to who claimed responsibility.

You may find the general trend surprising. The number of deaths from terrorist attacks was down in twenty-five of the thirty-four countries where we asked this question, and across the countries as a whole, terrorism-related deaths are about half the level they were.

The perception was quite different: overall, only 19 per cent of the public thought deaths from terrorist attacks were lower, 34 per cent thought they were higher, and 33 per cent thought they were about the same. Within that, some countries were very wrong. For example, 60 per cent of our respondents in Turkey thought that deaths from terrorism had increased over these time periods, whereas they had actually halved. This is not in any way to down-play the continued seriousness of the terrorist threat in Turkey: the number of deaths in Turkey remains one of the highest in the countries we've asked about, at 2,159 deaths over this most recent fifteen-year period. Nevertheless, the view of change is very wrong.

Some countries did get the trends right, usually when things have got worse: the majority of our French respondents correctly identified that the number of deaths in their country had in-creased. Some were even overly optimistic about recent changes: the majority of our Russian respondents thought the number of deaths from terrorism had either decreased or remained about the same, when they'd actually doubled.

Britain has experienced one of the steepest falls in deaths from terrorism when comparing these periods, largely as a result of the Northern Ireland peace process and the ceasefire declared in 1997. According to the GTD, there were 311 deaths due to terrorism in mainland Britain (we excluded Northern Ireland, as our survey was of respondents in Great Britain rather than the UK) in the fifteen years prior to 2001, whereas there were sixty-two in the fifteen years after that (the decline would have been even more dramatic if we had included deaths in Northern Ireland). However, that is not the perception in Britain: 47 per cent thought deaths from terrorism increased over these periods, 29 per cent thought they stayed about the same, and only 15 per cent thought they had declined.

Unsurprisingly, the explanations of why we're wrong are similar to those we saw with murder rates—our rosy retrospection colours our view of the past, and the coverage and rhetoric around terrorism enhance our sense of increased threat. Indeed, deaths from terrorist attacks are by definition more extreme and unusual than murders in general, and therefore they tick more boxes in the list of 'news values' that determines how much attention they're given, and equally their rarity means we have hardly any direct experience to draw on.

Q. In the 15-year period after the September 11th attacks (2002–2016) do you think there were more, fewer or about the same number of deaths caused by terrorist attacks in your country compared with the 15-year period before the September 11th attacks (1985–2000)?

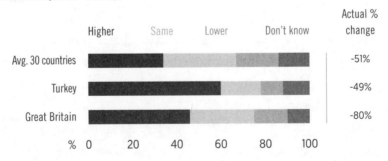

Figure 22. Very few people thought that deaths from terrorist attacks were lower in recent years, despite that being the case in most countries.

The lifetime odds of dying in a terrorist attack pale into insignificance in comparison with such mundane activities as bathing, driving, or climbing a ladder.[18] But as Steven Pinker, psychology professor at Harvard, puts it, 'Our intuitions about risk are driven not by statistics but by images and stories. People rank tornadoes (which kill dozens of Americans a year) as more dangerous than asthma (which kills thousands), presumably because tornadoes make for better television'.[19]

———

Looking back on my long study of misperceptions, it's no surprise at all that crime was where it started, because it has so many of the features that describe our system of delusion. We not only have a built-in bias towards focusing on the vivid and threatening, we also tend towards thinking things were better in the past, and therefore are worse now. Neither of these tendencies is dumb, as they have their roots in our strong sense of self-preservation, including in remembering our history more fondly than the reality justifies.

But they have consequences, which the media and politicians exploit. The media know we're drawn to these stories. Politicians often exploit them to provide a sense of threat or decline. But that's partly because both those groups are human too: journalists are interested in these stories themselves, and at least some politicians will genuinely believe their faulty facts because they 'feel' right.

It's an effective sales technique, whether it's clicks or votes you're after. But it has serious consequences and is perhaps the main reason why our delusions are so important and dangerous. When we feel this false sense of threat and decline, it opens a space for someone, anyone, to sell us an easy solution—which is often that the current system is broken and we need to tear it up.

Our own starting point should therefore be to understand that most things are getting better, not to kid ourselves into accepting the status quo, but to counter a deep trait that leads us to a greater danger. In *Enlightenment Now*, Steven Pinker shows endless charts with good things (mostly) going up, and bad things (mostly) going down. He quotes Barack Obama, who cuts through our biases to highlight that, when it comes right down to it, while our world today is very far from perfect, it is better than the past:

> If you had to choose a moment in history to be born, and you did not know ahead of time who you would be—you didn't know whether you were going to be born into a wealthy family or a poor family, what country you'd be born in, whether you were going to be a man or a woman—if you had to choose blindly what moment you'd want to be born, you'd choose now.[20]

CHAPTER 6

POLITICAL MISDIRECTION AND DISENGAGEMENT

'Do you even know the cost of a pint of milk?'

This was the 'gotcha' question posed by fearsome BBC interviewer Jeremy Paxman to the then mayor of London, Boris Johnson.[1] Paxman was grilling Johnson over his party's proposed tax cuts on the wealthy, and he'd asked about the cost of a pint of milk to show how out of touch Johnson was with the lives of the people he was supposed to be representing. When Johnson suggested that it was about 80p (about a dollar or euro), Paxman immediately corrected him: 'No, it's about 40-something'. Johnson tried to bluster his way out of it, saying that he was thinking of one of those 'biggish ones', but Paxman was having none of that, hitting back with:

'This is such typical Boris, trying to change the question, I asked about a *pint* of milk'.

Obviously, underneath the banality of the exchange, viewers at home were meant to understand Johnson shouldn't be fighting for a tax plan that cut the top rates if he had no idea what it cost for an ordinary family to buy the bare essentials.

The next day, the then prime minister, David Cameron, was asked the price of bread by a different reporter, just to mix up the shopping list a little. Cameron said, 'Well north of £1', and when told by the presenter it was only 47p (which was very wrong; it was more like £1.20 at the time), blustered that he had a bread maker and preferred to bake his own, getting lost in the nuances of the type of flour (Cotswold Crunch) and brand of bread maker (Panasonic) he uses.

Later that same day, Boris was asked about the price of bread and got it spot on. Clearly there had been a frantic briefing on grocery prices at the highest levels of UK government. (In fact, it was later revealed that David Cameron *did* have a crib sheet of facts and figures to swot up on, with crucial economic and policy data like the latest growth figures and minimum wage levels, alongside the price of twenty king-size cigarettes and a pint of lager. Bread was also on there at £1.27, so he'd remembered his figures pretty well.)

This series of events is hardly edifying for anyone involved, but it highlights just how desperate the media and others are to pin down skilled and slippery politicians to verifiable and understandable facts, something that all 'ordinary people' can be expected to know. But *do* ordinary people know?

We asked the public in Britain about the price of a pint of milk, and it turns out many of us can't afford to be too judgemental.[2] True, the average guess is pretty close to the 49p reality (at the time). But one in five of us said 80p or more (which must be the same sort of specialty yak's milk Boris is drinking), and one in nine of us said 29p or less (you should be worried about any milk that costs that little—remember that *Simpsons* episode about Fat Tony's 'rat milk scam'?).

Being 'in touch' with reality and fairly representing all their citizens are two of the key asks of politicians. But so often our impression is that they're misdirecting us, or just plain lying. They don't represent us on even the most basic factors (note how many are men and how many are women), and they play on the emotions of voters seemingly for their own gain rather than true concern. Politicians are often thought of as self-interested, out-of-touch elites who don't understand our concerns and don't intend to govern to our benefit.

DEMOCRATIC DEFICIT

It's no surprise, then, that many of us distrust the entire political process. Quite a few of us completely check out of politics as a result. But as it happens, not as many of us reject the polling booth as we think. When asked to guess what percentage of the eligible population voted in the last main parliamentary or presidential election, every country underestimated, and some—like France, Italy, and Britain—substantially so.

Even where the average guess was close to the actual level, such as in the United States, many people guessed much lower: for example, a quarter of Americans thought that 40 per cent or less of their fellow citizens voted in the 2012 presidential election.

The reason we underestimate voting levels is very likely to be related to the widespread coverage of declining voter turnout in general and at particular elections. It echoes our discussion in the previous chapter on newsworthiness. As summarized by Professor Mark Franklin in his book on voter turnout, 'Stable turnout is not news. Moderately increased turnout is not news. Low or declining turnout is newsworthy'.[3] Allied to this, turnout levels *have* declined in many established democracies in the post–World War era, although it's often more variable and *not* the wholesale

Q. Out of every 100 eligible voters in your country, how many do you think voted in the last election?

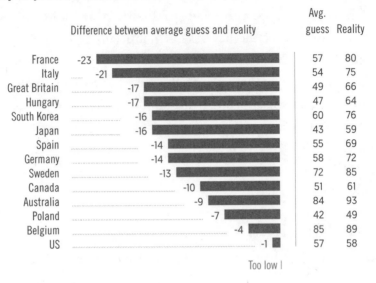

	Difference between average guess and reality	Avg. guess	Reality
France	-23	57	80
Italy	-21	54	75
Great Britain	-17	49	66
Hungary	-17	47	64
South Korea	-16	60	76
Japan	-16	43	59
Spain	-14	55	69
Germany	-14	58	72
Sweden	-13	72	85
Canada	-10	51	61
Australia	-9	84	93
Poland	-7	42	49
Belgium	-4	85	89
US	-1	57	58

Too low |

Figure 23. All countries underestimated the proportion of the population that voted in the last major national election.

rejection that you might think if you look at the coverage. As we can see from Figure 23, it is still mostly the norm to vote.

There are important social implications from our misperception of voting levels. As we've seen several times, if we think it's the norm to act in a particular way, we're more likely to act that way ourselves, due to our tendency to imitate the majority or follow the herd. In this case, our view of the norm is often wrong and, as with drinking alcohol at Princeton University, our 'pluralistic ignorance' could push us to think that active rejection of voting is the majority view, and that could affect our own inclination to vote.

Of course, we also do need to consider whether declining turnout rates are always such a bad thing, or the fault of citizens themselves. As Professor Franklin points out, in the early days of study of turnout levels in the twenties, researchers accepted as true that turnout would be higher in elections that hung in the balance or where 'issues of vital concern are presented'. Seen like this, lower turnouts could reflect the fact that politicians and parties have given us little meaningful choice. In this scenario, our lack of interest in voting or political issues more generally may be rational.[4]

'Rational ignorance' was coined as a term by economist Anthony Downs in the fifties, in *An Economic Theory of Democracy*.[5] He made the point that it's perfectly rational for us to be ill-informed about key political and social realities, because to be informed takes time and effort—and there is no point if we can't influence anything through our vote. Individual votes don't have any impact, so why would we expend the effort?

It is definitely true that the chances of any single person affecting the outcome of an election are very slim. It has been calculated for past US presidential elections that it's anywhere from one in 100 million to one in 1 billion if you happen to live in one of the more populous US states—many times less likely than winning most national lotteries. So effectively zero.

Rational ignorance is a fascinating area of study and provides us with many of the longest-standing measures of political ignorance we have, as it received a lot of attention in the United States in the forties, fifties, and sixties. These studies measured understanding of various 'taught facts' (how government works, who is responsible for what) and 'surveillance facts' (things we need to update, like which party controls the Senate, the current unemployment rate, etc.). This knowledge—or lack thereof—has barely changed over the decades: we're about as wrong now as we've always been. For example, a 1947 Gallup survey showed that just 55 per cent of people could tell you which party was in control of the Senate—and this was virtually unchanged in 1989, with only 56 per cent of Americans getting it right.[6]

There is some criticism of the theory—mainly that the sort of political facts focused on can seem like trivia. This means that some downplay its importance—if people can cope with broader concepts, maybe not knowing nitty-gritty facts is not that important for a well-functioning political system. But that seems a bit blasé. Ilya Somin, a professor at George Mason University, argues that it is difficult to hold governments to account if you don't know who's responsible for what.[7]

Another criticism is that the theory seems altogether *too* rational, which has some weight, given we've already seen how emotional and instinctive many of our thought processes are. However, this does not entirely undermine the theory's importance. As Somin and others argue, we may not be doing a conscious calculation about whether it's worth being informed—just a vague sense is enough—and we can probably identify that trait in many people we know.

The implication from having such a long series of survey data showing that political ignorance is pretty stable over time (and certainly not decreasing) is that it seems highly unlikely we're going to see any significant increase in political awareness in the future. So perhaps we should not be trying to increase knowledge, but rather to reduce the impact of ignorance. That, it is suggested, is mainly done through limiting and decentralizing government, putting more into the private sector, and allowing people to 'vote with their feet'—that is, move to areas that fit their preferences better. If you're an American who wants to pay less in taxes, you can relocate to Alaska or Delaware, where state taxes are at least 40 per cent lower than the average for the United States. Clearly this highlights some of the issues with the workability of 'footfall democracy'—that there are many motivations behind choosing a place to live, and some people will be more equipped or inclined than others to take advantage of such a system.

Nevertheless, rational ignorance raises an important point, in showing that our lack of political knowledge is a long-standing and unshifting issue. Therefore, it's not the supply of political information that's the main missing ingredient—there's loads of good, accurate information out there if we care to look. It's at least as much a demand-side issue, and citizens need to look to themselves too.

To bring it back to our discussion of voter turnout, some of those who argue that political ignorance is an important reality in our societies point out that one's likelihood to vote is highly associated with our level of political knowledge. Therefore, the logic goes, the more people who turn out, the less well-informed the average voter is. So should we be that focused on increased turnout in any case? Again, this is a relatively sound piece of analysis that is as old as democracy itself. In the *Gorgias*, Plato suggested that democracy is defective because it adopts policies based on the views of the ignorant masses, at the expense of better-informed and just smarter philosophers and experts. Aristotle was more optimistic, suggesting the masses have more information collectively than any individual—basically, none of us is as smart as all of us. But concern about ignorance persisted, with, for example, John Stuart Mill arguing that the better educated and more knowledgeable should be given more votes than the less well educated or ignorant. This view also points to important facts, such as how risky high-turnout referenda like the EU Referendum in the UK can be.

This logic also rather loses sight of the equality arguments, that all citizens should have an equal say, not just those we deem to have sufficient ability. It's easy to forget that women were excluded from voting until the mid-twentieth century or later in many countries: full suffrage was only granted in France in 1944, Italy in 1945, India in 1950, and Switzerland (incredibly) in 1971. The echoes of this suppression of women's political rights are still clearly impacting today, including in their woeful underrepresentation in leadership positions.

A MAN'S WORLD?

The theme for International Women's Day 2018 was '#Press forProgress', highlighting how far we still have to go to achieve gender equality. This theme was chosen partly in response to the World Economic Forum's 2017 Global Gender Gap Report, which suggested that, at the current rate of progress, gender parity across the world, on four key dimensions—economic opportunity, educational attainment, health outcomes, and political empowerment—will take another *217 years* to achieve![8]

We worked with the International Women's Day organizers to conduct a global poll on perceptions around these shocking realities—and our collective delusion was significant. The average guess was that economic gender equality would be achieved in around forty years, with, for example, the average Canadian thinking it would only take twenty-five years, the average Indian only twenty years, and the average Mexican only fifteen years. Our misperceptions reveal our complacency about the distance still left to travel.

That complacency is seen in our misperceptions of the woeful reality of representation of women in leadership roles globally. The percentage of female CEOs of Global Fortune 500 companies scrapes in at 3 per cent, but, again, people think things are more equal than they really are.[9] The average guess was that one in five CEOs of the world's largest companies is female.

Fair representation of women is not just about sending a signal that half of the world's population is an equal part of society; it also changes policies and practices in business and government, by uncovering often unconscious gender bias in decisions.

Take one example from local government in Sweden. It snows a lot in Sweden, and *how* the snow is cleared has a significant impact on people's lives. You might be wondering what this has to do with gender equality. Well, the way that snow clearing had traditionally been done prioritized the ring roads first, then the main roads, and only after that, the smaller roads, cycleways, and pavements. The areas cleared first also tended to be areas of male-dominated employment, in financial districts and the like.

On average women drive less, and walk, cycle, and use public transport more, and snow has a huge impact on walking and cycling, where smaller amounts are more disruptive and dangerous than with driving. This had a direct impact on the balance of injuries and accidents involving the different genders: in fact, in Sweden, pedestrians were three times more likely to be involved in snow-related accidents and injuries than motorists, and most of them were women.[10]

The decades of development of snow clearing approaches by politicians and officials, who were largely men, had unconsciously exacerbated gender inequality. Since then, a number of Swedish municipalities have completely shifted their approach. Pedestrian footpaths and cycleways are cleared first. Then routes to infant schools, because that's where parents (of both genders) go first on their way to work. Larger workplaces are given the next level of priority, with female-dominated workplaces, such as hospitals and municipal facilities, included. Only when this network is cleared are the remaining roads cleared of snow. Working in this new priority order costs no more, but it allocates resources more fairly, and, as a result, accident rates have gone down and fewer employees miss work, leading to broader economic benefits.

Sweden has a particular focus on gender equality in political representation, with 44 per cent of parliamentarians being women. Next best are South Africa and Mexico, where the figure is 42 per cent. Both are also examples of how national legislative and party-political commitment can significantly shift representation. In February 2014, after years of lobbying, Mexico passed an amendment to their Federal Constitution requiring that political parties develop 'rules to ensure gender parity in the nomination of candidates in federal and local congressional elections', and this has resulted in record numbers of female representatives. There is no national legislation of the same sort in South Africa, but there are significant voluntary commitments from the political parties, particularly the African National Congress (ANC), which holds over 60 per cent of seats. Again, the push for gender equality in the ANC has a long and fascinating history, and in 2006 they adopted a 50 per cent gender quota in local elections, and then extended that to national elections in 2009.[11]

Sadly, these countries are clearly the exception, and the average across the thirty-two countries included in the study is much more depressing, at only around 25 per cent. Within this, many are incredibly low: only 10 per cent of parliamentarians in Brazil, Hungary, and Japan are women.

When we asked people what percentage of parliamentarians in their country are women, the guesses weren't as far off as they were on most topics. In fact, across the countries as a whole, the average guess was 23 per cent, when the actual average is 26 per cent. But this hides a pattern where individual countries were very wrong in each direction. The most deluded on political gender equality were Russians, who thought that 31 per cent of national politicians were women, when it is only 14 per cent. But interestingly, Mexicans also did badly, unaware of how progressive they are—they guessed at 26 per cent, but, as we've seen, the reality is actually 42 per cent.

We shouldn't feel particularly good about being wrong in either direction. Not realising the scale of a problem (or overestimating progress) in countries like Russia will mean less focus on it as an issue and less pressure to achieve the change that other countries have. Equally, not recognizing that progress has been made, in countries like Spain and Mexico, can discourage other women from getting involved or trusting the legitimacy of political decisions, giving the false sense that nothing can be done. As we've seen, we're social animals and we imitate the majority, not the underrepresented minority.

A majority of the public do see the benefits of more equal representation: 61 per cent of people across twenty-seven countries agreed that things would work better if women held more positions

Q. What percentage of politicians in your country do you think are women?

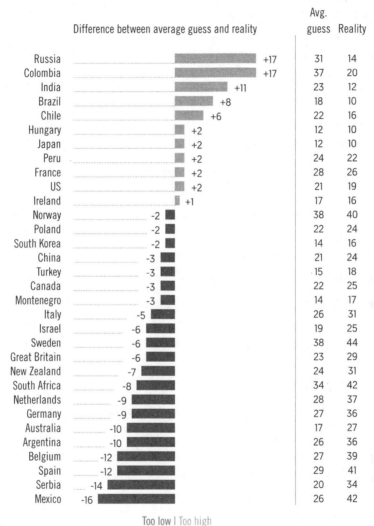

Figure 24. Accuracy was mixed on the proportion of female politicians: people in a number of countries were very accurate, whereas others significantly overestimated and underestimated.

of responsibility in government and business. This is even the view of a majority of men, although this was one of the few questions in which men and women had a notably different perspective, with only 53 per cent of men agreeing versus 68 per cent of women. In many countries, including Germany, Japan, South Korea, and, most markedly, Russia (where only 26 per cent of men agreed), it was only a minority of men that agreed. In that context, it is perhaps clear why (mostly male) politicians in a number of countries don't take bolder actions on equal representation.

Politicians are constantly calculating and balancing their appeal to different groups, not just between genders, but across all sorts of demographics. With sluggish economic growth and wage stagnation for large swathes of the population in much of the West, one group that has been particularly courted in recent years is the economically 'left behind'. Giving a sense that political parties and leaders 'feel the pain' this group has experienced has been a key objective of most election campaigns since the 2008 financial crash, and that included the 2016 US presidential election.

THE LEFT BEHIND

Donald Trump came back to US unemployment figures time and again during his presidential campaign, claiming they were actually anything up to 42 per cent, rather than the official figures at the time of around 5 per cent, prompting much derision from people who knew the numbers. It earned him four Pinocchios from the *Washington Post*'s fact-checker, which is their highest award, and translates in their scale as a 'whopper'.[12] 'Don't believe these phony numbers', Trump told supporters. 'The number is probably 28, 29, as high as 35 [per cent]. In fact, I even heard recently 42 [per cent]'.[13]

And there was a later campaign passage on it at a rally:

> The unemployment number, as you know, is totally fiction. If you look for a job for six months and then you give up, they

consider you give up [*sic*]. You just give up. You go home. You say, 'Darling, I can't get a job.' They consider you statistically employed. It's not the way. But don't worry about it because it's going to take care of itself pretty quickly.[14]

The figures may be spurious, but the *meaning* of the statement— what Trump is trying to say—is clear: *they give up on you.* You've fallen through the cracks because the system tries to hide bad news. Trump was tapping into an emotion, his specialty. When he was asked by David Muir, the anchor of ABC's *World News Tonight*, 'Do you think that talking about millions of illegal votes is dangerous to this country without presenting the evidence?' Trump replied, 'No, not at all! Not at all—because many people *feel* the same way that I do'.[15] The reality is secondary to the emotion. Or as British columnist Matthew d'Ancona puts it, 'He communicated a brutal empathy to [his supporters], rooted not in statistics, empiricism or meticulously acquired information, but an uninhibited talent for rage, impatience and the attribution of blame'.[16]

Of course, there are many measures of unemployment and underemployment monitored by the United States and other national statistics bureaus. The headline Trump picks out as phony conforms to an internationally recognized standard and is the one used most often by governments around the world. It is designed to give an idea of active job search rather than underemployment, and is useful for international comparisons, as most countries focus on a similar measure.

But the other accepted definitions do include many measures that have a broader understanding of unemployment, and that therefore put the percentage up. For example, some count people who would prefer full-time work but have been forced to settle for part-time work. But none of these get anywhere near the type of figures Trump was talking about.

In fact, the only way to get to 42 per cent in the United States is to include all caregivers for children, all students, and retirees.

That's clearly not a useful measure. Of course, Trump is not think-ing about the measure itself, more about the meaning people take from his statement.

What did the public think the unemployment level in their country was? Interestingly, the guesses across fourteen countries were often much closer to those of Donald Trump than reality! People in every single country went for an average guess that was much higher than the actual rate, with even Germans, the most accurate, saying 20 per cent, when the official figure was 6 per cent at the time.

Italy was the most wrong—Italians thought that 49 per cent of their population were unemployed and looking for work, when the actual unemployment rate at the time was 12 per cent. That's a very high real unemployment level, but not half the working-age population. US respondents were close to some of the (many) fig-ures Trump threw out, at 32 per cent—and this survey was con-ducted long before the presidential race.

Of course, as with any of the questions that ask people to pick a figure, our guesses on unemployment could be affected by the rescaling we do in our heads, where we hedge our bets and head to the middle of the range. Even taking psychophysics effects into account, Italy and South Korea were still way over what we would expect. Even in the United States, where the psychophysics model suggests our adjusted guesses are only a little larger than what we should expect, many people were much further out. For example, one in five Americans thought that 61 per cent or more of their population was unemployed!

It seems likely, then, that our emotional responses still play a major part, with some individuals overestimating something that they're worried about. And we know that unemployment *is* a real concern for people. Unemployment is the issue that tops our global poll of twenty-six countries that we track every month, asking what most worries them. This is ahead of all other issues and has

Q. Out of every 100 people of working age in your country, about how many do you think are unemployed and looking for work?

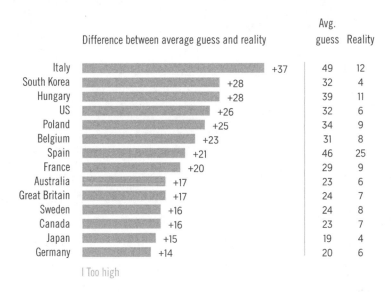

	Difference between average guess and reality	Avg. guess	Reality
Italy	+37	49	12
South Korea	+28	32	4
Hungary	+28	39	11
US	+26	32	6
Poland	+25	34	9
Belgium	+23	31	8
Spain	+21	46	25
France	+20	29	9
Australia	+17	23	6
Great Britain	+17	24	7
Sweden	+16	24	8
Canada	+16	23	7
Japan	+15	19	4
Germany	+14	20	6

I Too high

Figure 25. Unemployment levels were hugely overestimated in every country.

been since the financial crisis in 2008. In some countries, such as Italy and Spain, around two-thirds of the population says it's the most important issue facing the country.

Kathy Cramer, professor of political science at the University of Wisconsin–Madison, is the author of *The Politics of Resentment*, which she based on interviews with voters in rural Wisconsin and published in 2016, before many of the trends she identified became widely discussed. Cramer identified three key dimensions to political resentment in the United States, which can equally be applied to segments of the population in many countries. A significant proportion of people in these economically precarious communities don't think they get their fair share of decision-making power, of resources, or of respect (in the sense that the challenges they face and the contribution they make are not sufficiently recognized).

In an interview in the *Washington Post* before the results of the 2016 election were known, Cramer emphasized that, from her research, facts and policies were less important than the *feeling* that the concern was recognized:

> I think all too often we put energy into figuring out where people stand on particular policies. I think putting energy into trying to understand the way they view the world and their place in it—that gets us so much further toward understanding how they're going to vote or which candidates are going to appeal to them. . . . I don't think that what you do is give people more information. Because they are going to interpret it through the perspectives they already have. People are only going to absorb facts when they're communicated from a source that they respect.[17]

Cramer is describing the directionally motivated reasoning, with its associated confirmation and disconfirmation biases, that we've encountered throughout this book. There is long-standing evidence from other political analyses of how leadership can be more important to people than policy positions from politicians: we shift our views if our favoured politicians do, rather than changing our preferred leader.[18] It's a bit like our relationships with brands: it's too time-consuming and costly to keep reviewing and changing.

While these observations are vital, and still too often ignored, it's absolutist to suggest that people's identities are so set and overpowering that providing further information to them is pointless. People clearly do update their views of leaders and political parties, based on what they see and hear. Our preferences are formed through a balance between information and beliefs, and this is reflected in our attitudes to evidence and conviction.

We asked people in Britain how they thought they and other people make decisions about the different policies put forward by political parties—is their view based mainly on evidence, or is it based more on what they think is the right thing to do, or is it a mix? We asked people what they thought they and others actually did, and then how we think they *should* make decisions. Of course, this is a very simplistic presentation of a complex interaction, but we were interested in general perceptions of the balance. The pattern was pretty clear: we're more likely to think other people go on their gut, while we are balanced, trying to take both evidence and conviction into account. That's also what we think the ideal should be: 41 per cent said that decisions should be both on evidence and what we think is right, 26 per cent that it should be more about the evidence, and just 13 per cent that it should be more about our instincts for what's right.[19]

We went on to ask the same sort of questions about politicians, and views were pretty evenly split—we don't all think that all politicians are ideologues pursuing only what's right in the face of all evidence. Our ideal view of how politicians *should* act is pretty similar to our view for ourselves: more emphasis on basing decisions on facts than conviction, but nevertheless recognizing there is a balance.

Whether this is how we *actually do* come to judgements is clearly much more debatable, but it's a pretty sensible approach to aspire to: we need to get better at recognizing the importance of our identity in shaping how we see reality and our political preferences, but that doesn't entirely discount the importance of evidence and facts.

The discussion of the perilous state of politics over the last few years has often been about how this balance has been lost, focusing on the growth of identity politics and how we are increasingly polarised into groups, blind to the failings of our chosen parties or leaders. However, it's important to recognize that we are *not* actually becoming steadily more wedded to party political blocs. We can see this from Figure 26, based on trend data from the

Netherlands. The question asks whether people feel attached to one particular political party—not whether they're interested in politics overall or vote in elections, but just whether they feel a strong attachment to just one party. We've split the answers by different generations, not looking at age groups, but cohorts— tracking people based on when they were born. This is a really useful way to predict how the future might look: the balance of the population is slowly shifting from a steadily ageing (and dying) cohort at the top, to the youngest at the bottom.

The pattern couldn't be clearer: younger generations are less likely to say they feel attached to one particular political party. More than that, these generational lines are pretty flat, which suggests that this is an attitude we're largely socialized into at a young age and take with us. In fact, if we were looking for a time when people were set in their political ways, unshakeable in their support of their own party, this would be well in the past, when these

Q. Do you feel closer to a particular party than all other parties?

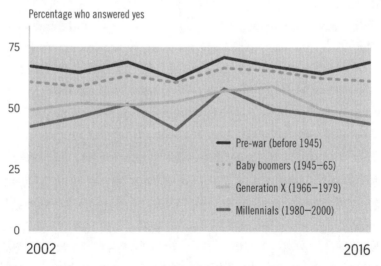

Figure 26. Younger generations in the Netherlands are less likely to feel attached to one particular political party.

older cohorts made up more of the population. The present and future look more fluid.

Of course, that's not the same as saying that identity politics is not on the rise or important, but it does mean that parties cannot count on the unquestioning support of the public quite as much as they once could. Employment and social structures, like trade unions and religion, that once made political affiliation an easy choice are dissolving or changing, and so younger generations are freer to actively choose. It's not just in the Netherlands that we see this pattern; nearly every country we've looked at—across Europe and wider—shows a similar pattern to varying degrees. Rather than a future of unbridgeable divides between identity groups, we may actually see more movement, forming and reforming of political allegiances, than in the past.

———

Emotions are vitally important to how we see political realities and politicians. This was, to some extent, underrecognized in some past discussions of politics that imagine people coolly weighing up policy preferences before choosing parties and leaders, and it's right that we've rebalanced. It highlights the extent to which politicians can and do appeal to our emotions, with little reference to realities, and significant misdirection.

Things are also not changing as much as some portray, or we imagine. The headlines and political discourse encourage a sense of threat and decline. But we're not checking out of politics at the rate we think, we're not dumber on politics than we were in the past, and, although polarisation is an issue in some countries, we're not ossifying into great ideological blocs any more than we did in the past.

But we're also not making progress in representation as quickly as we think. We've heard about the focus on gender equality for a number of years, we've seen some examples of success, and we therefore assume much greater progress than the reality. That women *still* make up, on average, only a quarter of our political representatives across such a wide range of countries is shocking. The variety of situations in different countries also has the power to startle, both with how ludicrously low female representation is in some, but also, more encouragingly, how much and quickly it can be shifted with focus and action. We need to guard against the complacency that representation and equality are improving more quickly than they actually are—knowing where we are is vital to understanding how far we still have to go, and what can be achieved.

CHAPTER 7

BREXIT AND TRUMP: WISHFUL AND WRONGFUL THINKING

It would be downright negligent to write about misdirection and delusion without mentioning the 2016 EU Referendum in the UK and US presidential campaigns. There have been endless studies of what was true or false, reasonable or misleading, and there will be many more for years to come.

This chapter is the closest we get to taking a straight look at whether we're living in a 'post-truth' era. In his book on post-truth politics, journalist and author Matthew d'Ancona builds a passionate case that something is different about now, when he argues that the shift is not so much the behaviour of politicians, but rather more about our reaction: 'What is new is not the mendacity of politicians, but the public's response to it. Outrage gives way to indifference and, finally, collusion'.[1]

I'm not sure we have decent evidence that our reactions are qualitatively different today, that we are quicker to outrage and action than in the past—that view has a hint of rosy retrospection. Still, these two seismic political events provide vital case studies for understanding our delusion and how it is driven by our preexisting beliefs and wishful thinking.

THE EU REFEREN-DUMB

'Who pays most into the EU budget: the UK, Germany, France, or Italy?' I'd wager very few of you think it's the UK. Whenever I present these findings, I get a couple of people, at most, picking out the UK, probably because they misheard the question.

However, among the British public as a whole, nearly a quarter (23 per cent) said they thought the UK paid in the most. They were, of course, wrong, and the answer is Germany, which contributes twice what the UK pays. In fact, the UK is last on the list, with France and Italy also contributing more. Not even a technical misunderstanding of the question (which obviously has complexity behind it) can explain this. No matter how you cut it—even the pre-rebate contribution (the UK receives a rebate from the EU each year, negotiated by Margaret Thatcher in 1985), even if you work it out per capita or look at net contribution—the UK is miles behind Germany in terms of what it pays in.

'Just give us the facts and we'll decide' was the call from the general public at the start of the EU Referendum campaign. We asked people whether they agreed with that in surveys and, because we like to think of ourselves as rational actors, they said they did.[2] But regardless of your view of the outcome, the campaigners clearly failed to get the facts across, and this is especially true on the crucial issue of the UK's payments to the EU, which always came near the top of the list of aspects of EU membership that irked British people the most.

Of course, the idea that the decision was all about 'facts' is naïve. The responses from people who thought the UK pays in more are, once again, a very clear example of 'directionally motivated reasoning', driven by deeper emotional reactions. Brexit was always as much about emotion as facts—as the great psychologist Daniel Kahneman spotted before the result of the vote was known. 'Irritation and anger' may lead to Brexit, he said, in the weeks running up to the vote. 'The major impression one gets from observing the debate are that the reasons for exit are clearly emotional'.[3] How prescient that view turned out to be.

There are all sorts of reasons why we're 'fooled' into believing things that aren't true. We get some things wrong because others have fooled us—the media, our peers, politicians. But just as often, we're 'fooling' ourselves, leaning on wrongful or wishful thinking rather than the facts when considering the world around us. We are motivated to use those facts in a particular way, and it's harder to resist that urge than it may seem.

One of the more startling proofs of this comes from Yale law professor Dan Kahan, who asked more than one thousand Americans to review the data from a scientific study and extrapolate the meaning of the results. Some subjects were shown a table of numbers that purported to show the effectiveness of a 'new cream for treating skin rashes', whereas others were shown the same table labelled as showing the effectiveness of a 'new law banning private citizens from carrying concealed handguns in public'. In some of the charts, the cream or law improved things; in others it made things worse.

Lots of people made mathematical mistakes in both cases (proving again how our brains struggle with statistics), but it is striking that with the handgun data, far more people were likely to misinterpret the data. Even those who were highly 'numerate'— having taken a greater number and higher level of mathematics classes, or working in a mathematically based field—were *more* likely to get the maths wrong. Why? Their political persuasions were overriding their mathematical abilities: more left-leaning Democrats said that the gun control law worked when the chart said it didn't, and many more right-leaning Republicans said the gun control law didn't work when the chart said it did.[4]

This aligns with other research showing that when people are asked about an issue on which they disagree with their political party's official position, they take longer to answer—suggesting that it takes 'additional cognitive effort' to go against our beliefs.[5]

Kahan's analysis has profound implications—that our statistical or critical reasoning abilities alone are not always a sufficient guard against our motivated reasoning, and in fact may even make the situation worse, as we have more tools to torture the data to fit with our worldview.

Again, while this is a vital insight, it's also important to say that not everyone acted like this: it's just they were slightly more likely to. You sometimes see the findings discussed as if this landmark experiment proves that we're entirely slaves to our beliefs, and critical thinking is no guard at all, when the actual findings and conclusions are more nuanced.

In the EU Referendum, we saw more wishful thinking, beyond guesses about what the UK pays into European budgets. We asked a sample of British people to estimate how much out of every £100 invested in the UK comes from Europe—and how much from China.

The public were not entirely incorrect on the amount EU countries invest in the UK. On average they guessed at 30 per cent, when the actual figure is 48 per cent. People underplayed the importance of close economic ties with Europe, but they understood that it's the biggest chunk of the UK's foreign investment income. This guess was lower (25 per cent) among those who said they were going to vote Leave, but not massively so. As Kahneman's interpretation of the vote suggests, there was not complete blindness to the possibility of economic impact, it was just outweighed by other more emotional concerns, as we'll come back to.

There was a much bigger error on the China question. People thought that nearly £20 of every £100 coming into the UK in direct investment came from China—when in reality it's only £1. The importance of China as a future partner was played up during the campaign. We may sacrifice some of the closeness of our links with the EU, the Leave campaign messages went, but that will free us up to strike trade deals and investment from other, faster-growing global economies. This was the tone set, but even if people didn't hear that, they would have a general sense of the scale and growth of the Chinese economy.

There have also been some very high-profile investments in the UK from China, particularly in infrastructure and energy, that made the national news. These were usually presented as partially a threat or risk to the UK's sovereignty, but this sticks with people all the more because of that, given the greater impact of 'negative information'. Ironically, that threat probably reinforced the message that China is more important to the UK economy than it really currently is, and therefore that Britain is less dependent on Europe than it really is.

Q. In 2014, international investment in the UK was £1034bn. To the best of your knowledge, what share of this total amount do you think comes from the following?

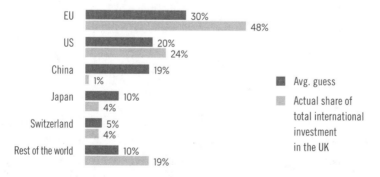

Figure 27. The general public underestimated investment into the UK by the EU, overplaying investment by China in particular.

BENDY BANANAS

UK misperceptions concerning the EU even stretch to subjects that may seem insane to anyone from outside the UK (and many of those within it). Few would have expected that bananas would become a campaign issue for several days over the course of the EU Referendum. But there is (sadly) a long history of claim and counterclaim on whether the EU *really* banned bendy bananas across the continent, and therefore denied Britons their God-given right to eat whatever-the-hell-shaped yellow fruit they like. It goes back to *The Sun* newspaper's catchy headline in 1994: 'Now they've really gone bananas—Euro bosses ban too bendy ones', with the article providing a 'banana hotline' for concerned readers to call.[6]

It passed in and out of tabloid newspaper attention over the years, until it was brought into the EU Referendum campaign, mainly by former London mayor Boris Johnson. He brought it up robustly, with his usual bombast, at a rally in Stafford:

> It is absurd that you cannot sell bananas in bunches of more than two or three, you could not sell bananas with abnormal curvature of the fingers . . . this is not a matter for a supranational body to dictate to the British people![7]

In the days after, bananas became a focus around Boris—he was followed by a man in a gorilla suit, but also quizzed in various interviews and debates. His response shows what he was getting at:

> Do you know how many directives there are on bananas from the EU? There are four. Do we need them?

Boris's take on the number of fingers in a bunch was completely misleading, if based on a kernel of truth. The directive in question says that if you are a wholesaler, you are not allowed to pack bananas in bunches of two or three—they have to either be single bananas or bunches of four or more. But that doesn't affect retailers, who can sell bunches of any size they like.

On the curvature question, this is based on a real regulation, Commission Regulation 1333/2011, which sets out minimum standards for imported bananas—including that they should generally be 'free from malformation or abnormal curvature'. But 'abnormal curvature' wasn't intended to mean more bendy than average. The aim of the regulation was to stop importers from sending boxes of bananas that are so malformed that fewer fit into a standard size package for transport, or are so weirdly shaped that no one would buy them.[8]

I never thought my career would reach a peak of researching banana regulations, but in some ways, that's exactly the point. What Boris was highlighting was the apparent absurdity of the detail that EU regulations go into. It's such a heady combination of a vivid anecdote, told with customary zeal (related to what social scientists call the 'fluency heuristic', which means we pay more attention to well-told stories), but also linked to a real, broader concern (Britain's sovereignty) and triggering the question: if the EU is meddling in high-potassium fruits, what else is it mucking about with?

Of course, there is significant misdirection here. These sorts of measures may seem absurd, but they exist in UK regulations as much as in the EU, and often for good practical reasons. The public are (rightly) utterly unaware of the intricacies of the regulatory controls that touch most areas of life and therefore have no baseline for what's reasonable or not. So the point stuck with many: when we checked in a survey of 'euro myths', a quarter of the public believed the ban exists.[9] One audience member in the BBC's political show *Question Time* cited straight bananas as the signal issue that made her switch from Remain to Leave.[10]

Perhaps the most famous of all 'facts' that formed a key part of the referendum campaign was that Britain sends £350 million per week to the EU. It was plastered on buses and posters, and often behind the key campaigners (including Boris in Stafford) as they spoke. That led to amazing recall for the figure throughout the campaign: our polling showed that 80 per cent had heard it.[11] More than this, there was incredibly high belief for such a contested figure—half thought it was true. And more important, different groups saw this figure entirely differently, depending on whether they supported remaining in the EU or leaving. In fact, Leave supporters were twice as likely to believe it was true (around two-thirds) than Remain supporters (one-third). The same reality, seen vastly differently depending on your political identity.

After being asked for a response by politician Norman Lamb, the UK Statistics Authority broke the calculation down in great detail: starting with the gross contribution, which is the £350 million; then outlining what that is after the rebate, £280 million; then what that is net, after we take away what public sector bodies in the UK get back in direct funding from the EU, £180 million; and, finally, what it is after similar payments from the EU to non–public sector bodies in the UK, £120 million.[12]

This last figure is arguably a much fairer representation of what the UK 'sends to the EU each week', as the rest of the £350 million flows directly back. But Boris Johnson continues to have very little concern about this, so much so that he brought up the £350 million again in September 2017. This prompted another letter from the UK Statistics Authority saying it was 'surprised and disappointed'.[13] But Boris came back, *again*, in January 2018, saying, 'There was an error on the side of the bus. We grossly underestimated the sum over which we would be able to take back control'. This was in response to projections that the UK's gross contribution could rise to £438 million by the time it fully exited the EU in 2021. He went on to qualify that about half of that could be used for public services, with the NHS 'at the top of the list'.[14]

This focus on the spuriousness of the figure is important, but it misses the point. When Nigel Farage, then leader of the UK Independence Party, was challenged on its use after the campaign, he said,

> When you've got your army and you're facing their army, what you don't do is shoot your own side in the back given the significance of what we were facing. But net it's £250m a week. Had he just used that net figure that would have been big enough to convince voters that actually we were wasting an awful lot of money.[15]

Farage was entirely wrong about the net figure, but right about the sentiment. These figures are unimaginable for nearly all of us anyway. They reflect a truth that Britain pays in more than it gets directly back out. Of course, this is only a partial picture, as other economic benefits flow back from EU membership, but that is much less tangible, and difficult to communicate.

The Remain campaign and the Treasury hit back with a key figure that tried to capture this wider economic impact, stating that each household could be £4,300 a year worse off by 2030 if the UK did leave the EU. In theory, it seems like this should be a strong figure. It's a personal impact on our own finances, and it focuses on loss—and we know we have a strong loss aversion, where we feel those more keenly than we celebrate gains. But it didn't have anything like the traction of the £350 million figure. In fact, only 17 per cent believed it was true,[16] a paltry figure compared with the half that said they believed the £350 million figure.

This may be for a number of reasons. First, it was prospective, rather than something that was currently happening. It is always harder to convince people of predictions, particularly when they are over a decade away, and there is suspicion that a vested interest exists behind them. Second, it just wasn't a believable amount for most people. It was based on a model that suggested the economy could be 6.2 per cent smaller by 2030 than it would be if Britain remained in the EU, and then divided that amount by the total number of households, even though that burden would clearly not fall evenly. In a country where the average salary is around £25,000 per year, this average amount seemed incredible.

Overall, the EU Referendum campaign was supposed to be about facts, but it was nothing of the sort. We shouldn't kid ourselves that either side particularly thought it would be. The Remain campaign was called 'Project Fear' by opponents, for good reason—because focusing on potential costs is often a good tactic when you're campaigning against change. For the most part, social scientists expect some 'status quo bias' in these types of decisions, for this exact reason—our built-in fear of the unknown. Arguably, such an effect worked in the Scottish Referendum in the UK two years before the EU Referendum—and there is a perception that it usually does, although evidence from more thorough reviews shows this is less clear than some think. Polling academics Stephen Fisher and Alan Renwick collected data on over 250 national referendums held since 1990 and found that the change option actually won seven in ten of the votes (although only 40 per cent actually passed, due to the presence of additional requirements for a result to be counted as valid). They also looked at the relationship between final polls and the eventual result and found that, although there was, on average, a small swing to the status quo, there was no reason to believe that a late swing would have shifted things significantly towards Remain. That was the assumption of models from many forecasters, and that's why they were more wrong than the polls they were based on: they factored in this bias, and it didn't really happen.[17]

The criticism of the Remain campaign mainly focused on its overuse of facts. Arron Banks, one of the leaders of the Leave campaign, said, 'The Remain campaign featured fact, fact, fact.

It just doesn't work. You've got to connect with people emotionally'.[18] This is a vitally important point, but only half the story: it's certainly true that they failed to build an emotional connection into the case for staying in the EU, and this was the most important weakness in the campaign. But the contingent and uncertain nature of their facts also hurt them: 'There are no facts about the future', one academic put it at the time.[19]

It's understandable, even sensible, that we should be sceptical about politicians' predictions. It's maybe less forgivable how easily many of us are duped by utterly fabricated 'fake news' stories about the past.

REAL FAKE NEWS

Donald Trump is inextricably linked to discussions of 'fake news', and not just because he (bizarrely) appeared to claim he invented the word 'fake' in a television interview in 2017.[20] He is also connected to a lot of the truly made-up stories that brought attention to the fake news phenomenon. We conducted a poll for BuzzFeed (which has done some of the best research on the reality of fake news) on what Americans had seen and believed from the highest profile fake news stories of 2016—and it was no coincidence that there were more about President Trump and the presidential race than any other issue.[21]

These stories hit home with decent proportions of the US population. For example, around one in five Americans saw three stories that were utterly fabricated: that Pope Francis endorsed Trump; that a protestor was paid $3,500 to protest against Trump; and that Trump sent his own plane to rescue two hundred marines.

The papal endorsement was particularly inventive. It first appeared on a now-defunct site called WTOE 5 News, which claimed to be satirical, and was then picked up by fake news website Ending the Fed. It had nearly 1 million Facebook engagements according to BuzzFeed, although all sources have since been taken down. It was actually a pretty bland and straight statement—there were no satirical twists or obvious attempts at absurdity. The pope was supposed to have said he was endorsing Trump not in his duties as the Holy See, but as 'a concerned citizen of the world', linking this to a need for a strong and free America.

Americans didn't just see the stories, they believed them: 64 per cent believed in Trump's papal endorsement (including 46 per cent of Clinton supporters), 79 per cent believed an anti-Trump protestor had been paid, and 84 per cent believed his private plane had rescued marines.[22] These are not misestimations of social realities or belief in statistics or statements that have at least a kernel of truth in them—they are belief in completely made-up nonsense, and therefore more akin to belief in conspiracies and urban myths, and 'placebo misperceptions', which have been the subject of a huge number of academic studies.

Placebo misperceptions are where respondents claim some knowledge of or view on fictional claims that they couldn't previously have been exposed to (because they're made up). For example, in one study, 33 per cent of Americans said they believed that the US government was covering up the 'North Dakota Crash' (a completely made-up event by researchers at Chapman University).[23] Another study, by Delroy Paulhus, a psychology professor at the University of British Columbia, asked respondents to rate their knowledge of 150 different topics, everything from Napoleon to 'double entendre', but sprinkled in were completely made-up examples, such as 'choramine' and 'El Puente'. Respondents claimed to have at least some knowledge of 44 per cent of real topics, but also claimed to know something about 25 per cent of the made-up ones.[24]

It seems like one of those cruel tricks my younger self would have hated; but as with the other experiments I objected to, it has an important purpose, not least in highlighting how blurred the lines are between ignorance and delusion that we discussed in the Introduction. In fact, for decades we've run similar studies in our political polling. Periodically since the eighties, alongside real politicians, we've asked people to rate 'Stewart Lewis', a now-retired research director at our company. Around 20 per cent always claimed to have some view on Stewart, even though he never went near a candidate list.

Of course, playing with our willingness to react to completely invented facts has long been the focus of satirists, using it to highlight the gullibility of the famous and powerful, our tendency for moral panic, and the need to have an opinion on things we know nothing about. The series of satirical shows developed in the UK by Chris Morris and various collaborators over twenty years ago, from *On the Hour* through *The Day Today* to *Brasseye*, were masterpieces in highlighting and predicting the growth of these trends. The most infamous examples involve duping politicians and celebrities to sign up to invented campaigns. They earnestly read to camera about the dangers of 'Cake', a synthetic (or 'made-up') drug that allegedly affected a part of the brain called 'Shatner's Bassoon' and made users 'cry all the water out of their body'. One politician even asked a parliamentary question about how Britain could deal with this growing menace.[25]

Of course, such examples are deliberately absurd. But the broader point is that we've known for a long time that we'll accept things that are utterly false if we have sufficient motivation.

'Post-truth' was the Word of the Year in 2016, and 'fake news' was the Word of the Year for 2017—but it is now thirteen years since Stephen Colbert picked 'truthiness' as his first word of the day in the late-night American TV show *The Colbert Report*. 'Truthiness' had been around for a while before this, but it was defined more precisely then as the belief or assertion that a particular statement is true based on the intuition or perceptions of some individual or individuals, without regard to evidence, logic, or facts.

Colbert's full quote from an interview at the time explains why he saw it as so important:

> Truthiness is tearing apart our country, and I don't mean the argument over who came up with the word. I don't know whether it's a new thing, but it's certainly a current thing, in that it doesn't seem to matter what facts are. It used to be, everyone was entitled to their own opinion, but not their own facts. But that's not the case anymore. Facts matter not at all. Perception is everything. It's certainty. People love the President [George W. Bush] because he's certain of his choices as a leader, even if the facts that back him up don't seem to exist. It's the fact that he's certain that is very appealing to a certain section of the country. I really feel a dichotomy in the American populace. What is important? What you want to be true, or what is true?[26]

Colbert was in part reacting to a 2004 *New York Times* magazine article by Ron Suskind, who attributed a quote to an anonymous aide in the White House—whom people have since identified as Karl Rove, President Bush's senior advisor, although he denies it. Here's an extract from his article, which highlights there is nothing new about 'alternative facts':

> The aide said that guys like me were 'in what we call the reality-based community,' which he defined as people who 'believe that solutions emerge from your judicious study of discernible reality.' [. . .] 'That's not the way the world really works anymore,' he continued. 'We're an empire now, and when we act, we create our own reality. And while you're studying that reality—judiciously, as you will—we'll act again, creating other new realities, which you can study too, and that's how things will sort out. We're history's actors . . . and you, all of you, will be left to just study what we do.'[27]

It became infamous, with liberals proudly adding to their websites that they're part of the 'reality-based community'. And it's been given a timely boost by US rock group The National, including it in their song 'Walk It Back'. They promised a cut of royalties to Suskind, but really want to give them to Rove, to remind him that 'we know he said that'.

The point is this is not new or unique to our time. Kurt Andersen's excoriating article in the *Atlantic* in 2017, 'How America Lost Its Mind', outlines how long our lax attitude to facts has been in the making:

> Mix epic individualism with extreme religion; mix show business with everything else; let all that ferment for a few centuries; then run it through the anything-goes '60s and the Internet age. The result is the America we inhabit today, with reality and fantasy weirdly and dangerously blurred and commingled.[28]

While we shouldn't think there was a golden age of truth and reason in the past, there is much about the current communications environment that *is* different and brings new threats, precisely because they work with so many of our known biases, but at a previously unimaginable scale. We'll return to this point in the next chapter when we discuss the impact of the growth of communications technology.

This increasingly confusing communications environment is an important part of the reason why we're often so bad at accurately identifying what's real and fake in past and present political issues, and why we are deeply sceptical of politicians' predictions. But are we any better at predicting political futures ourselves?

THE WISDOM OF THE CROWDS AND WISHFUL THINKING

There is a very rich literature on how the mass of the general public can be better predictors of outcomes than experts, most notably in *The Wisdom of Crowds* by James Surowiecki. In that, Surowiecki outlines the classic example of how the average guess from a large number of people trying to identify the number of jelly beans in a jar will be more correct than those of its individual members.[29] This idea has a long history and can be traced at least as far back as Francis Galton's famous experiment at a county fair in 1907, in which competitors entered a competition to guess the weight of an ox—with the average 'voter' guessing the weight of the ox almost perfectly, as the errors of individual guesses cancelled out.

To be fair, Surowiecki also points out how crowds get it wrong and are easily swayed. But there is some weight to the idea that the crowd is worth paying attention to when it comes to predicting political outcomes—with claims that the betting markets, made up of real people risking real money, are a more accurate measure than polls or models.

It's not surprising that, following the publication of *The Wisdom of Crowds,* there was interest in the political polling world on whether asking people what they thought *would* happen could be a more accurate predictor than asking them what their own voting intentions were. There were some early encouraging signs, with an experiment by a pollster in the 2010 election in the UK showing that a 'wisdom of the crowds'–based approach would have provided the most accurate final poll from any conducted. But as is so often the case with political polling, new methods that happen to hit on the right electoral outcome can't keep it up across several elections—as endless examples of one-off successes of models based on analysis of Twitter chat or surveys of Xbox gamers testify. It was the same with wisdom-based approaches: when similar approaches were used in the UK's 2015 election, they fell foul to the same sort of errors as regular polling, missing that the Conservatives would be the largest party. It's easy to understand why: unlike estimating the weight of an ox or counting jelly beans, people are subject to the same sort of messages in the media about likely outcomes, and so our estimates are not completely independent. This predictive approach has gone a little quiet in recent years.

The results from our study (across forty countries) on views about whether Trump would win reinforce that caution and echo some of the explanations for why. As Figure 28 shows, only two countries had notably more people saying Donald Trump would win than Hillary Clinton—Russia and Serbia, with China pretty evenly split. So unless you're from one of those countries, your fellow citizens mostly didn't see a Trump victory coming.

All other countries had significant leads for Clinton, including in the United States itself, where 50 per cent said Clinton, and only 26 per cent Trump. Mexico was the extreme case, with 86 per cent saying Clinton would win, and only 6 per cent Trump.

Of course, it was an incredibly close election, with Clinton actually winning the popular vote, so we shouldn't judge people too harshly. But our collective failure to predict the outcome illustrates the impact of both what we're told and how we think. In this case, media coverage will have affected our perceptions of a contest tipped in Clinton's favour, but also our wishful thinking is a factor: we partly answer what we think will happen, and partly what we want to happen. The large majority of countries will have been affected by the generally negative view of Donald Trump, as we saw in international polling at the time and since.

The stance of Russian media outlets on Trump and, in particular, their negative portrayal of Clinton is well documented. It may be less obvious why Serbians were so sure of a Trump victory, but they have close links with Russia, including in media consumption. The Serbian people are also generally negative about the Clintons, following the role of President Clinton in the bombings of Kosovo and Bosnia. Indeed, a story appeared during the 2016 campaign claiming that Donald Trump apologized for the bombings carried out under Bill Clinton. It was later denied, but the story took hold in the country.

Q. Thinking about the upcoming US presidential election, do you think that Donald Trump or Hillary Clinton will be elected as president?

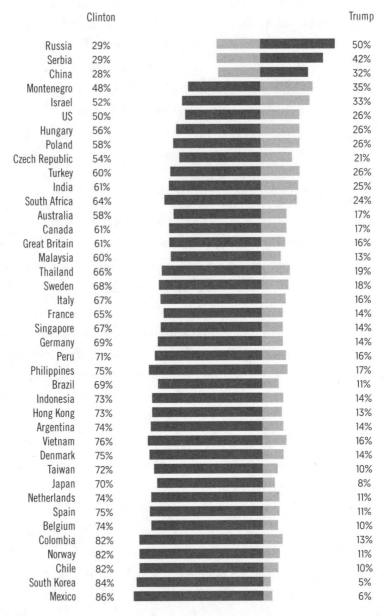

Clinton / Trump

	Clinton	Trump
Russia	29%	50%
Serbia	29%	42%
China	28%	32%
Montenegro	48%	35%
Israel	52%	33%
US	50%	26%
Hungary	56%	26%
Poland	58%	26%
Czech Republic	54%	21%
Turkey	60%	26%
India	61%	25%
South Africa	64%	24%
Australia	58%	17%
Canada	61%	17%
Great Britain	61%	16%
Malaysia	60%	13%
Thailand	66%	19%
Sweden	68%	18%
Italy	67%	16%
France	65%	14%
Singapore	67%	14%
Germany	69%	14%
Peru	71%	16%
Philippines	75%	17%
Brazil	69%	11%
Indonesia	73%	14%
Hong Kong	73%	13%
Argentina	74%	14%
Vietnam	76%	16%
Denmark	75%	14%
Taiwan	72%	10%
Japan	70%	8%
Netherlands	74%	11%
Spain	75%	11%
Belgium	74%	10%
Colombia	82%	13%
Norway	82%	11%
Chile	82%	10%
South Korea	84%	5%
Mexico	86%	6%

Figure 28. Only Russia, Serbia, and China predicted a Trump victory in the US presidential election.

At the other end of the spectrum, it's no surprise that Mexicans were the least likely to see Trump as the winner, given his extremely strong rhetoric against Mexico, including regular run-ins with Mexico's former president, Vicente Fox (including Fox's memorable tweet 'I am not paying for that fucken wall!').

———

We saw in the previous chapter how powerfully our emotional reactions and identity shape our views of politicians and issues. This chapter has built on that, showing in turn how our political identities colour our views of reality and how we react to information—and this is a vital point to understand more broadly, not just in the context of Brexit and Trump.

We can see it in political movements and social trends across many countries. We may not have experienced the tidal wave of populism that some expected or feared at the start of 2017, but the rise of identity politics is still a real trend. This does not guarantee blocs of votes for established parties. Indeed, given the generationally driven decline in connection to just one political party for your whole life, we should expect more emergent parties, as with Five Star in Italy and En Marche in France. As we saw in the previous chapter, it's as much about who you believe really feels your pain, rather than historical connections, the veracity of what they say, or carefully weighing up the unknowable outcomes of political and economic decisions.

We need to guard against the idea that our apparent disregard of evidence is entirely new, ubiquitous, or insurmountable. Satirical magazine *The Onion* had this as a headline in 2017: 'Fearful Americans Stockpiling Facts Before Federal Government Comes to Take Them Away'.[30] It captures a sense of dangerous times, but the reality is that headline would have had just as much satirical bite over many decades. Of course, it also (playfully) underplays our role in our own ignorance and delusion: this is a long-standing issue because it reflects not only our politics or media, but also how our brains work.

There are implications for us, too, on a more personal level—in particular, being aware of the emotional stance we bring to both our decisions and our predictions of what will happen—our own wrongful and wishful thinking. The level of surprise at both Trump's victory and Brexit among the losing halves of the population reflect how pervasive these tendencies are on both sides of ideological divides, and how filtered our understanding of the world can be.

CHAPTER 8

FILTERING OUR WORLDS

The chief economist at Google—Hal Varian—has said many times that 'the sexy job in the next 10 years will be statisticians. And I'm not kidding'.[1] The fact he needs to *keep* saying it and reassure us that he's not kidding suggests that not everyone is convinced. And he'd be right in thinking that we undervalue statistical thinking: we're three times more likely to say we'd be embarrassed about our lack of skill at reading and writing than at maths.[2] Varian goes on to explain that the rise of the stats nerd (happy days for me!) is a reflection of our changing world, driven by technology that is working its way into every aspect of our lives:

> The ability to take data—to be able to understand it, to process it, to extract value from it, to visualize it, to communicate it— that's going to be a hugely important skill in the next decades.[3]

The new technology around us brings with it huge volumes of data, in a way we couldn't have imagined even a couple of decades ago. Previous technological advances did not result in anything like this quantum leap in the amount of information available for re-use and analysis, from every sphere of life.

These technological advances don't just provide a passive stream of data, to be analyzed neutrally, if we have the skills. This information is actively used to shape what we see and experience, again in a way that would have been unimaginable even a few years ago. The original view of the open, collaborative, sharing phase of the Internet was quite different. It was assumed that with so much access to information, the truth would out. Those assumptions now look incredibly naïve, given what we know about our built-in biases and heuristics: it provided the perfect environment for the opposite to happen, for our automatic impulses to take control of our better intentions, without us even really noticing.[4]

OUR ONLINE ECHO CHAMBERS

The term 'filter bubble' was coined by Upworthy chief executive and Internet activist Eli Pariser, and it refers to the interaction between our tendency to favour data that supports our worldview and the invisible algorithms that dictate what we encounter online. According to Pariser, those algorithms create 'a unique universe of information for each of us . . . which fundamentally alters the way we encounter information and ideas'.[5]

Pariser explains how Google searches bring up vastly differing results depending on the history of the user: when two people searched for 'BP' (British Petroleum), one saw news related to investing in the company, whereas the other received information about a recent oil spill. Look up a word like 'depression' on dictionary.com, and the site installs up to 223 tracking beacons on your device so that other websites can send you ads for antidepressants. At its core, surveillance is the business model that supports our largely free-of-charge Internet.[6]

Of course, we can overplay the unseen sophistication of this—which is itself an issue. Entrepreneur and author Margaret Heffernan says that part of the block that stops us tackling the very real impact that technology companies have on our lives is the sheen of complexity and precision that we mere mortals couldn't possibly hope to understand.[7] As this piece in the satirical online website *The Daily Mash* makes clear, it's not as laser-guided as is often claimed:

> The internet, we're told, is a sinister force harvesting our data to create a complete picture of our lives, precision-targeting us with adverts and all but controlling our minds. Well, all I can say is when it comes to me, they're severely underestimating what a cheap bastard I am. The sidebar on my Facebook page is basically one long avenue of over-expensive trees they're barking up. I keep seeing decking adverts. Nice try. I live in a fourth floor flat.[8]

While technology companies don't yet have full access to our innermost thoughts, the wider threat is still real: from all we've seen so far about our biases and heuristics, the possibility of distorting our view of reality is very clear. We're less bothered here about advertisements for blue pills that embarrassingly pop up when you're sharing your phone with friends.

There are much bigger issues—when our view of what's real is being shaped by algorithmic programs and our own selection of social media individuals and groups to follow, our filter bubble becomes an 'echo chamber', and we only hear ourselves and what we want to hear; we lose the shared facts that a functioning society depends on. In these circumstances, it doesn't matter whether we're thinking 'fast' or 'slow'—we are trapped in a system that feeds us only one biased version of reality.

These human tendencies are not new, and we filter our world all the time by surrounding ourselves with people and information that provide us with lovely, comforting 'cognitive consonance', as Leon Festinger called it in the fifties. But the capabilities of ourselves and others to filter reality are a million miles from his original tests that show we'll avoid magazine reviews that are critical of the car we've already chosen.

In 1962, Jürgen Habermas, a German sociologist and philosopher, argued that a healthy 'public sphere'—the real, virtual, or imagined spaces where social issues could be discussed and opinions formed—was essential for democracy, and that it needed to be inclusive. But as early as 2006 he acknowledged that 'the rise of millions of fragmented chat rooms across the world had tended instead to lead to the fragmentation of large but politically focused mass audiences into a huge number of isolated-issue publics'.[9]

This can have real consequences. Jacob Shapiro from Princeton University conducted an experiment manipulating search engine rankings on political issues and showed that biased search rankings can shift the voting preference of undecided voters by 20 per cent, without their knowing what they've seen has been manipulated.[10]

It's partly due to this potential impact that there was such concern about the revelations in March 2018 that Facebook data from millions of users may have been used, without their knowledge, in key political contests. A whistle-blower working at political consultancy Cambridge Analytica outlined how a simple personality quiz developed by a University of Cambridge academic provided a shell to allow researchers to access not just the data from the 270,000 Facebook users who took the quiz, but also *all* their Facebook friends and connections, providing a dataset of over 87 million people. This was then sold to Cambridge Analytica, which created 30 million 'psychographic' profiles from the information, which could then be used to design targeted political ads in both the EU Referendum vote and the 2016 US presidential election, working with the campaign teams in each.

Despite investigations on both sides of the Atlantic, which included Mark Zuckerberg being called to testify before the US Congress, we're unlikely to ever fully determine whether the targeting of information had any material impact on the results of these two political events—and at least some inside the Trump camp cast doubt on whether the communications strategy Cambridge Analytica built around it was as accurate or useful as claimed.[11]

However, it is just one part of a broader trend and concern, as outlined in a brilliant but terrifying paper from the Council of Europe titled 'Information Disorder'. The real concern extends well beyond election ads to 'the long-term implications of disinformation campaigns designed specifically to sow mistrust and confusion and to sharpen existing sociocultural divisions using nationalistic, ethnic, racial and religious tensions'.[12]

BuzzFeed's Craig Silverman outlined how 'in the final three months of the US presidential campaign, the 20 top-performing false election stories from hoax sites and hyper-partisan blogs generated 8,711,000 shares, reactions, and comments on Facebook. Within the same time period, the 20 best-performing election stories from 19 major news websites generated a total of 7,367,000 shares, reactions, and comments on Facebook'.[13] The relative weight of real and fake is perilously balanced.

The EU's StratCom Task Force analysis of Russian propaganda across the EU shows the strategy is to send as many conflicting messages as possible, to convince people that there are too many versions of events to find the truth. This information warfare uses all sorts of sources, from established media outlets to fringe players, with Russian generals openly admitting that 'false data' and 'destabilising propaganda' are legitimate tools in their kit. The Russian minister of defence described information as 'another type of armed forces'. Other countries are catching up on the centrality of these techniques to national security, with many, including Australia and the UK, launching or retargeting their own information warfare units.[14]

Of course, the tools may be new, but the theory is not. In 2017, Hannah Arendt's classic 752-page magnum opus from 1951, *The Origins of Totalitarianism*, temporarily sold out on Amazon, prompted partly by the widespread sharing of this quote on social media:

> The ideal subject of totalitarian rule is not the convinced Nazi or the dedicated communist, but people for whom the distinction between fact and fiction, true and false no longer exists.[15]

Arendt's analysis is much broader than the quote suggests, but she does pick out some of the current risks we face, echoing our focus on confirming our already held views and the ability of technology to provide that at a frightening scale: in totalitarian rule, the *consistency* of what we see, regardless of its veracity, determines what we believe.

The modern tool of 'digital astroturfing'—campaigns that use troll factories, click farms, and automated social media accounts—is far from only a Russian or totalitarian regime approach. One report tracked this activity and sourced it to twenty-eight countries, and for all sorts of purposes.[16]

The volume of misinformation (the inadvertent sharing of false information) and disinformation (the deliberate creation and sharing of information known to be false) is therefore a problem, for a number of reasons. First, the sheer weight of it means we are too distracted by the deluge to find the most accurate stories. But more than this, repetition brings its own credulity through the illusory truth effect of seeing the same information more than once.[17]

WE CHOOSE OUR FRIENDS TOO CAREFULLY

We know from all we've seen so far that it doesn't take these sinister interventions to lead to problems with our views of reality—we have a natural tendency to surround ourselves with information that reinforces our already held views. One of the reasons academics find it hard to identify a causal effect on opinion from the traditional media we consume is because we choose newspapers and channels that reflect our preexisting opinions. The same applies online, with endless studies showing we herd together in how we follow and friend.

It's such a concern that even Barack Obama used part of his presidential farewell speech to highlight the risks:

> Increasingly, we become so secure in our bubbles that we start accepting only information, whether it's true or not, that fits our opinions, instead of basing our opinions on the evidence that is out there.[18]

In many ways, our online existence is designed with this confirmation bias at its heart: it strives to give us the pleasure we feel in seeing information that confirms our already existing views. It does its best to strip out anything that causes the discomfort of dissonance—otherwise we'll click away and on to the next thing.

James Carey, a communications theorist at the University of Illinois, emphasizes the 'ritualistic' function of communication, that it plays a fundamental role in representing shared beliefs between people and groups. We often focus on the 'transmission' role of communication—imparting information—when it has an equally important ritualistic function in which a particular worldview is portrayed and confirmed, saying as much about who we are.[19]

It's this ritualistic aspect of communication that is critical for understanding how and why individuals react to messages in different ways. As the Council of Europe paper outlined, the types of information we consume, and the ways in which we make sense of them, are significantly impacted by our self-identity and the 'tribes' we associate with. In a world where what we like, comment on, and share is visible to our friends, family, and colleagues, these 'social' forces are more powerful than ever.

We are encouraged to 'perform' to be rewarded by 'likes', comments, and shares. We tend to like or share things on social media that our friends or followers would expect us to like or share. We are social animals, where our perceptions of norms have a powerful effect on our own views and behaviours, even where we're wrong in thinking it *is* the norm, as we saw with examples of our pluralistic ignorance. We have social desirability biases, where we unconsciously engage in 'impression management', presenting an image of ourselves that we think will result in others' approval.

The results from the questions we asked on technology provide clear evidence of how skewed our view of the world can be, because we generalize from what we see. This is not only on fevered issues of identity politics; even our estimation of basic facts, like how many of us have access to the Internet, betrays how filtered our view of the world really is.

ONLINE, ALL THE TIME

The social and economic value of Internet access is hard to overstate. Every sphere of life is affected, and it is embedded so far into most of our lives that its centrality has become difficult to see. One study showed that closing the access gap between countries in the less developed world and the rest of the world would add 140 million new jobs and save 2.5 million lives, due solely to the link between health literacy and mortality.[20] In that context, it is easy to lose sight of the fact that around half the world still does not have access to the Internet.

What would you answer to this question: 'Out of every 100 people in your country, about how many have access to the Internet?' As we'll see, in Figure 29, there is real variety in access around the world, and that's mirrored in the errors in our guesses. In fact, the countries are about evenly split between those guessing too high (sometimes ridiculously high) and those guessing too low.

India stands out as particularly deluded about Internet access. The average guess was that 60 per cent of all Indians had access to the Internet, when the reality at the time (in 2016) was just 19 per cent. Internet use is, of course, expanding quickly in such a fast-developing country, and at the time of writing, it's up to about 25 per cent. But that is still a long, long way from 60 per cent. Other countries, particularly in less developed markets like Peru and China, also overestimated Internet access significantly.

At the other end, Israel guessed too low at 60 per cent, when it was actually 76 per cent, and then a series of countries with close to universal access also guessed a bit too low, thinking it was more around 80 per cent.

This latter group of errors is likely to be most related to psychophysics explanations: that people think they're picking a big number, but it's just not quite big enough because of our tendency to underestimate big things and hedge back towards the middle.

However, the more interesting and important points are at the other end of the chart, and particularly with the Indian data. No amount of psychophysics hedging can explain the average guess in India—there is a different explanation for this significant bias. Our survey was conducted online, so, by definition, everyone who answered it had Internet access, even in countries with low Internet penetration. Therefore, respondents in places like India were more unusual and less representative of their full populations than

Q. Out of every 100 people, about how many do you think have access to the Internet at home either through a computer or mobile device?

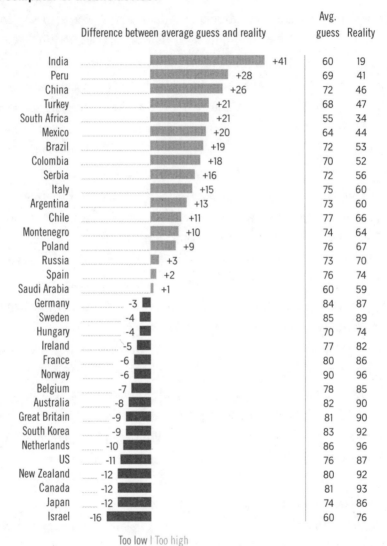

	Difference between average guess and reality	Avg. guess	Reality
India	+41	60	19
Peru	+28	69	41
China	+26	72	46
Turkey	+21	68	47
South Africa	+21	55	34
Mexico	+20	64	44
Brazil	+19	72	53
Colombia	+18	70	52
Serbia	+16	72	56
Italy	+15	75	60
Argentina	+13	73	60
Chile	+11	77	66
Montenegro	+10	74	64
Poland	+9	76	67
Russia	+3	73	70
Spain	+2	76	74
Saudi Arabia	+1	60	59
Germany	-3	84	87
Sweden	-4	85	89
Hungary	-4	70	74
Ireland	-5	77	82
France	-6	80	86
Norway	-6	90	96
Belgium	-7	78	85
Australia	-8	82	90
Great Britain	-9	81	90
South Korea	-9	83	92
Netherlands	-10	86	96
US	-11	76	87
New Zealand	-12	80	92
Canada	-12	81	93
Japan	-12	74	86
Israel	-16	60	76

Too low | Too high

Figure 29. People in less developed countries overestimated the proportion of people who have Internet access, whereas in more developed countries the opposite was true.

places where Internet access is more widely available. (Focusing on this connected group is much more of interest to many of the businesses we work with, not just because of their greater affluence, but because they set the trends that ripple out. Of course, this is not at all to dismiss that bulk of the population who are not yet online, whom we regularly survey in our social research studies.)

While this means we need to be clear that the Indian survey data is only representative of this emergent, connected middle class, this has a helpful side effect in pointing to another important bias in how we think. This subset of the Indian population thought that the rest of the country was much more like them than they really are: our respondents all had access to the Internet, and the people they interact with regularly were more likely to have access to the Internet—and so they assumed that many more of the general population had access to the Internet than actually did.

This is related to what social psychologists call the 'false consensus effect'—people tend to see their own behavioural choices and judgements as relatively common, while viewing alternative responses as uncommon. We generalize from our own situation, thinking others are more like us than they really are. This effect is usually applied to beliefs and attitudes—that we think others agree with our opinions more than they really do—but it applies to behaviours too.

The effect was demonstrated brilliantly by Lee Ross at Stanford University in the seventies. He asked students to wear mildly embarrassing signs that read 'Eat at Joes' or 'Repent' (wonderfully evocative of the time!) and walk round a route on campus, on the pretence that they should make notes of reactions. The task was explained to the students, and they were told they didn't have to do it; they would still get course credit either way.

Some did and some didn't (I would have fled; I was way too cool and/or insecure), but then the real experiment took place.

He asked the students to rate whether they thought other people would do the task, and 60 per cent to 70 per cent of the students thought that others would agree with their choice, regardless of what that choice was.

This might seem an elaborate way to demonstrate that people tend to think others are like them, but Ross needed people to make a real choice about a behaviour that had some consequences, not just a theoretical one.

In our example, the influential Indian middle class appears to have no idea just how rare Internet access is for the bulk of their fellow citizens. This sort of miscalculation will inevitably affect how they view the urgency of expanding Internet access more widely, and how important an issue it is to ensure that people who currently have no access are not left behind from the opportunities these connections bring.

It also links to a broader point—that we struggle to realise that not all groups have access to the same information as us. For example, immigrants coming to the United States and UK do not see nearly as much coverage of the 'hostile environment' that has been created as residents in those countries do. Immigrants' decisions to still come can therefore seem strange, even suspicious to some. Of course, decisions to migrate are based on a complex set of factors, not least a desperation that may trump any information, but our misplaced assumption of equal knowledge is still an important driver of misunderstanding.

BRINGING THE WORLD CLOSER TOGETHER?

The importance that humans place on social connection is core to the success of Facebook. Its first mission statement was 'Making the world more open and connected'. Mark Zuckerberg changed this in 2017 to 'Give people the power to build community and bring the world closer together', to provide a greater sense of purpose and explain why connection is beneficial.[21]

This urge to connect has helped make Facebook a barely imaginable behemoth. There are around 2.2 billion monthly users, which is approaching 30 per cent of the world's entire population, and 1.4 billion log in *each day*. And this is still growing—daily use at the end of 2017 showed a 14 per cent increase over 2016.[22] Zuckerberg himself has said, 'In a lot of ways Facebook is more like a government than a traditional company'.[23]

The Cambridge Analytica scandal, along with others in 2018, put Facebook in the headlines for all the wrong reasons.[24] But the #deletefacebook movement did not catch on as strongly as it seemed it might early in the year. It is completely unsurprising that even this level and consistency of scandal had a limited impact on overall global usage of the platform, given how intertwined it is with many of our lives.[25]

Does this dominance affect our view of how many people are Facebook users? As Figure 30 shows, it seems that's very much the case, with huge overestimations in every country. This scale of error is not the result of automatic rescaling, but our biased view of the prevalence of Facebook.

The more extreme errors tend to be in countries similar to those that overestimated Internet access. Most remarkably, online Indians thought that 64 per cent of all Indians had a Facebook account, when it was really only 8 per cent. Clearly, this will be directly related to the image they have of Indians as being much more online than they really are, but still this was one of the largest gaps in perceptions we've measured.

The eagle-eyed among you may have spotted that this means Indians think that more people have Facebook accounts than have Internet access, which clearly isn't possible. But this may be partly because the two sets of findings were taken from different surveys, with the Facebook question asked a year later. Our Indian respondents may have picked up on the rapid expansion of online access, even if they're completely wrong on its scale.

However, it's not just low Internet access countries that were very wrong. Germans, for example, thought 72 per cent of their fellow citizens had a Facebook account, when the reality was barely half that at 34 per cent. No country was within 15 percentage points of the real figure for their country.

There are some interesting particular cases—for example, in Russia and China. Russia has its own version of Facebook in vk.com, which, among other advantages, works with the Cyrillic alphabet, and so Facebook itself hasn't taken hold in quite the same way: our Russian respondents estimated that around half of Russians had a Facebook account, when actually only 6 per cent did. The situation in China is quite different, as Facebook has been banned in the mainland since 2009, with some linking that move to the riots that broke out in the northwest province of Xinjiang in July that year. Despite years of Facebook courting Chinese officials, this is still the case, with senior Facebook managers saying they no longer see a way forward in China, and as Facebook pivots the platform to be more focused on ensuring privacy. In that context, it's fascinating that our respondents thought that as many as 20 per cent were getting round that ban, when the real figure was (supposedly) only 0.1 per cent.

Aside from these very particular circumstances, the explanations for how wrong we are will be similar to those for our misestimations about Internet penetration—we have a tendency to think that 'all we see is all there is', and so we generalize from our experience to others'.

There is more going on here, though—in particular, the utter dominance of Facebook in social networks, mirroring Google's dominance in Internet searches. Between them, these two sources account for 75 per cent of referral traffic to top digital publishers (e.g., news, sports, 'lifestyle' articles).[26]

We saw in earlier chapters how we're generally likely to think we're luckier and more skilled than the average when we think

Q. Out of every 100 people aged 13 and over in your country, about how many do you think have a Facebook account?

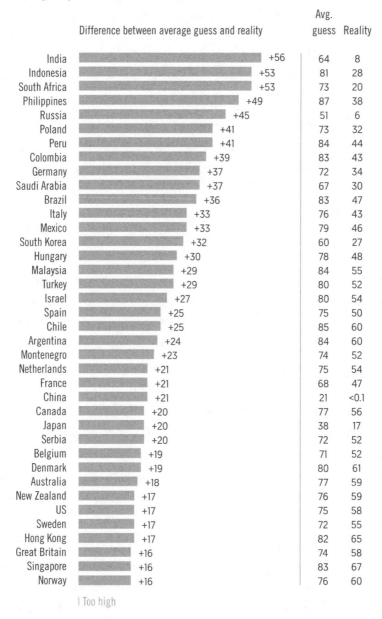

	Difference between average guess and reality	Avg. guess	Reality
India	+56	64	8
Indonesia	+53	81	28
South Africa	+53	73	20
Philippines	+49	87	38
Russia	+45	51	6
Poland	+41	73	32
Peru	+41	84	44
Colombia	+39	83	43
Germany	+37	72	34
Saudi Arabia	+37	67	30
Brazil	+36	83	47
Italy	+33	76	43
Mexico	+33	79	46
South Korea	+32	60	27
Hungary	+30	78	48
Malaysia	+29	84	55
Turkey	+29	80	52
Israel	+27	80	54
Spain	+25	75	50
Chile	+25	85	60
Argentina	+24	84	60
Montenegro	+23	74	52
Netherlands	+21	75	54
France	+21	68	47
China	+21	21	<0.1
Canada	+20	77	56
Japan	+20	38	17
Serbia	+20	72	52
Belgium	+19	71	52
Denmark	+19	80	61
Australia	+18	77	59
New Zealand	+17	76	59
US	+17	75	58
Sweden	+17	72	55
Hong Kong	+17	82	65
Great Britain	+16	74	58
Singapore	+16	83	67
Norway	+16	76	60

| Too high

Figure 30. Every country significantly overestimated the proportion of their population with Facebook accounts, with some incredibly high estimates, particularly in India, Indonesia, and South Africa.

about positive outcomes and attributes. This chapter points to the dangers of the mirror effect: we need to be careful to avoid thinking that what we do and what we see is the norm, or all there is.

BURSTING OUR BUBBLE

This brings us back to the bigger challenge of how our world has become so filtered, and the implications of this on how we see reality. The most terrifying aspect is that we're only at the beginning: the real challenge is the accelerating pace of change, and how far behind the curve we are in mitigating its impact.

For example, much of the concern among politicians and the media has been focused on text-based disinformation, controlling and correcting claims in 'fake news' articles. But we already know that visuals are often the most shared, and that we process them at much greater speed than text. For example, a team of neuroscientists at the Massachusetts Institute of Technology found that we can process entire images that we see for as little as thirteen milliseconds—and as a result, our critical reasoning skills are less likely to engage when we see rather than read.[27]

The video and sound manipulation approaches that are coming will dwarf the simple photo editing features offered by Photoshop-like apps and meme factories. For example, researchers at the University of Washington used artificial intelligence programs to create completely fake but visually convincing videos of Barack Obama. The researchers fed a neural network seventeen hours of footage from the former president's weekly addresses as 'training data'. The resulting algorithm can generate mouth shapes from Obama's voice and overlay them onto Obama's face in an entirely different video.[28] Similar technology, including an extremely simple tool called FakeApp, is already freely available, and its main use so far has (predictably) been to manipulate pornographic videos, replacing actresses' faces with those of more famous celebrities, and (also predictably, given this is the Internet) to insert Nicolas Cage into films he's not actually in.[29]

Audio can be manipulated even more easily than video. Adobe has prototyped a program called VoCo (nicknamed 'the Photoshop for voice'), which enables users to feed short clips of someone's voice into the application, and then allows them to generate new words in a sound-alike voice.

Taken together, these developments clearly have more serious political implications than faked 'revenge porn' videos. The ability to entirely fabricate what people say and do it in a convincing way could take disinformation to another level.

Of course, we're not utterly helpless in the face of these technological leaps preying on our built-in biases. Actions are being taken by governments, platforms, and others—and more serious actions seem possible in light of the Facebook–Cambridge Analytica revelations, and others that came to light over the course of 2018. By controlling access to their advertising rosters and embedding third-party fact-checking approaches, Facebook and Google have taken some steps to discourage manipulative disinformation. They have both tried to prick our filter bubbles with 'related articles' features and similar approaches, and we know this can help to some extent. Experimental research by Leticia Bode and Emily Vraga at the University of Wisconsin–Madison in 2015 suggested that when a Facebook post that includes misinformation is immediately contextualized in their 'related stories' feature underneath, its influence is significantly reduced. Identifying misleading information quickly, getting in early, and providing alternative narrative accounts really can help.[30]

Ultimately, though, it's difficult to imagine social media platforms voluntarily making such substantial changes to their approaches that these alone will pop our filter bubbles. More challenging material, forcing us to reconsider some of our established worldviews, is likely to make us spend less time on their platforms, which in turn means less advertising revenue. In fact, Facebook has admitted that when they have attempted to deliver more content from an opposite view, people tend not to click on it.

We have undoubtedly seen an explosion of 'fact-checking' more generally in recent years: the Council of Europe report listed thirty-four permanent fact-checking operations in twenty countries in Europe alone.[31] It is important work. Certainly, evidence suggests that fact-checks do tend to nudge individuals' knowledge in the direction of the correct information, particularly when this is done well, providing not just facts but explaining the broader context, telling us more of the story.

Of course, providing the correct information after the event is not the sole, or increasingly even the main, ambition of fact-checking. This is what fact-checkers call 'first generation'. Full Fact, the largest independent fact-checker in the UK, has described the move towards 'third generation fact-checking'. The second generation, where we mostly are now, is more focused on behaviour change, attempting to get producers and publishers to correct the information at source, using the evidence from previous fact-checks to campaign for changes, and training for journalists, politicians, and others in how to use information accurately. The third generation is nascent and, as well as the above, is focused on getting fact-checks embedded in real time, ensuring they can be used and reused easily, such as through their and others' work with Google.[32] The key aim is to change the system and, failing that, get in first. In a report on Russian propaganda, researchers argue that one of the most effective ways of tackling misinformation is to inoculate users, or to 'forewarn audiences of mis-information, or merely reach them first with the truth, rather than retracting or refuting false "facts."'[33]

Even this broader push won't be enough on its own. The complexity of the challenge is reflected in the fact that the Council of Europe report included thirty-four recommendations for action, calling on technology companies, governments, media organisations, education ministries, funding bodies, and researchers all to play a role. The range of actions will need to be multifaceted, too, not just relying on technological solutions. No one approach will do it.

For example, regulation may seem underused and a tempting lever to pull. Billionaire investor and philanthropist George Soros gave a speech at Davos in 2018 that pulled no punches on the impact of social media companies and the need for regulatory action. He described them as a 'menace', with no real inclination to protect society, and that they

> influence how people think and behave without them even being aware of it. This has far-reaching adverse consequences on the functioning of democracy, particularly on the integrity of elections. . . . It takes a real effort to assert and defend what John Stuart Mill called 'the freedom of mind'. There is a possibility that once lost, people who grow up in the digital age will have difficulty in regaining it.[34]

But there are also dangers of overregulation. Governments may end up controlling who sees what or arbitrating 'the truth'. This rightly gives people reason to pause. As social media and Internet companies' increasing focus on self-regulation might suggest, there are routes to put more pressure on them without necessarily legislating what is true. For example, in a key piece of US regulation, there is one sentence that says, 'No provider or user of an interactive computer service shall be treated as the publisher or speaker of any information provided by another information content provider'.[35] And James Naughton wrote in *Prospect* magazine, 'Careful redrafting of this Section could—at a stroke—oblige social media companies to accept some degree of responsibility for what appears on their sites'.[36]

We will never be able to entirely regulate away disinformation. So another approach is to encourage 'news literacy' programmes, including integrating core elements into national curricula. These would not just focus on technical skills and knowledge (on what to look for in reputable and less reputable sources, how algorithms work, or statistical numeracy), but the much more important and difficult to deal with tendency of allowing our emotional responses and tribal identities to override our critical faculties.

Although training in these critical thinking abilities—to override many of our evolutionary biases—is incredibly difficult and, by itself, insufficient, it's impossible to see how we can improve the situation without it. Our delusions are as much about how we think as what we're told, and all current and coming dangers to our grip on reality make improving our skills one of the most important and urgent social challenges of our time.

To be effective, this needs to start early, in schools. And there are some encouraging moves being made. For example, Italy has introduced 'detecting fake news' as an addition to the national curriculum in a pilot of 8,000 schools, alongside reading, writing, and language classes in secondary school.[37] In the UK, the BBC is working with 1,000 schools to guide and mentor children in news literacy, promoting online materials and classroom activities, alongside a Reality Check Roadshow that will tour the country.[38] These moves are encouraging, but not nearly enough, particularly when there is emerging evidence that better techniques can be learned.

For example, a recent study at Stanford University reviewed how ten PhD historians, ten professional fact-checkers, and twenty-five Stanford undergraduates evaluated live websites and searched for information on social and political issues. They found that the historians and students often fell for the easily manipulated features of fake websites, such as professional-looking logos. Even though these were well-educated groups, they tended to stay within websites, while fact-checkers took a much more lateral approach, opening multiple tabs to quickly gather external views of the veracity of the information. The fact-checkers came to the correct conclusions in a fraction of the time it took the other groups. It can seem that 'popping' your filter bubble is just a high-minded ideal, for people to boast at dinner parties about their new app that pulls stories from both the *New York Times* and Fox News and shows they're keeping an open mind. But it's much more than that: using multiple sources is the best way to quickly sniff out deluding information.

Of course, we can't all be fact-checkers in all aspects of our lives (that would be exhausting), and it will not work for everyone, but these sorts of new practical skills and habits will become increasingly important in the future. The scale of the disinformation challenge and the threats it brings mean we will undoubtedly need action from everyone involved in online communication, but given the issue has a lot to do with how we think, we can't rely on others to do it all for us.

CHAPTER 9

WORLDWIDE WORRY

International development is beset by confusion, angst, and contradictions, among those who work in the sector, let alone the public. Even what you call it is controversial and laden with meaning: 'aid' and 'development' suggest a patrician-like one-way relationship, where richer countries are helping out poorer countries, with no benefit flowing the other way and no reference to the historical exploitation of poorer countries by 'donors'. This complexity is part of the reason why the general population view development activities with a mix of sympathy, suspicion, and resentment, as seen in polling of our attitudes and misperceptions.

'Foreign aid' is regularly the first item of government spending that people want to see reduced: it's no surprise politicians regularly use threats to cut it to show that they are focusing on their 'own people' first. The general sense is that nothing much is changing as a result of the money being spent: repeated appeals and new crises lead to doubts about the impact of aid. This is despite us having an overblown sense of what is actually being spent. For example, in the United States the public think that foreign aid spending takes up 31 per cent of the federal budget, when it's well under 1 per cent, and in the UK, 26 per cent of people thought that spending on overseas aid was one of the three largest areas of the government's budget, when it was in fact one of the smallest.[1]

So far we've been almost exclusively looking at our understanding of country-level realities, but we can also apply the same approach to global realities, to help understand how we see the world and how it's changing. Given the evident confusion, it's no surprise that we're very wrong about global trends in lots of important ways.

Our delusions about global development have been a particular focus for Gapminder, an independent Swedish foundation set up by Anna Rosling Rönnlund, Ola Rosling, and Hans Rosling in 2005. There's a very high chance you've seen Hans or Ola present some of this data in truly inspiring ways. Hans's TED Talk, 'The Best Statistics You've Never Seen', is (ironically) now one of the most viewed ever, and helped him become one of the first bona fide statistical stars of the modern age before his death in early 2017. The combination of statistical analysis and storytelling is a joy to watch, and the tactics to reduce our delusions, which Gapminder continues to champion, remain vitally important.[2] A sense that nothing can be done or everything is getting worse leads not only to apathy and inaction, but also to rejecting things that are working to at least some extent.

GLOBAL POVERTY AND HEALTH

This undue negativity is very much the pattern suggested by our view of some key trends, including how extreme poverty is changing around the world. What would be your answer to whether the percentage of people living in extreme poverty over the last twenty years has almost doubled, remained more or less the same, or almost halved? If you are anything like the population across the twelve countries we asked this in, you were probably very wrong. On average, only 9 per cent correctly said it had halved.

Sweden stood out as the best informed, with 27 per cent getting it right. Is it a coincidence that Sweden is the home of Gapminder, where the Roslings are national figures? It is very possible that it's part of the explanation, as their analysis does get incredible coverage in their home country. They regularly take free teaching materials into schools and workplaces to 'dismantle misconceptions and promote a fact-based worldview'.[3] It would be a remarkable achievement to shift delusion on a national scale, but there is evidence that this is a factor: in a follow-up survey among those Swedes who got various facts correct, when asked how they knew the right answers, 'Hans Rosling' was a common response.[4] Of course, as we've seen, the Swedes are often pretty good at estimating all sorts of realities.

Most countries, however, are hopelessly wrong, with Spain and Hungary at the other end of the spectrum: only 4 per cent of Hungarians thought that extreme poverty had halved, and 71 per cent of Spaniards thought it had doubled. In some ways these are easier questions than many we've looked at so far, as we give people only three options to choose from. As the Gapminder team points out, that means that if people were just choosing randomly, 33 per cent should pick the right answer. In fact, as Hans and Ola have so memorably presented, this suggests we know 'less about the world than chimpanzees', because 'if for each question I wrote each of the possible alternatives on bananas, and asked chimpanzees in the zoo to pick the right answers by picking the right bananas, they'd just pick bananas at random'.[5] The point this makes, of course, is that we're wrong not just because we're uncertain and choose blindly; we're wrong because we have a biased

Q. What has happened to the percentage of people living in extreme poverty over the last 20 years?

Figure 31. Just one in ten correctly identified that extreme poverty has halved in the last twenty years.

view. And that bias is almost always in a negative direction for the majority of the population in all countries (even Sweden).

That's the root of the explanations for this delusion. We have all heard terrible stories about poverty, and no matter how much progress is made, the same individual and mass tragedies seem to be happening. Our attention is drawn to these harrowing examples of negative information, and we don't notice the positive—or we are not able to find it, because progress doesn't get reported nearly as much as disasters.

The same applies to our perceptions of key aspects of global healthcare, including the extent to which children around the world have access to vaccinations. There has been a very quiet revolution in the reach of vaccines, with incredible benefits for global health. In 1980, when measles vaccination was down below 20 per cent of the population, the number of cases globally each year was over 4 million. But by 2009, when immunisation was around 80 per cent to 90 per cent (depending on which figures you believe), the number of cases fell to around 250,000.[6]

However, we are still way too pessimistic about vaccinations' reach. When asked what percentage of the world's one-year-old children today have been vaccinated against at least some diseases, the average guess across twenty-five countries was under 40 per cent, when it's actually 85 per cent—over twice the average guess.

Many countries were miles out. The average guess in Japan was just 19 per cent, and in South Korea and France the average guess was barely a quarter. Even if we adjust these sorts of guesses for our tendency to hedge towards the middle of the range, as suggested by psychophysics, we're still (mostly) miles out.

Some countries were significantly closer to the reality, though—most notably African countries like Senegal, Kenya, and Nigeria, as well as India. They still guessed too low in their raw estimates, but it's interesting that they were the least wrong. This is probably partly because the stereotypical mental image of poor availability of all medicine in poorer countries is countered by reality in these countries. Respondents in Japan were no doubt partly thinking that vaccinations are rarer in countries that are at an earlier stage of development, and that they make up a lot of the world's population—and therefore the leap was made to a very low figure.

Part of the explanation for our low guessing could be that the question asked about vaccination against 'some' disease, not what proportion of one-year-olds have had *all* the vaccinations that could be available. We all remember tragic cases where disease has spread because vaccinations are not available in poorer countries, and how the prices charged by pharmaceutical companies has meant some can't be afforded.[7] These true and compelling stories will help us to miss what we're actually being asked.

As we've seen, negative information is attention-grabbing—it is literally processed differently in our brains—whereas positive progress is mostly gradual and incremental. We're not nearly as adept at spotting these trends as sudden and eye-catching disasters. Max Roser from the University of Oxford points out that newspapers could have legitimately run the headline, 'Number of people in extreme poverty fell by 137,000 since yesterday' *every day* for the last *twenty-five years*.[8] But, as we've seen from academics' detailed analysis of news values and criteria, the predictable isn't newsworthy, because that's how our brains work: we get the media we deserve and, to some extent, crave.

This is the negative payoff of rosy retrospection—it may protect us against obsessing over past failings or bad experiences, but it makes us overly negative about the present. Steven Pinker, a psychology professor at Harvard, explains:

> Time heals most wounds: the negative coloring of bad experiences fades with the passing of years. . . . As the columnist Franklin Pierce Adams pointed out 'Nothing is more responsible for the good old days than a bad memory.'[9]

Indeed, this is likely to be part of the explanation for why we're more wrong on global characteristics and change than on facts about our own countries. Our distance from direct information leaves space not only for uncertainty but bias, based on stereotyping and all the other mental quirks and external prompts that push us towards thinking the worst.

As Pinker outlines in his book *The Better Angels of Our Nature,* our standards also shift.[10] We judge governments or economic systems as falling short of standards we expect *now,* but this loses sight of the fact that those standards are shifting all the time. For example, we're outraged by examples of torture that were commonplace not that long ago.

Our incorrect view that things are getting worse has consequences. As Gapminder points out, it is stressful, causing us misplaced anxiety, and often leads to bad decisions on a global scale.

IT'S ALL GOING WRONG

Our negativity is writ large in responses to a question on whether people think the world is getting better or worse. Given all we've seen so far, you are probably not surprised that it's not a hugely optimistic picture. But if you hadn't been through this book, your first thought might have been that this is such a ludicrously broad question that people would prevaricate. They might legitimately say 'I don't know' and query how to come to one view of this 200 million square mile planet with 7 billion inhabitants. Or they could wonder which particular aspects we're thinking of—economics, the environment, politics, social issues, etc.

However, people didn't fence-sit at all—their verdict was clear: we're screwed. Only one in ten thought the world was getting better, one in five were not sure, but 68 per cent thought it was getting worse. The Swedes were the most positive (again), but my god, pity the Belgians, only 3 per cent of whom thought the world was getting better, with 83 per cent thinking it was getting worse.

It became something of a trope in 2016 (when we asked this question) to suggest and then endlessly list why that particular year was the worst year ever. The catalogue of woes was

Q. Which of these is closest to your views? The world is...

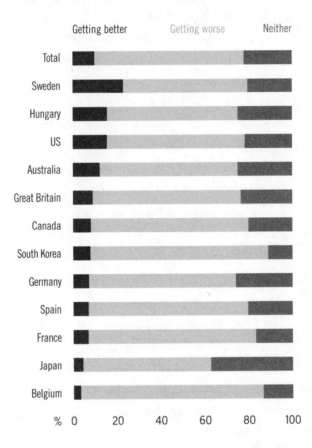

Figure 32. Only 10 per cent thought the world was getting better, but the Swedes were more positive.

significant, from unsettling political shifts and horrific terrorist attacks to failed coups and a catalogue of celebrity deaths (leading to one memorable tweet: 'I'm not saying that David Bowie was holding the fabric of the universe together, but *gestures broadly at everything*').[11]

There is a lot more to be cheerful about now than we might immediately think. Deaths from terrorist attacks are lower in recent years than at the end of the twentieth century in the vast majority of countries. It's the same for murder rates. The proportion of the world's population living in extreme poverty fell below 10 per cent for the first time in the last couple of years. Global carbon emissions from fossil fuels have failed to rise for the third year running (okay, that doesn't mean climate change is solved, but it's still a positive shift). The death penalty has been removed from more than half of countries. Child mortality is roughly half what it had been as recently as 1990. Looking further back, in 1900 worldwide life expectancy was only thirty-one due to early adult death and rampant child mortality; now it's seventy-one. Three hundred thousand people are gaining access to electricity each day. Even the giant panda has been removed from the list of endangered species.[12]

It's this sense that we've become too pessimistic that's given rise to a 'new optimist' countermovement—a disparate group that is trying to present a more positive picture of how the world is changing, and how it can be shifted further.

The media's reaction to this new optimism is (ironically) often pretty negative. The key criticisms are (1) that pointing to progress lets us off the hook on how much further we still have to go, and (2) imagine what could have been achieved if we had changed things more radically: global poverty may have declined significantly, but we could surely have eradicated it if we'd really tried. The charge is that this optimism leads to a sense of complacency that progress is guaranteed, which is particularly risky in an increasingly interconnected and dangerous world.

From all we've seen so far on how people actually perceive social realities and change, this seems much less of a risk than the opposite—our tendency to overly focus on the negative, and feel overwhelmed by the sense that nothing can be improved.

ONE VERSUS MANY

Paul Slovic, a professor of psychology at the University of Oregon, has studied what he termed 'psychic numbing' for decades, which is where the scale of tragedies or need for help drives us to inaction:

> Most people are caring and will exert great effort to rescue 'the one' whose plight comes to their attention. But these same people often become numbly indifferent to the plight of 'the one' who is 'one of many' in a much greater problem. Why do good people ignore mass murder and genocide? Specifically, it is our inability to comprehend numbers and relate them to mass human tragedy that stifles our ability to act.[13]

This taps into the connection we feel with an individual and how distant and powerless we can feel when confronted with tragedies at scale. Slovic explored the practical impact of this in groundbreaking experiments, which involved asking people to donate to help children in West Africa. One of his groups was asked to give aid to a seven-year-old girl named Rokia. A second group was asked to donate to help millions of hungry children. And a third group was asked to help Rokia, but was also provided with statistical information that set out more context on the situation in the country. Given what we've already seen, we're probably not surprised that people donated more than twice as much to help Rokia as to help millions of children. What's maybe more surprising and distressing is that providing the background information on African hunger diminished willingness to help Rokia.[14]

It isn't just adding millions to the equation that affected willingness to donate; adding just one extra child did. In a different experiment, some people were asked again to donate to Rokia and some were asked to donate to a boy, Moussa, in the same situation. In each case, people donated generously to both. But when people were asked to donate to them *together*, with their pictures side by side, donations decreased. Slovic found that our willingness to help decreases when the number of victims moves from one to two. As he puts it, 'The more who die, the less we care'.[15] There are similar findings from many other variants of these experiments.

We respond more to emotion than facts. So we should not be surprised that sadness also works as a motivator for us. Sad facial expressions in pictures of victims produced much greater donation responses than happy or neutral images. Researchers suggest this is achieved through 'emotional contagion', where viewers 'caught' vicariously the emotions on the victim's face.[16]

People use distinct processes to make judgements about specific instances as opposed to general targets. Our processing of the needs of individuals is more emotionally engaging, whereas statistics elicit a more deliberative response. The greater the deliberative thinking, the more emotional engagement is overridden and donations go down.[17]

This is the double edge that charities working with the most in need struggle with. They know they can push sadness buttons to get people to donate, but it can be a fleeting response. They need the money to do good, so it's tempting to keep pushing that button. However, once people are flooded with pictures of desperate children, it can leave long-term engagement and more active support cold: that needs to be reinforced with a sense of progress and success.

For example, another experiment showed that people are willing to pay for a water treatment facility to save 4,500 lives in a refugee camp with 11,000 people in it—but they are much less willing to pay for the same sort of facility, saving the same number of lives, when it's in a camp with 250,000 refugees. Saving a large proportion feels like success, and saving a small proportion, a failure. And failure doesn't feel good. We know from a large body of other research that one of the key drivers of altruism is this personal reward of satisfaction.[18] Doing good can literally be its own (psychic) reward, but only if we feel we've achieved something.

FEEL THE FEAR

This is not to say that some sense of fear for the future is always a bad thing, for all forms of action and all people. This was highlighted in the reaction to a 2017 article on climate change by David Wallace-Wells in *New York* magazine. 'The Uninhabitable Earth' painted a horrifying worst-case scenario for the impact of global warming.[19] It was the most read story in the magazine's history, which may not be surprising when you remember our deep-seated attraction to negative information and then look at the headings of the subsections: The Bahraining of New York, The End of Food, Climate Plagues, Unbreathable Air, Perpetual War, Permanent Economic Collapse, and Poisoned Oceans.

A lot of the reaction to the piece from climate change experts was that stoking fear was unhelpful. One *Washington Post* op-ed by climate scientists, headlined 'Doomsday scenarios are as harmful as climate change denial', said, fear 'does not motivate, and appealing to it is often counter-productive as it tends to distance people from the problem, leading them to disengage, doubt and even dismiss it'.[20] At first glance, this seems to broadly align with what we've seen—a sense of efficacy and agency is important to action, particularly when we're distant from the issue and therefore have to rely on reports rather than see and experience the impact ourselves. But there are three points that qualify this. First, social psychology suggests that emotions are not separate states experienced distinctly; they are instead always in interplay with one another and the context. And this shifts over time, depending on what we see and the reinforcement or contradictory information we receive (which is why repetition is so important in communications). We don't fully understand how emotions impact on action in the real world, and that's reflected in some mixed evidence: concluding that 'fear is bad' and 'hope is good' is way too simplistic.

Second, part of the reason for the contradictory evidence will be, as we've seen throughout this book, that it's not possible to generalize to everyone—people react in different ways to facts, emotions, and the mix between the two. I agree with David Roberts, a writer on climate change, that it's not been demonstrated that fear has no role at all to play in action: 'humans are complicated and diverse and need all sorts of narratives, images, facts, tropes and other forms of group reinforcement to really get something this big'.[21] One size does not fit all.

And third, many of us are still not getting the message on how extraordinary recent climatic conditions have been. In our 2018 study, we asked people how many of the last eighteen years have seen the hottest global temperatures since records began in 1961. The frightening reality is that the correct answer is seventeen. But the average guess across the thirty-seven countries we asked the question was only nine. We could do with a little more fear.

This is not contradictory with the view that we should generally be more positive about the change that has happened, and what might be possible in the future. Wallace-Wells's piece was deliberately a worst-case scenario, but drawn from verified expert analysis—and he concludes by noting that most of the climate change scientists he talked to were, despite everything, optimistic about our ingenuity in ensuring we find a way to avoid that doomsday.

———

I believe the 'new optimism' movement is an important balancing factor and that a lot of the criticism of the perspective misses the point, by questioning whether we should really be so content about what has been achieved. The idea is the opposite: to encourage more action, by countering an overblown sense that all is already lost, as we've seen in so many of our findings. This does not mean that only hope works, and people are incapable of reacting positively to fear. But, as we've seen, on many issues, we already have a strong sense of the challenges we face. It's not at all surprising that in a global poll we conducted, 61 per cent of people agreed they 'hear much more about the negative impacts of climate change than I do about progress towards reducing climate change', whereas only 19 per cent disagreed with this.[22]

There are other important reasons to have a more realistic and fact-based view of how far the world has improved. First, because in many respects it's true. Rather than trying to socially engineer responses based on a shaky understanding of the precise connection between different emotional reactions and our actions, being open about the progress we've made is altogether more ethical and doesn't rule out that we still face massive challenges, particularly on climate change.

Second, a bit more understanding of the good that's been achieved is a benefit to our own psychic health.

CHAPTER 10

WHO'S MOST WRONG?

> 'We graciously accept this medal on behalf of the
> Italian people. We are a proud nation, but we are
> not offended by this award. Because we're also an
> emotional nation, one that lives in bright colours and
> with big gestures. And that, I think, partly reflects why
> we're so often so wrong. But we do it with style'.

We're at the dog-end of our annual conference of Ipsos social scientists in London. There are around fifty heads of research teams from around the world in a stuffy conference room, and we've been here for two days straight. It doesn't feel, or smell, great—that unique odour of over-breathed air mixed with curling sandwiches from lunch.

It's safe to say, you'd be hard-pushed to find a room full of more jaded international social scientists anywhere in London at that point. But there is at least the prize-giving to look forward to. We don't give a prize for the best research project. No, we give a prize for the most wrong country on our Perils of Perception study. It's the first year we've run the study, and I've come fully prepared with a gold (plastic) medal and a bottle of cheap fizzy wine. (This is not the Oscars.)

I'd be lying if I said the atmosphere in the room was electric, but there was at least some interest in who'd come 'top'. We're so-cial scientists who deal a lot in perceptions, so we are genuinely fascinated when people get things wrong, and where we're most wrong. But more tactically, the media love a league table: coming top, being the most wrong country in the world, guarantees media interest (much more so than being the most correct).

So the audience is waiting for the big reveal (which is a jpeg of the national flag pasted into a PowerPoint slide, shown on a forty-two-inch television—again, not the Oscars). And the win-ner of our first ever Misperceptions Index is . . . Italy! The head of our Italian team, Nando Pagnoncelli, whose charming acceptance speech you saw at the start of the chapter, is delighted.

That was our first award, and we've repeated it a few times since, with winners from Mexico, India, and South Africa.

The Misperceptions Index performs an important function, allowing us to identify which countries are most wrong (and right) by summarizing the gaps between perception and reality across all the questions for each country. You'll have noticed that some countries tend to come out better or worse throughout the differ-ent questions we've looked at. But it's not always consistent, and some are terrible at one question and great at another. The index is just a fair way to summarize this by standardizing the errors across questions and then adding them up.

We've calculated a mega-index for this book, looking across all the studies we've done. This means we can draw on around thirty questions, with data from around 50,000 people across thirteen countries over four years. We narrowed it down to thirteen, as we had data for every question we've asked for each of them. This is fairer in any case. These thirteen are the countries where Internet access is high enough that we can think of the surveys as broadly representative of their entire populations.

The full list of where countries rank provides a fascinating run-down of relative wrongness. After Italy comes the United States, with the second highest level of delusion across the population. At the other end of the spectrum, the most accurate countries are, not surprisingly given what we've seen, Sweden and then Germany. Britain does not do too badly, as fifth least wrong, behind these two countries and South Korea and Japan.

Misperceptions Index

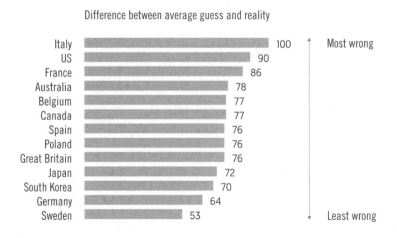

Difference between average guess and reality

Italy	100	Most wrong
US	90	
France	86	
Australia	78	
Belgium	77	
Canada	77	
Spain	76	
Poland	76	
Great Britain	76	
Japan	72	
South Korea	70	
Germany	64	
Sweden	53	Least wrong

Figure 33. Italy and the United States have the highest levels of misperception across the population, whereas Sweden and then Germany are the most accurate countries.

While this is an interesting summary measure, people can't help immediately moving on to ask why. Why are some countries better informed than others? What can we learn from elsewhere? These are the questions I'm most often asked by journalists.

But can we explain the pattern? Can we find factors that are associated with the relative position of countries? If we think back to all of the explanations for why we're wrong that we've discussed throughout the book, can we match up data to each of these to see which correlates?

We have attempted to do that, and I'll run through what we found next. First, it's important to recognize a bias in ourselves that we touched on earlier. We are programmed to look for causation; it's in our nature as storytelling animals. That's why a journalist's first question is always 'Why?'. But we also confuse correlation with causation—we naturally look for patterns and bestow them with meaning when there may well be none. The examples of this are multifold, and you see it endlessly in media articles. Take one example of an article that draws together two of our previous themes: 'More Buck for Your Bang: People Who Have the Most Sex Make the Most Money'. Apart from the lurid pun, that's actually a pretty neutral headline, just stating a relationship. But the commentary in the article goes on: 'Scientists . . . found that people who have sex more than four times a week receive a 3.2 percent higher paycheck than those who have sex only once a week. God forbid you don't have sex at all'. The (slightly tongue-in-cheek) causal implication is clear: if you want to be better off, you need to get it on.[1]

Of course, the academics behind the serious research paper the article was based on were more circumspect. A review of the piece in *Scientific American* says, 'It's likely that health influences both sexual activity levels and income, and sex may improve certain aspects of health as well. The causal chain is likely very complicated and filled with loops'.[2]

This human fascination with ascribing cause has led to the brilliant Spurious Correlations website and book of the same name by Tyler Vigen, which shows, for example, the spooky relationship between the number of people who've drowned by falling into a pool in America each year and the number of films Nicolas Cage has appeared in, or the per capita cheese consumption and the number of people who've died by becoming entangled in their bedsheets, or the divorce rate in Maine and the per capita consumption of margarine (Vigen's work heavily features odd means of dying and dairy products).[3] Of course, it is hard to imagine a causal relationship behind such examples.

We need to guard against similar tendencies in explaining our delusions. We do at least have some theoretical framework on which to base our expectations of effect. We have good reason to think that our delusions could have some relationship with education levels, and particularly statistical or news literacy, the political and media contexts in different countries, or factors more associated with national culture, such as how openly people express their emotions.

The challenges in even proving a simple association are significant. First, we only have thirteen countries where we have sufficient data to calculate a fair overall index. Sure, that's based on a big study, of tens of thousands of interviews, but when we're looking for explanatory patterns we still only have those thirteen aggregate observations, and so have to be cautious. Of course, even having double that amount of countries would still mean the power of our findings would be limited—which is one of the challenges of cross-national comparative studies.

Second, finding data on these possible explanatory factors is tough. We spend a good chunk of our time at Ipsos sourcing real facts—about individual countries and the world—to run the Perils of Perception studies in the first place, so we're aware of lots of sources, but we struggle to get data that meaningfully measures these concepts. It's relatively easy to get figures on ratings of education levels across countries, but these are broad-brush metrics, not focused on the type of critical literacy we would ideally like to measure. For example, the OECD's Programme for International Student Assessment (or PISA) data is a great indicator of the relative abilities of high school students in maths, reading, and science, but it tells us little about the whole population of each country's critical ability. The same applies to so many of the measures we would like to study, including the political context, media quality and plurality, how people in different countries use social media, and how it is controlled. On the personality characteristics of different populaces, how do you measure in a rigorous way how 'emotional' a country is? As we've seen, there are real challenges in defining even apparently simple concepts, like what counts as 'sex' or how 'fat' we are—so capturing these factors is clearly going to be tricky.

In spite of these challenges, we've attempted to bring together as much data as we can. In fact, we identified dozens of indicators across many domains, everything from the PISA ratings, through indices that measure general social progress in a country, to measures of media pluralism, independence and freedom, validated indices of different values systems in different countries, measures of online activity, to more attitudinal factors like trust in institutions, how emotionally expressive countries see themselves, the values we think are important for our children, and how people think things are going in their country. A full list of the data we used is given in the references.[4]

Maybe not surprisingly, given my Introduction, and in the spirit of not wanting to add to the industry of spurious correlations, we have found no magic answer, and claim little more than broad indications from the patterns we have observed. What we've found does, however, have some value—there are three domains where we find sufficient evidence of a relationship, at a country or individual level.

1. EMOTIONAL EXPRESSIVENESS

My colleague Nando's instincts seem to be partially correct, as there is a relationship between the scale of our error at a national level and measures of how emotionally expressive nations are, as developed by Erin Meyer in her book *The Culture Map*.[5] Her emotional expression measure is based on factors such as whether people in that culture tend to raise their voices, touch each other (not like that), or laugh passionately when talking. If our emotional reactions are part of the reason we exaggerate or downplay reality, it makes sense that our delusions may relate to how emotionally expressive we are.

On Erin's measure, for example, Italy and France are at one end of emotional expressiveness, with Korea, Japan, and Sweden at the other. Britain is towards the cooler end. The anomalies that don't fit the relationship are the United States, which Meyer places in the middle of the range, and Spain, which is counted at the emotionally expressive end of the spectrum.

So it's far from a perfect match, but the general pattern suggests there is something there.

2. EDUCATION LEVELS

At a country level, we can find little direct evidence of a link between ratings of national education levels and how wrong we are—although there are some patterns with some of the PISA rankings. For example, from our list of countries, Italy and the United States are among those that perform worst on reading and maths, whereas South Korea and Japan do best. But again, Sweden is not particularly highly rated on PISA, and Canada, which does badly in our index, is near the top of the PISA ratings. So there is some correlation, but it is far from powerful.

The relationship between education and accuracy in our questions is different at an individual level, though. Throughout our Perils of Perception studies, one of the clearest patterns has been

214 | WHY WE'RE WRONG ABOUT NEARLY EVERYTHING

that the higher the education level of the individual, the more accurate their perceptions are likely to be. For example, looking across the entire thirty-eight-country survey in 2017, those with low education levels (no qualifications or only basic ones from the minimum level of required schooling) guessed that 29 per cent of teenage girls in their country gave birth each year, whereas those with high levels of education (degree and above) guessed a more accurate, if still not great, 21 per cent. Similarly, on the proportion of prisoners who are immigrants in their country, those with a low level of education guessed way too high at 35 per cent, whereas those with higher levels of education guessed 24 per cent, which was substantially closer to reality. Again, we need to note this is an association, and we cannot conclude that it is a causal relationship—but from all we've seen across many years, it seems safe to suggest that education has some relationship with accuracy.

3. MEDIA AND POLITICS

We found no relationship between the extent of delusion in countries and national measures of press freedom, media pluralism, or objective measures of how open governments are with their data. There is no apparent link between our index scores and how highly people rate their government, how positive they are about the direction the country is going in, or how much trust they have in national institutions.

However, there is one finding that does correlate strongly with our Misperceptions Index at a national level, which is agreement with the statement, 'I wish my country was run by a strong leader instead of the current government'. The country least likely to agree with this statement was Sweden, with about half the level of agreement seen in Italy and the United States (at the time; the survey was from 2016). Other countries that ranked highly as wrong about realities in our measures also agreed they wanted a strong leader, including Spain, France, and Australia. Obviously we need to be careful in how we interpret these results: it will mean different things in different national contexts, and any causal relationship is clearly very difficult to untangle. But it does perhaps give a sense that countries where citizens feel confused and angry are more likely to want simple solutions from strong leadership.

As with education levels, there is also clearer evidence of a relationship between our delusions and our political preferences and media consumption at an individual level, but we only see it on a small number of questions. In our most recent studies in 2017 and 2018, we asked about party political support and media consumption in the UK and United States, to allow us to explore how these characteristics interact with delusion. It turned out that very few of the issues we asked people about related to their political allegiances or media consumption. In fact, only three showed any significant relationship: the extent to which guns were responsible for violent deaths, the proportion of prisoners that people thought were immigrants, and trends in the number of deaths from terrorist attacks.

All three questions showed patterns we may have expected. For example, around eight in ten Democrats identified that guns were the main source of violent deaths in the United States, significantly ahead of knives or other violence—which was the correct answer, as guns accounted for 68 per cent of violent deaths in the United States in 2017. But Republicans saw the same reality very differently, with only 27 per cent of strong Republicans picking guns as the main source of violent death. Similarly, Republican supporters guessed that 39 per cent of the US prison population were immigrants, whereas Democrats guessed 28 per cent (the actual figure was 5 per cent). In the UK, Conservative supporters also guessed 39 per cent, whereas Labour supporters guessed 31 per cent (the actual proportion was 12 per cent). In the United States, 47 per cent of viewers of the more right-leaning Fox News (incorrectly) thought that deaths from terrorism had

increased in the last fifteen years compared with the fifteen before that, whereas those who watched other news sources guessed
34 per cent. However, we found no differences in guesses in the
UK based on broadcast media consumption.

These were the only differences we found in this study—there
were no other patterns on such issues as teen pregnancies, diabetes levels, suicide rates, or changes in the murder rate. The conclusion, then, is much as we'd expect and echoes the very strong
relationship between newspaper readership and concern about immigration that we saw earlier: that on some highly identity-driven
issues, such as immigration and terrorism, political support and
media consumption do seem to have a relationship with our delusions, but they do not solely determine our broader worldview and
how accurate we are.

—

There is one final cross-country comparison that is worth making that relates to another bias: the Dunning–Kruger effect. This
comes from the work of social psychologists David Dunning and
Justin Kruger, who identified that the illusory superiority bias—
our tendency to think we're better than others—has an interesting
relationship with our cognitive abilities. They discovered that people with low abilities are less able to identify that they're struggling
and therefore are more likely to view themselves as competent than
people with higher abilities.[6] It's a very intuitive idea, reminiscent
of a famous dialogue from Plato in which Socrates attests that he
is wise, precisely because he knows that he knows nothing. Dunning and Kruger illustrated the effect vividly in their article with a
brilliant example.

In January 1995, a 1.7-metre (5 feet 7 inches) and 122-kilogram
(269 lb.) middle-aged man named McArthur Wheeler robbed
two Pittsburgh banks in broad daylight. Just to set that scene a little more (and because we've looked at the scourge of obesity), that

height and weight convert into a BMI of 43: this is very clearly in the 'morbidly obese' territory, and Wheeler was not an inconspicuous guy. He didn't wear a mask or make any other attempts to blend in—in fact, he smiled at the surveillance cameras before walking out of each bank. Later that night, police arrested a surprised Wheeler and showed him the tapes. He stared at the video, dumbfounded: 'But I wore the juice', he said. Wheeler's misplaced confidence in his understanding of physics meant that he thought that rubbing lemon juice on his skin would render him invisible to the cameras. After all, he reasoned, lemon juice is used as invisible ink, so he should have been unseen.

This story encouraged Dunning and Kruger to examine many other such effects, from low-ranking students' higher confidence that they had scored well, to uninformed gun enthusiasts' overconfidence in their understanding of firearm safety.

Do we see the same effects with our confidence in our own estimations of realities, at a country level? Are the poorer performing countries more confident than they should be? The answer, as Figure 34 on page 218 shows, seems to be a pretty resounding yes. We've only asked this question, on how confident people are in their answers, in our most recent 2017 survey, so this is for a larger group of countries than our overall Misperceptions Index. But for the purposes of showing overconfidence, it's useful.

It's an incredibly satisfying chart from the Dunning–Kruger perspective, with a (mostly) strong linear relationship between confidence and being wrong. At one end you have India, which scored among the least accurate countries in the 2017 study, but where an incredible 38 per cent of respondents said they were confident in *all* their answers. In the bottom left-hand corner are Sweden and Norway, where only 7 per cent and 2 per cent, respectively, said they were completely confident in their answers, despite these being among the best-performing countries in the study. We really are wrong about nearly everything, including what we're wrong about!

Q. Thinking about all the answers you have given, how confident would you say you are...?

Percentage who say they are confident in all their answers

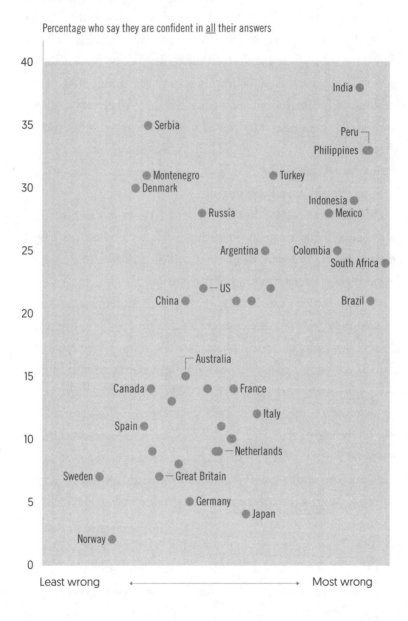

Figure 34. There is a strong relationship between confidence and being wrong, with poorer performing countries more confident than their more accurate counterparts.

Of course, the relationship is not perfect, and countries like Serbia, Montenegro, and Denmark had more cause for their confidence. As with people, it seems there are countries more likely to be hit by the Dunning–Kruger effect than others. Given that these tend to be low Internet penetration countries, like India, the Philippines, and Peru, this will be partly because they assume their quite unusual life experience and comparison sets are more normal for their countries than they really are. This is a useful warning of the dangers of assuming 'all we see is all there is', as we move to our final section and some suggestions on what we can do to improve the perils of our perceptions.

CHAPTER 11

DEALING WITH OUR DELUSIONS

The starting point for most discussions of why we're so wrong is to view the answer as solely *out there,* in what the media, social media, and politicians tell us. We're wrong only because we've been misled, rather than it being how we think, the repeated errors we make.

As we've seen, there is no single cause, and there is definitely sufficient evidence to conclude that we're not just wrong about the world because our media or politics are misleading us. Rather, our delusions need to be seen as arising from a complex system of forces, both in our heads and in the world, that reinforce each other. Our ignorance and misperception of facts are long-standing and they persist in very different conditions over time and across countries. We ignored the reality of crime statistics in 1950s Britain, and political knowledge was no better in 1940s America than it is today.

222 | WHY WE'RE WRONG ABOUT NEARLY EVERYTHING

We tend to think of our current era as uniquely ill-informed and beset by 'fake news' in a new 'post-truth' age. But disinformation in politics didn't start with the 2016 US presidential election, or with dodgy claims about EU budgets on the sides of buses, or with the entirely spurious claim, which emerged during the 2017 French presidential election, that the French state was replacing Christian holidays with Muslim and Jewish ones.[1]

Trends on levels of trust in our political dialogue across countries show there was no recent golden age of trust. Even in the summer of 1944, as the D-Day landings were hitting the beach, only 36 per cent of the British people thought the government could be trusted to put the country's interest above their own individual or party's interest. The widely asserted view is that this new collapse of trust has driven us towards our post-truth world.[2] But it's difficult to support that from the evidence based on our stated views. For example, looking across all European Union countries, the aggregate level of trust in country governments was barely different at the end of 2017 (with 38 per cent saying they trust their government) compared with 2001 (with 36 per cent trusting their government). Sure, within this, trust in some individual countries has tanked—trust levels have fallen from 55 per cent to 22 per cent in Spain, for example—but this is balanced with increases elsewhere (for example, in Sweden and Germany).[3]

In fact, in our polls in the UK dating back to 1983, the most common pattern we observe is an *increase* in trust, in all sorts of professions, from civil servants to trade union officials to the police. One of the most famous sound bites of the Brexit campaign was from politician Michael Gove, who stated, 'People in this country have had enough of experts'.[4] However, what we've actually seen is huge increases in trust in scientists and professors. Indeed, the only profession that has significantly dropped in trustworthiness in recent years is the clergy. We clearly shouldn't think of ourselves as in a new 'age of enlightenment', but we're also not seeing a wholesale rejection of the veracity of experts.

Politicians and journalists, on the other hand, fight it out to be the least trusted profession, with politicians currently 'winning' in the UK. But the point is this is nothing new: trust levels are virtually identical to when we started the series in 1983. Every year there are studies that purport to show a 'new crisis of trust', but the evidence for that is scant and more likely to reflect our rosy retrospection, looking back to a mythical time of respect and deference.

Any study of trust will quickly show you that it's a nebulous concept that is context-specific—what are you trusting someone to do, and under what circumstances? And more important for our focus on delusions, which particular experts do you trust on which topics? The massive shift in communications technology has changed our ability to pick and choose beyond recognition. The explosion of information sources and social media has combined with our natural tendencies to seek information that

Q. For each of the following professions, would you tell me if you generally trust them to tell the truth, or not?

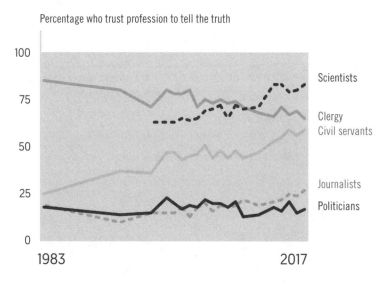

Figure 35. Key moves in public trust over time.

confirms our views and avoid those that don't, encouraging us towards experts who support our existing views.

There are many, many other tendencies in both the context and how we think that lead us astray and distort our view of the world. As I outlined in the Introduction, and in Figure 36, these run on a spectrum from things that are internal to us, our capabilities and how we think (our mathematical and statistical abilities, critical literacy, our biases and heuristics, including emotional innumeracy, and our 'hedging' related to psychophysics), to those that are externally driven (the media, social communications technology, politics, and what we see and experience directly).

Obviously this is a simplification, and each element interacts. Each works differently for different issues, and not all are of equal weight or importance. In particular, our biases and heuristics cover a huge range of distinct explanations, with emotional innumeracy on its own explaining a significant portion of the patterns we see.

However, it provides a checklist to consider against each error: understanding the dominant reasons for why we're wrong on particular issues points to what we might be able to do about it.

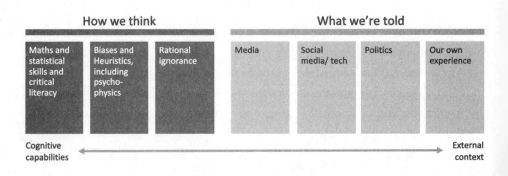

Figure 36. The sources of our delusions about social realities.

WHAT CAN WE DO?

**'I've been studying this stuff for about 45 years
and I really haven't improved one bit'.[5]**

Daniel Kahneman was talking here about a much broader set of situations, and how our thinking can go wrong in all the decisions we make, but his caution applies equally to how we think about realities in the world. Biases are hardwired into us and prove difficult to evade.

So what hope is there? If the most famous and revered Nobel laureate of behavioural science, who probably knows more about the mental traps we fall into than anyone alive, hasn't managed to improve one bit, has this whole book been a massive waste of time?

Of course that's not the entirety of what Kahneman said. A fuller extract of the interview it's taken from gives us a glimmer of hope:

> **DK:** I'm really completely pessimistic about this [*Thinking Fast and Slow*] as a self-help book. And I know that from experience—as you say, I've been studying this stuff for about 45 years, and I really haven't improved one bit. In fact, the work began that way . . . it started when we [Daniel Kahneman and his long-term collaborator Amos Tversky] examined our wrong intuitions. We were both teaching statistics and we both had intuitions that were not in accord with what we were teaching and that was the game actually—of understanding where our intuitions diverged from the rules. Nothing happens to system 1 [fast, instinctive thinking].
>
> **Interviewer:** So the point is, you can't teach system 1 basically, you can exercise system 2 [slower, more deliberative

thinking] and you can make system 2 more aware of when not to trust system 1?

DK: That's it. You can recognize cues that tell you 'oh here I'm likely to be making a mistake'. And it's a rare event that you do it. And then the answer typically is to slow yourself down, that is to bring system 2 into the picture.[6]

Kahneman and Tversky backed up this advice with a very practical example in their seminal 1973 paper, that related directly to how we see the world. They pointed out that the apparent distance of an object is determined in part by its clarity—the more sharply an object is seen, the closer it appears to be. So distances are underestimated on clear days—and we cannot control this perception, as it happens automatically.[7]

However, it is possible to learn when our initial perceptions are likely to be biased. We can slow down and consider whether we're being led astray. So when we're making a decision on whether to climb a hill, we should stop to think whether that summit looks much closer than it really is because it's a clear day.

Rolf Dobelli, author of that great compendium of cognitive errors, *The Art of Thinking Clearly,* makes a similar point. He offers no 'Seven Steps to an Error-Free Life'. But he also says that after making his list of pitfalls that he'd fallen into, he felt calmer and more clear-headed, and it helped him recognize his errors sooner.[8] All of the evidence I've seen confirms we're not going to rid ourselves of these errors—in fact, we wouldn't want to, as many are useful clues to how we think and feel. But knowing the common traps will help us evade the worst excesses of having an entirely biased view of the world.

In pointing out these traps, I've also been at pains to establish that we're not entirely slaves to them. Look at some of the findings from the classic studies we've outlined throughout the book: only a third of people fell for the extreme peer pressure in Asch's line comparison experiment; only 60 per cent to 70 per cent thought others would respond the same as them in Lee Ross's sandwich board experiment—not masses more than a 50:50 chance on this binary option; the average bid for wine increased somewhat for those who had high numbers for the last two digits of their social security number in Ariely's anchoring experiments, but not everyone was significantly influenced.

Sometimes, even where we do seem to be driven by our automatic thought processes, as seen in the psychophysics explanations for why we overestimate or underestimate different social characteristics, this has a 'good news' slant: it suggests that a chunk of our incorrect views of the world is just how we rescale numbers; it doesn't always reflect deeply biased attitudes.

As well as tackling these delusions individually, the communications environment is also important. While we shouldn't think there was ever an age of perfectly neutral information, we also shouldn't kid ourselves: we're travelling towards a world where disinformation has more opportunity to be created faster and travel faster. The revolution in communications technology has had many massively positive impacts on our lives, including in politics, where connecting people and highlighting issues has led to real change, not just in the Arab Spring, but in myriad ways: the hashtags #MeToo and #BlackLivesMatter demonstrate the centrality of communications technology to key social movements. But when combined with the growth of identity politics, this technology plays to our natural tendency to reinforce our existing views and ignore conflicting information.

WHY ARE WE NOT BECOMING *MORE* DELUDED?

There is an apparent contradiction in two themes outlined above and throughout the book: if our information environment is changing so much, increasingly playing on our biases and feeding us more disinformation, why are we not getting more wrong about social realities?

As outlined in the Introduction, there is very little long-term trend data on our delusions—but what there is shows very little change in how wrong we are on things like unemployment levels, all the way back to 1940s America. And the studies that I've run with Ipsos over the past decade, when we'd expect the effects of our changed information environment to have most taken hold, reinforce this view of stubbornly consistent errors. In every survey I've done, Americans and Brits think immigration is roughly twice its actual level.

Does this mean we're worrying too much about the threat from our increasingly filtered lives and the growth of disinformation? Unfortunately, I think we're still right to be concerned, as these new forces do have the potential to throw a relatively stable system of delusion out of balance.

First, we're only at the start of this new communications and disinformation context. It may be that it will just take some more time to work through into our delusions. More than this, we need to keep a very clear eye on the future, not just the current technological capabilities to manipulate and target information. These are evolving at an accelerating pace, and their impact is difficult to predict and could tip us quickly into even deeper delusions. We need to avoid the mistakes of the past, in assuming only the best outcomes from our increasingly unfettered and fractured information environment, ignoring how this will interact with our human characteristics. Equally, we need to break out of our current trap of responding to present capabilities and threats—because the technology constantly adapts before we can act.

Second, we may be looking in the wrong place, if we're focused solely on our misperceptions. I've always thought of our delusions about key social realities as important indicators, not as the key concern in themselves. They show us what we're worried about, what messages we're hearing or not hearing, and what we're willing to express to others. But they are only one part of how we see and think about the world.

The impact of this information shift may not, therefore, be on our estimates of realities, but how certain we are of our worldview—and how wrong we think others are. In other words, how polarised our perspectives are becoming.

There is significant evidence of this polarisation across societies, suggesting we're fragmenting into 'tribes'[9] with highly divergent views. For example, evidence from the Pew Research Center for the United States is compelling. This outlines how the partisan gap in political values in the United States has widened dramatically in the past twenty years, and particularly since the early 2000s. In 2004, there was only a 17 percentage point gap between the average Democrat and average Republican on ten political values, such as whether the government should do more to help the needy, or whether racial discrimination is the main reason why black people can't get ahead these days. By 2017, this gap had more than doubled to 36 percentage points.[10]

Between 1994 and 2017, we moved from a position where 65 per cent of Republicans were more 'conservative' in their attitudes than the average Democrat, to almost entirely distinct tribes where 95 per cent of Republicans have more conservative views than the average Democrat.[11]

Fighting this rising tide of polarisation may seem impossible—but I'm not defeatist about our individual abilities either to avoid these traps or to collectively improve the 'information pollution' in our environment. Far from it—there are reasons for hope.

Distribution of Democrats and Republicans on a 10-item scale of political values

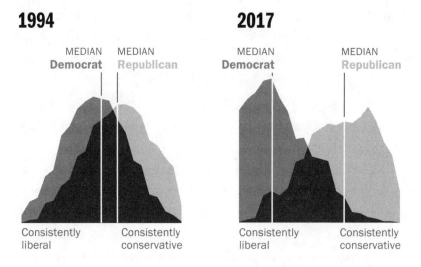

Figure 37. The US public has become more politically polarised over the past two decades (Pew Research Center).

Below I look at ten ideas for how we can form more accurate views of the world. This isn't just relevant for those rare occasions where you're asked questions about social realities in quizzes or on one of our surveys, or to impress people at your table during wedding receptions with your knowledge of teenage pregnancy rates around the world (although I do that). They have much broader applications for how we see the world, what we prioritize, and how we approach new information. I've started with points more related to how we think as individuals, moving through to society-wide actions we need to take.

1. THINGS ARE NOT AS BAD AS WE THINK— AND MOST THINGS ARE GETTING BETTER

Emotional innumeracy is one of the most important concepts in explaining why we're so wrong on so many social realities. Our concern causes our overestimation, as much as being the result of it. This makes misperceptions a useful clue to what really does concern us—but it also means that we can control our delusions if we recognize what we're worried about.

This is related to a broader point: most social realities are getting better. This isn't true of everything, and those that are improving are often not getting better as quickly or as much as we'd like. But starting with the assumption that most things are improving over time is more likely to be accurate than the opposite.

This shortcut is not just useful because we miss the great strides that are being made. It's important because we're wired to think the opposite. We tend to suffer from 'rosy retrospection', in which we edit out the bad from the past and emphasize the good. This is a useful human characteristic, as it stops us dwelling on our historical pain, and it frees up more mental space. But it also encourages a faulty view that today is worse than ever. It's crucial we avoid this perception, as we know that some sense of success is an important motivator for how we both act and feel. More than this, too pessimistic a view of how things are changing can cause extreme reactions, where we rip up what's been achieved because we're blind to the progress we have made.

2. ACCEPT THE EMOTION, BUT CHALLENGE THE THOUGHT

I realise this reads like an 'inspirational' Facebook thought for the day. It's true, this quote is based on a line from a self-help book on midlife crises by Andrew G. Marshall (not that I've read it, and every other title in the series, you understand), but it also works perfectly for how we see realities.[12]

Denying that we have an emotional reaction to, for example, immigration (whether positive or negative) is pointless and impossible, but accepting these emotions and trying to understand them is not. Tempering our immediate emotional reactions with more deliberative, contemplative thought is much more difficult—but that's the key. This is a parallel of Kahneman urging us to give up on changing our System 1 reactions, but rather training ourselves to get System 2 to kick in when we need it.

3. CULTIVATE SCEPTICISM BUT NOT CYNICISM

In *Annals of Gullibility: Why We Get Duped and How to Avoid It*, Stephen Greenspan suggests we cultivate scepticism but not cynicism because there are dangers in being too far on either end of the spectrum.[13] It's a difficult line to tread, but a vital one.

We've seen throughout the book that one of the fundamental challenges in building an accurate view of the world is our deep desire to avoid cognitive dissonance, to let go of things we already believe. This leads to all sorts of quirks of confirmation bias, directionally motivated reasoning, and asymmetric updating that allow us to dismiss contrary information and only take the points that support our case.

However, some scepticism is valuable, and attitudes should have some inertia—otherwise we would be flopping around, always believing the last thing we heard.[14] Cynicism allows us to dismiss contrary information too easily, but being too open allows us to be easily duped. The media environment is full of extremes we need to guard against. It's not just about the gore implied in the journalistic cliché 'If it bleeds, it leads'. Evan Davis, a BBC journalist, in his book on post-truth tells of another old adage in the media: 'First simplify, then exaggerate'. As he describes it, those who work in the media have to sell their programmes to editors and audiences, and that sometimes means trying to make them sound big even if the material is 'small or medium'. He outlines how a fact is reported, a legitimate interpretation is placed on the fact, but then it is 'puffed up to a magnitude beyond anything it deserves'. It's much easier to get pulled into this much more common trap than by anything concerning 'fake news'.[15]

James Pennebaker is a US social psychologist, most famous for his experiments that show how just writing about our emotions can improve our health. He also suggests a more active way of interacting with the media, advising that we change how we consume news, from passive receptivity to actively thinking about the information and trying to make sense of it. In our online world, this is akin to the lateral reading strategies used by fact-checkers, verifying as we go. This may be too exhausting to do all the time, but a little more could help.[16]

4. OTHER PEOPLE ARE NOT AS LIKE US AS WE THINK

When there is so much confusing and apparently contradictory information around, it's understandable that we have a natural tendency to fall back on our own direct experience and assume that all we see is all there is. Some of the biggest errors we see in our estimations can be traced back to thinking that we, and our circle of friends, are absolutely typical. This is a problem not just because we are often not as typical as we think (as with online Indians), but also because we are often very wrong about our own characteristics (for example, when we underestimate our own weight or sugar consumption). An appreciation of how different other people are, and how misguided we can be about ourselves, is important in forming a more accurate view of the world. (If nothing else, I hope the factual data about the world I've presented in this book makes that point.)

5. OUR FOCUS ON EXTREME EXAMPLES ALSO LEADS US ASTRAY

On the other hand, there are also many examples where we stereotype others, often assuming the worst. We need to consider the extent to which our views are affected by that one vivid anecdote that we remember. We're naturally drawn to extreme examples, which means that true but vanishingly rare events or populations take up more of our mental capacity than they deserve. We think of destitute asylum seekers when asked about immigration, we think of the one vivid story on teenage mums, and we are distracted by the horror of the most lurid terrorist incident. But these are not representative—most things are not so remarkable. The norm is usually more boring than our mental image.

Combatting this is partly just about knowing where you sit within your society, appreciating its diversity, but also about opening yourself up to different perspectives.

6. FIGURE OUT WHAT'S REAL

In our increasingly online existence, opening up our perspective means trying to pop our filter bubble and distinguish accurate from misleading information. We outlined the society-wide effort it is going to take to achieve this at scale. There are no easy answers, but there are answers that governments, media, technology companies, educators, and researchers all need to engage in.

The actions required, particularly when they may involve legislation or regulation, need to be considered extremely carefully, not as a knee-jerk response to moral panics about 'fake news' or 'echo chambers'. There is a risk that the cure is worse than the disease, if government-sanctioned crackdowns result in states regulating what is 'true'.

This can be seen in the varied and sometimes ill-considered reactions around the world. For example, in 2018 the Indian government withdrew its controversial plan to blacklist journalists judged to be writing fake news, after widespread concerns about freedom of speech.[17] France, however, passed another hotly contested law allowing judges to remove fake news during election campaigns, but only after it was twice rejected by the French senate.[18]

The European Commission has taken a different route, developing a voluntary code of conduct for self-regulation by the platforms, including Facebook and Google, with commitments to disrupt the advertising incomes of companies that spread false information, close fake accounts, and make political advertising more transparent. But this has come in for criticism from the other direction—that it needs to go 'much further, much faster'.[19]

These varied experiences show how difficult a line it is to tread between legitimate control of bad actors and state censorship. The immediate focus should be on where it counts most: updating election laws and regulations to reflect the new capabilities of political campaigning. In an environment where the Trump campaign ran 5.9 million variations of ads in the run-up to the 2016 election, we need greater, quicker transparency over what is being said to which groups by whom. Moves are under way to bring election advertising up to date in a number of countries, but we need to move more decisively.

But the much broader actions on controlling disinformation and how filtered or fractured our worlds are becoming is going to take time and careful thinking. Rather than piecemeal responses to particular threats, this will need some clarity on the principles we're applying, to ensure they are 'fit for purpose' for the future.

In the meantime, on a personal level there are very practical things we can do, using the tools that are increasingly available to help us break out and techniques to help us sort the real from the fake. For example, FlipFeed allows you to randomly see the Twitter feed of someone with a diametrically oppositional view to your own. The Read Across the Aisle app positions itself as a health aid for our confirmation bias: 'This app will notice when you've gotten a little too comfortable in your filter bubble—and it'll remind you to go see what other folks are reading'.[20]

Mainstream media outlets are trying similar approaches. The *Wall Street Journal* created 'Blue Feed, Red Feed' to reflect the different political slant of content. BuzzFeed's 'Outside Your Bubble' pulls in opinions from across the spectrum of views, and the 'Burst Your Bubble' weekly column in the UK's *Guardian* curates 'five conservative articles worth reading' for the paper's more left-leaning audience.[21]

7. CRITICAL, STATISTICAL, AND NEWS LITERACY ARE GOING TO BE DIFFICULT TO SHIFT, BUT WE CAN DO MORE

I once had a fascinating discussion with a government statistician and an academic working on misperceptions. We talked about how wrong people frequently were about the world, and how this had long been a concern for the statistician. When it came to discussion about what we could do, we quickly got to statistical literacy and critical thinking, and the need to start that early, through the education system, as it was too late by the time people were adults. We argued that we needed statistical and news literacy and critical thinking courses that used real-world examples and encouraged children to challenge what they were told. The statistician nodded sadly and said,

> When I was looking at the misrepresentation of statistics and how this affects perceptions, I thought there were three routes to affect change: through changes to the school curriculum, by engaging politicians to use statistics better or by focusing on the media. I chose trying to change politicians and the media. That will give you an idea of how hard it is to influence the school curriculum.

This may sound defeatist, but it is deeply frustrating how abstract statistical teaching can be. It turns children off statistical and critical thinking, and this is tragic when there is such an array of brilliant real-world examples that we could use instead to pique their interest.

However, I believe the growing focus on news literacy can break this deadlock: the new skills we need to deal with the hugely changed flow of information provide a focus for our efforts, and there have already been significant moves to build this into the core of the curriculum in countries like Italy. It really is becoming the social, cultural, and political challenge of our time, and these actions are a key response.

Of course, we need to be cautious about the notion that we can change our nature or that improving our skills will be a panacea: we won't be able to teach the human out of our kids, and critical thinking is not a universal guard against delusion. But creating 'walking encyclopaedias' is not the aim; rather it's to provide people with tools that are becoming increasingly core to effective citizenry, including recognizing our inherent biases.

8. FACTS AREN'T CURE-ALLS, BUT THEY STILL MATTER

The academic literature on the use of facts to correct delusions shows very mixed results. It sometimes works, it sometimes works in a limited way, and it sometimes doesn't work at all. The effects sometimes seem to last over a longer period, and sometimes they don't. It depends a lot on the issue being tested, how it's done, and what we're expecting to shift, from factual knowledge to policy preferences to beliefs.

That makes perfect sense when we bear in mind the theory of cognitive dissonance and consider what we know about how we think. We naturally look for confirming information, and discount disconfirming information. When the evidence reaches a tipping point and there is sufficient weight against our current view, we switch. The dissonance is emotionally unpleasant, and while we're attached to our current opinions, it becomes less unpleasant to shift than to cling on to them.

The message is that we can't always solve delusions with more facts alone, but that we definitely shouldn't give up on them entirely. People are marvellously varied, and different approaches work with different people in different situations. Of course, facts don't exist entirely outside of their context: as we've seen, many measures are more complex than they seem, require cautious interpretation, and selection of other, equally valid facts can paint a very different picture. But this is not an excuse to give up on the value and power of the best facts we can muster. They can indicate an underlying truth that we shouldn't carelessly discard because they are imperfect.

Regardless of the effectiveness of correcting people or information, there are ethical considerations. It's just wrong to misuse facts, and there should be accountability, particularly when disinformation has such significant consequences, as with vaccine take-up. It's easy, but incorrect, to conclude that people are just stupid when they're actually being exploited or failed by those creating and controlling information.

Without deterrents and without the threat of being picked up and corrected, the extent of disinformation will be much worse. Fact-checking may be a minor deterrent to those who don't really care, but some do—and being pulled up has already shifted behaviour. For example, the head of statistics at a major UK government department has been set a formal objective: that they should not get criticized by Full Fact, a UK fact-checker.[22]

Of course, fact-checking is about more than correcting disinformation that is already out there, or shaming those who create or propagate it. It is increasingly about getting in first, building fact-checking into the system, and stopping the disinformation before it starts. We need to invest in these approaches with commitment and ingenuity that at least equal those who are developing tools and content to spread disinformation.

9. WE ALSO NEED TO TELL THE STORY

Although facts are important, they are not sufficient given how our brains work. We need to be aware of how people hear and use them, turning them into stories that might not always lead to the right conclusions. This echoes psychologist Robert Cialdini's concern about the dangers of using descriptive norms (that is, what the majority are thinking or doing) to illustrate how serious an issue is. Telling people that most people are overweight or obese is a useful fact to shock us out of complacency, but as well as hearing that obesity is a big problem, there is a real risk that people hear *it's normal*. As we know, we follow the herd: if we hear that other people are doing something, we are more inclined to do so too—even if it's bad for us.

This is why campaigners on contentious issues have learned to focus on a story, rather than statistics. In terms of changing people's concept of the typical immigrant, for example, it's pointless to argue the case on numbers alone. Instead the focus should be on presenting real examples, with real individuals who happen to be immigrants, to change the stereotypical mental image people hold.

Michael Shermer, the science writer and founder of the Skeptics Society, highlights steps you can take to convince people of errors in their beliefs, including the importance of discussing (not attacking), acknowledging that you understand the basis for an opinion, and trying to show how changing our understanding of the facts doesn't necessarily mean changing our entire worldview.[23]

There is no contradiction between facts and stories; you don't need to choose only one to make your point. The power of stories over us means we need to engage people with both.

10. BETTER AND DEEPER ENGAGEMENT IS POSSIBLE

The 'rational ignorance' school of thought argues that we can't shift raw political and social knowledge that much—it's been such a long-standing and consistent pattern that it is difficult to see why it would change. But rational ignorance proponents also point to the potential of more informed deliberation. American political scientists Bruce Ackerman and James Fishkin suggested a rather radical idea in 2012 of national 'deliberation days', in which citizens would be invited to participate in public community discussions.[24] Prior to each election, there would be a national holiday, and people would be gathered in groups of 500 or so to hear presentations and ask questions of experts or representatives. Attendance at such events would be incentivized, and there would be penalties for employers who compel people to work. It's clearly not a cheap approach, but it would quite possibly be money well spent.

There are, of course, many challenges with this: the practicalities and cost; its susceptibility to manipulation and perceived manipulation; the huge range of things that people would need to know—would a day, a week, or even a year even be enough?

I've seen first-hand the potential for similar ideas. We've run our own deliberative events for government and others for a day, a weekend, or sometimes longer, on some extremely complex topics, from the future of cities, to the future of social care, to the acceptability of genetically modified foods, concerns about artificial intelligence—and even incredibly dull topics like how to engage people in the government's legislative programme. Without fail, you see people's opinions develop as they hear more and challenge their own and others' thinking. People are more open to evidence, more willing to listen, and, yes, even shift their opinions in such environments. People rarely, if ever, completely upend their worldview, but that is not the objective. Of course, how quickly it decays outside the artificial environment of a deliberation day or public dialogue event is unclear. The full impact of the approach has not been measured, because it has never been fully implemented.

However, the potential is there, and arguably growing, as new technologies make virtual approaches to these techniques more viable and robust. There are numerous exciting fledgling approaches to digital dialogue and engagement being trialled in all sorts of environments, connecting people to a much wider variety of ideas, conversation, and evidence than has previously been possible. These are supplements to, rather than replacements for, democratic accountability—most people don't have the skills, time, or inclination to run governments—but they can still play an important role in informing and engaging.[25]

— — —

There is no magic formula to deal with our delusions: they are widespread, long-standing, and legion. But there are real practical things we can do, particularly once we realise that it is a system of delusion that no single solution aimed at any one of the causes can fix. Admitting the issue is complex and contingent opens up our options.

We don't need to give up on facts in order to admit that emotions are important. Indeed, it's a false distinction, because the two are inextricably linked.[26] We are far from perfectly informed or rational beings, as this book hammers home, but we're also not automatons, blind to evidence, unchanging in our views, or driven solely by protecting a single fixed identity. Our media, social media, and politics are also not solely to blame for our delusions, and, although the risks to our reality-based view of the world are growing, there are things we can do to improve them.

I hope this book outlines that things are not as bad as they're sometimes portrayed—in two ways. First, the world, while marvellously (and sometimes less marvellously) varied, is frequently not anywhere near as bad as we think. Second, although we may make mistakes, we're not all as dumb, obstinate, or narrow-minded as we imagine. We do change our minds, even if it doesn't happen easily. A better understanding of our foibles doesn't mean we're slaves to them or completely predictable. I really didn't need to be so adolescently defensive in my psychology classes.

Just as our delusions will never be entirely managed away, they shouldn't be ignored. They're valuable in their own right, for what they tell us about how we think, what we're worrying about, how we see ourselves relative to others, where we think the norm is, and therefore how we're likely to act ourselves. We can learn a lot by understanding why we're so often so wrong.

ACKNOWLEDGEMENTS

This is my first book, and it's been a struggle. Not just for me, but for those around me, particularly my partner, Louise, who has been incredibly understanding about my obsessive need to get it written. This book would not have been possible without her support, which included hiding away (from the kids) in a bedsit on the other side of London for weeks at a time.

It's hard to slip the habits of writing more academic reports and journal articles, and I'm sure I've not wholly succeeded. But it would have been a whole lot worse without the brilliant guidance and sometimes forceful intervention from my collection of editors: Mike Harpley, Julia Kellaway, and Robin Dennis. Any remaining turgid passages or disconnected thoughts are down to me.

There are so many other people who have made this book possible, particularly Rebekah Kulidzan, my always upbeat and encouraging research assistant, who covered so much ground so quickly.

Then there is the incredible team of people at Ipsos who have developed and run all of the studies this book is based on. In particular: James Stannard, Leila Tavakoli, Charlotte Saunders, Rosie Hazell, Galini Pantelidou, Hannah Shrimpton, Kully Kaur-Ballagan, Suzanne Hall, Gideon Skinner, and Michael Clemence; colleagues who collected the data: Paul Abbate, Kevin Zimmerman, and Nik Samoylov; and those who ran the clever statistical analysis: Pawel Paluchowski, Fintan O'Connor, Peter Hasler, and Kevin Pickering.

I also want to thank Ipsos's amazing graphics and communications team, which has been key to the success of our series of Perils of Perception studies, reaching millions of people, particularly Sara Gundry, Julia Nurse, Hannah Williams, Duncan Struthers, Hannah Millard, Claire Wortherspoon, Aalia Khan, and Jim Kelleher. Thanks, too, to all the other Ipsos offices around the world for putting the results in context in their country.

None of that would have been possible without the support from my bosses and their bosses—who've let me obsess over misperceptions for years, only vaguely rolling their eyes when I work it into every situation—particularly Ben Page, Darrell Bricker, Nando Pagnocelli, Henri Wallard, and Didier Truchot.

Many thanks to the people outside Ipsos who've been so generous with their time and expert advice: David Landy at Indiana University for introducing me to psychophysics; Brendan Nyhan from Dartmouth College for talking through his excellent research; Max Roser for pointing me to great sources of data about how the world is improving; Ola Rosling for some brilliant conversations on the importance of facts; Will Moy and Amy Sippitt at Full Fact for invaluable insight into the changing nature of fact-checking; David Spiegelhalter at the University of Cambridge for discussions on measuring perceptions of risk; Matt Williams at Save the Children for his insights on the challenges charities face in getting us to donate and act; Lisa O'Keefe at Sport England for the thinking behind their sports participation campaigns; and Owain Service and David Halpern at the Behavioural Insights Team for pointers to some great examples of why we misperceive reality.

NOTES

All the latest Perils of Perception data can be found at https://perils
.ipsos.com/, and a full archive of all Perils of Perception works can
be found at https://perils.ipsos.com/archive/index.html

Duffy, B., & Stannard, J. (2017). The Perils of Perception
2017. www.ipsos.com/ipsos-mori/en-uk/perils-perception-2017

Duffy, B. (2016). The Perils of Perception 2016. www.ipsos
.com/en/perils-perception-2016

Duffy, B., & Stannard, J. (2015). The Perils of Perception
2015. www.ipsos.com/ipsos-mori/en-uk/perils-perception-2015

Duffy, B. (2014). Perceptions Are Not Reality: Things
the World Gets Wrong. www.ipsos.com/ipsos-mori/en-uk
/perceptions-are-not-reality-things-world-gets-wrong

INTRODUCTION: PERILS EVERYWHERE

1. Dylan, S. (2015). Why I Give My Students a 'Tragedy of
the Commons' Extra Credit Challenge. Retrieved April 11, 2018,

from www.washingtonpost.com/posteverything/wp/2015/07/20
/why-i-give-my-students-a-tragedy-of-the-commons-extra-credit
-challenge/?utm_term=.605ed5e5401a

2. Poundstone, W. (2016). *Head in the Cloud: The Power of Knowledge in the Age of Google.* London: Oneworld Publications.

3. The Local Europe AB. (2018). From Flat Earth to Moon Landings: How the French Love a Conspiracy Theory. Retrieved April 11, 2018, from www.thelocal.fr/20180108/fro-flat-earth-the ory-to-the-moon-landings-what-the-french-think-of-conspiracy -theories; McKinnon, M., & Grant, W. J. (2013). Australians Seem to Be Getting Dumber—but Does It Matter? Retrieved April 11, 2018, from https://theconversation.com/australians-seem-to-be -getting-dumber-but-does-it-matter-16004; Rudin, M. (2011). Why the 9/11 Conspiracies Have Changed. Retrieved April 11, 2018, from www.bbc.co.uk/news/magazine-14572054; Wireclub Conversations. (2014). Conspiracy Theories That Were Proven True, Conspiracy Poll Results. Retrieved April 11, 2018, from www .wireclub.com/topics/politics/conversations/UZ5RfgOnSgewgJ3e0

4. Somin, I. (2016). *Democracy and Political Ignorance: Why Smaller Government Is Smarter.* Stanford, CA: Stanford University Press; Delli Carpini, M. X., & Keeter, S. (1991). Stability and Change in the U.S. Public's Knowledge of Politics. *Public Opinion Quarterly, 55*(4), 583–612. https://doi.org/10.1086/269283

5. Flynn, D. J., Nyhan, B., & Reifler, J. (2017). The Nature and Origins of Misperceptions: Understanding False and Unsupported Beliefs About Politics. *Political Psychology, 38*(1), 127–150. https://doi.org/10.1111/pops.12394

6. Schultz, J. (2017). How Much Data Is Created on the Internet Each Day? Retrieved April 11, 2018, from https://blog .microfocus.com/how-much-data-is-created-on-the-internet -each-day/

7. Reas, E. (2014). Our Brains Have a Map for Numbers. Retrieved April 11, 2018, from www.scientificamerican.com/article /our-brains-have-a-map-for-numbers/

8. Wells, H. G. (1903). *Mankind in the Making.* London: Chapman & Hall.

9. RSS Web News Editor. (2013). New Data Reveals Mixed Public Attitudes to Statistics. Retrieved April 11, 2018, from www.statslife.org.uk/news/138-new-data-reveals-mixed-public-attitudes-to-statistics

10. Laplace, P. S. (1814). *Théorie Analytique des Probabilités, Volume 1.* Paris: Courcier.

11. Ipsos MORI. (2013). Margins of Error: Public Understanding of Statistics in an Era of Big Data. Retrieved April 11, 2018, from www.slideshare.net/IpsosMORI/margins-of-error-public-understanding-of-statistics-in-an-era-of-big-data

12. Duffy, B. (2013). In an Age of Big Data and Focus on Economic Issues, Trust in the Use of Statistics Remains Low. Retrieved April 11, 2018, from www.ipsos.com/ipsos-mori/en-uk/age-big-data-and-focus-economic-issues-trust-use-statistics-remains-low

13. Kahneman, D. (2011). *Thinking Fast and Slow.* New York: Penguin.

14. Facebook, by all accounts, had a pretty awful 2018, with multiple data issues, staff departures, and stock market woes—but while growth stagnated in established markets, global users continued to rise. The death of Facebook has again been exaggerated, the short-term. However, some vital signs for its future health are taking a serious dip, particularly the growing generational divide in usage. A 2018 US survey found that an incredible 44 per cent of eighteen- to twenty-nine-year-old Facebook users did indeed delete the app from their phone in the previous twelve months, although this was a result of a much broader set of drivers than data concerns.

15. Kiernan, L. (2017). 'Frondeurs' and Fake News: How Misinformation Ruled in 17th-Century France. Retrieved April 11, 2018, from www.independent.co.uk/news/long_reads/frondeurs-and-fake-news-how-misinformation-ruled-in-17th-century-france-a7872276.html

16. Braun, S. (2017). National Archives to White House: Save All Trump Tweets. Retrieved February 6, 2018, from www .chicagotribune.com/news/nationworld/politics/ct-trump-tweets -national-archive-20170404-story.html

17. Beckett, L. (2017). Trump Digital Director Says Facebook Helped Win the White House. www.theguardian.com /technology/2017/oct/08/trump-digital-director-brad-parscale -facebook-advertising

CHAPTER 1: A HEALTHY MIND

1. *The Times*. (2017). A Goat Yoga Class Has Started in Amsterdam. Retrieved May 5, 2018, from www.thetimes.co.uk/travel /article/goat-yoga-amersterdam/

2. Poulter, S. (2017). Now Baby Food and Biscuits Are Linked to Cancer: Food Watchdog Issues Alerts for 25 Big Brands After Claiming That Crunchy Roast Potatoes and Toast Could Cause the Disease. Retrieved April 16, 2018, from www.dailymail.co.uk /news/article-4149890/Now-baby-food-biscuits-linked-cancer .html

3. Inman, P. (2016). Happiness Depends on Health and Friends, Not Money, Says New Study. Retrieved April 11, 2018, from www.theguardian.com/society/2016/dec/12/happiness -depends-on-health-and-friends-not-money-says-new-study

4. Centre for Health Protection, Department of Health, Government of the Hong Kong Special Administrative Region. (2010). Body Mass Index (BMI) Distribution. Retrieved February 2, 2018, from www.chp.gov.hk/en/statistics/data/10/280/427 .html

5. Nuttall, F. Q. (2015). Body Mass Index: Obesity, BMI, and Health—a Critical Review. *Nutrition Today*, *50*(3), 117–128. https://journals.lww.com/nutritiontodayonline/Fulltext /2015/05000/Body_Mass_Index__Obesity,_BMI,_and_Health _A.5.aspx

6. NHS. (2017). Being Overweight, Not Just Obese, Still Carries Serious Health Risks. Retrieved February 1, 2018, from www.nhs.uk/news/2017/06June/Pages/Being-overweight-not -just-obese-still-carries-serious-health-risks.aspx

7. Schwartz, N., Bless, H., Fritz, S., Klumpp, G., Rittenauer-Schatka, H., & Simons, A. (1991). Ease of Retrieval as Information: Another Look at the Availability Heuristic. *Journal of Personality and Social Psychology, 61*(2), 195–202. https://dornsife .usc.edu/assets/sites/780/docs/91_jpsp_schwarz_et_al_ease.pdf

8. Christakis, N. A., & Fowler, J. H. (2013). Social Contagion Theory: Examining Dynamic Social Networks and Human Behavior. *Statistics in Medicine, 32*(4), 556–577. https://doi .org/10.1002/sim.5408

9. Bailey, P., Emes, C., Duffy, B., & Shrimpton, H. (2017). *Sugar: What Next?* London: Ipsos MORI. Retrieved April 11, 2018, from www.ipsos.com/ipsos-mori/en-uk/sugar-what-next

10. Ipsos MORI. (2015). Major Survey Shows Britons Overestimate the Bad Behaviour of Other People. Retrieved April 11, 2018, from www.ipsos.com/ipsos-mori/en-uk/major -survey-shows-britons-overestimate-bad-behaviour-other-people

11. Health and Social Care Information Centre, Lifestyle Statistics. (2009). Health Survey for England—2008: Physical Activity and Fitness. Retrieved February 1, 2018, from http://digital .nhs.uk/catalogue/PUB00430

12. Public Health England. (2016). National Diet and Nutrition Survey. Retrieved February 2, 2018, from www.gov.uk /government/collections/national-diet-and-nutrition-survey

13. Harper, H., & Hallsworth, M. (2016). *Counting Calories: How Under-Reporting Can Explain the Apparent Fall in Calorie Intake.* London: Behavioural Insights Team. Retrieved April 11, 2018, from http://38r8om2xjhhl25mw24492dir.wpengine .netdna-cdn.com/wp-content/uploads/2016/08/16-07-12 -Counting-Calories-Final.pdf

14. Cialdini, R. B., Reno, R. R., & Kallgren, C. A. (1990). A Focus Theory of Normative Conduct: Recycling the Concept of Norms to Reduce Littering in Public Places. *Journal of Personality and Social Psychology*, *58*(6), 1015–1026. www-personal.umich.edu /~prestos/Downloads/DC/pdfs/Krupka_Oct13_Cialdinietal 1990.pdf

15. Asch, S. E. (1952). Effects of Group Pressure upon the Modification and Distortion of Judgements. *Swathmore College*, 222–236. Retrieved April 11, 2018, from www.gwern.net/docs /psychology/1952-asch.pdf

16. Just, D., & Wansink, B. (2009). Smarter Lunchrooms: Using Behavioral Economics to Improve Meal Selection. *Choices Magazine*, *24*(3). Retrieved May 28, 2019, from https://ideas .repec.org/a/ags/aaeach/94315.html; Thaler, R. H., & Sunstein, C. R. (2009). Nudge. *Nudge—Business Summaries*, 1–5. Retrieved May 28, 2019, from http://connection.ebscohost.com/c /book-summarys/60448472/nudge

17. Offit, P. A. (2006). *The Cutter Incident: How America's First Polio Vaccine Led to the Growing Vaccine Crisis*. New Haven: Yale University Press.

18. Reagan, R. (1985). Proclamation 5335—Dr. Jonas E. Salk Day, 1985. Retrieved April 11, 2018, from www.presidency.ucsb .edu/ws/index.php?pid=38596

19. Global Citizen. (2013). Could You Patent the Sun? Retrieved April 16, 2018, from www.youtube.com/watch?v=er HXKP386Nk

20. Taylor, L. E., Swerdfeger, A. L., & Eslick, G. D. (2014). Vaccines Are Not Associated with Autism: An Evidence-Based Meta-Analysis of Case-Control and Cohort Studies. *Vaccine*, *32*(29), 3623–3629. https://doi.org/10.1016/J.VACCINE .2014.04.085

21. The National Autistic Society. (2017). Our Position on Autism and Vaccines—There Is No Connection. Retrieved February

2, 2018, from www.autism.org.uk/get-involved/media-centre /news/2017-02-15-trump-vaccines.aspx

22. Spiegelhalter, D. (2017). Risk and Uncertainty Communication. *Annual Review of Statistics and Its Application*, 4(1), 31–60. https://doi.org/10.1146/annurev-statistics-010814-020148

23. BBC *Horizon*. (2005). Does the MMR Jab Cause Autism? Retrieved April 16, 2018, from www.bbc.co.uk/sn/tvradio /programmes/horizon/mmr_prog_summary.shtml

24. Sunstein, C. R., Lazzaro, S. C., & Sharot, T. (2016). How People Update Beliefs About Climate Change: Good News and Bad News. *SSRN Electronic Journal*. https://doi.org/10.2139/ssrn .2821919

25. McCarthy, J., & King, L. (2008). Jenny McCarthy's Autism Fight—Transcript of Interview with Larry King. Retrieved February 2, 2018, from http://archives.cnn.com /TRANSCRIPTS/0804/02/lkl.01.html

26. Gross, L. (2009). A Broken Trust: Lessons from the Vaccine–Autism Wars. *PLoS*, 7(5). https://doi.org/10.1371 /journal.pbio.1000114

27. The National Autistic Society. (n.d.). Our Position—MMR Vaccine. Retrieved February 2, 2018, from www.autism .org.uk/get-involved/media-centre/position-statements/mmr -vaccine.aspx

28. Jones, S. (2011). *BBC Trust Review of Impartiality and Accuracy of the BBC's Coverage of Science*. Retrieved April 11, 2018, from http://downloads.bbc.co.uk/bbctrust/assets/files/pdf/our _work/science_impartiality/science_impartiality.pdf

29. Inglehart, R. (1990). *Culture Shift in Advanced Industrial Society*. Princeton: Princeton University Press; Inglehart, R. F., Diener, E., & Tay, L. (2013). Theory and Validity of Life Satisfaction Scales. *Social Indicators Research*, 112(3), 497–537; Kahneman, D., & Krueger, A. B. (2006). Developments in the Measurement of Subjective Well-Being. *Journal of Economic Perspectives*, 20,

3–24; Layard, R., Clark, A. E., Cornaglia, F., Powdthavee, N., & Vernoit, J. (2014). What Predicts a Successful Life? A Life-Course Model of Well-Being. *The Economic Journal*, *124*(580), 720–738. https://doi.org/10.1111/ecoj.12170

30. Brickman, P., Coates, D., & Janoff-Bulman, R. (1978). Lottery Winners and Accident Victims: Is Happiness Relative? *Journal of Personality and Social Psychology*, *36*(8), 917–927. http://dx.doi.org/10.1037/0022-3514.36.8.917

31. Kahneman, D. (2010). Daniel Kahneman: The Riddle of Experience vs. Memory. Retrieved February 2, 2018, from www.ted.com/talks/daniel_kahneman_the_riddle_of_experience _vs_memory

32. CBS News. (2013). Everyone Thinks They Are Above Average. Retrieved April 11, 2018, from www.cbsnews.com /news/everyone-thinks-they-are-above-average/

33. Ipsos MORI. (2013). Margins of Error: Public Under-standing of Statistics in an Era of Big Data. Retrieved April 11, 2018, from www.slideshare.net/IpsosMORI/margins-of-error -public-understanding-of-statistics-in-an-era-of-big-data

34. Marsden, P. D., & Wright, J. D. (2010). *Handbook of Survey Research*. Bingley: Emerald Group Publishing.

35. The British Election Study Team. (2016). BES Vote Validation Variable Added to Face to Face Post-Election Survey. Retrieved April 11, 2018, from www.britishelectionstudy.com /bes-resources/bes-vote-validation-variable-added-to-face-to -face-post-election-survey/#.Ws4M0C7waUl

CHAPTER 2: SEXUAL FANTASIES

1. Binkowski, B. (n.d.). Dangle Debate. Retrieved April 11, 2018, from www.snopes.com/fact-check/hand-size-trump-debate/

2. Mustanski, B. (2011). How Often Do Men and Women Think About Sex? Retrieved February 1, 2018, from www .psychologytoday.com/blog/the-sexual-continuum/201112 /how-often-do-men-and-women-think-about-sex

3. Poundstone, W. (2016). *Head in the Cloud: The Power of Knowledge in the Age of Google.* London: Oneworld Publications.

4. Spiegelhalter, D. (2015). *Sex by Numbers: What Statistics Can Tell Us About Sexual Behaviour.* London: Wellcome Collection.

5. Ibid.

6. Gottschall, J. (2013). *The Storytelling Animal.* New York: Houghton Mifflin Harcourt.

7. McCombs, M. E., & Shaw, D. L. (n.d.). The Agenda-Setting Function of Mass Media. *The Public Opinion Quarterly.* Oxford University Press American Association for Public Opinion Research. https://doi.org/10.2307/2747787

8. Gavin, N. T. (1997). Voting Behaviour, the Economy and the Mass Media: Dependency, Consonance and Priming as a Route to Theoretical and Empirical Integration. *British Elections & Parties Review*, 7(1), 127–144. https://doi.org/10.1080/13689889708412993

9. Glynn, A. (2010). Pit Bulls' Bad Rap: How Much Is the Media to Blame? Retrieved April 11, 2018, from https://blog.sfgate.com/pets/2010/09/09/pit-bulls-bad-rap-how-much-is-the-media-to-blame/

10. Delise, K. (2007). *The Pit Bull Placebo: The Media, Myths and Politics of Canine Aggression.* Sofia: Anubis Publishing.

11. U.S. Department of Health and Human Services. (2016). Trends in Teen Pregnancy and Childbearing. Retrieved April 11, 2018, from www.hhs.gov/ash/oah/adolescent-development/reproductive-health-and-teen-pregnancy/teen-pregnancy-and-childbearing/trends/index.html

12. Heath, C., & Heath, D. (2007). *Made to Stick: Why Some Ideas Take Hold and Others Come Unstuck.* London: Random House.

13. Bacon, F. (1620). *Novum Organum.* Retrieved February 2, 2018, from www.constitution.org/bacon/nov_org.htm

14. Festinger, L. (1962). *A Theory of Cognitive Dissonance.* Stanford, CA: Stanford University Press.

15. Killian, L. M., Festinger, L., Riecken, H. W., & Schachter, S. (1957). When Prophecy Fails. *American Sociological Review*, *22*(2), 236–237. https://doi.org/10.2307/2088869

16. Ibid.

17. Taber, C. S., & Lodge, M. (2006). Motivated Skepticism in the Evaluation of Political Beliefs. *American Journal of Political Science*, *50*(3), 755–769.

18. Dobelli, R. (2014). *The Art of Thinking Clearly: Better Thinking, Better Decisions*. New York: HarperCollins Publishers.

19. This Girl Can. Retrieved February 2, 2018, from www .thisgirlcan.co.uk/

20. Coupe, B. (1966). The Roth Test and Its Corollaries. *William & Mary Law Review*, *8*(1), 121–132. http://scholarship.law .wm.edu/cgi/viewcontent.cgi?article=3035&context=wmlr

21. Strum, C. (1991). Brew Battle on Campus—Ban the Can or the Keg? Retrieved February 1, 2018, from www.nytimes .com/1991/10/08/nyregion/brew-battle-on-campus-ban-the-can -or-the-keg.html

CHAPTER 3: ON THE MONEY?

1. Duffy, B., Hall, S., & Shrimpton, H. (2015). On the Money? Misperceptions and Personal Finance. Retrieved April 11, 2018, from www.ipsos.com/ipsos-mori/en-uk/money -misperceptions-and-personal-finance

2. Duffy, B. (2013). Public Understanding of Statistics Topline Results. Retrieved April 11, 2018, from www.ipsos.com /sites/default/files/migrations/en-uk/files/Assets/Docs/Polls/rss -kings-ipsos-mori-trust-in-statistics-topline.pdf

3. Thaler, R. H., & Sunstein, C. R. (2009). Nudge. *Nudge— Business Summaries*, 1–5. Retrieved May 28, 2019, from http:// connection.ebscohost.com/c/book-summarys/60448472/nudge

4. Liverpool Victoria. (2016). Raising a Child More Expensive Than Buying a House. Retrieved February 1, 2018, from www .lv.com/about-us/press/article/cost-of-a-child-2016

5. Duffy, B., Hall, S., & Shrimpton, H. (2015). On the Money? Misperceptions and Personal Finance. Retrieved April 11, 2018, from www.ipsos.com/ipsos-mori/en-uk/money -misperceptions-and-personal-finance

6. Bullock, J. G., Gerber, A. S., Hill, S. J., & Huber, G. A. (2015). Partisan Bias in Factual Beliefs About Politics. *Quarterly Journal of Political Science*, *10*, 519–578; Prior, M., Sood, G., & Khanna, K. (2015). You Cannot Be Serious: The Impact of Accuracy Incentives on Partisan Bias in Reports of Economic Perceptions. *Quarterly Journal of Political Science*, *10*(4), 489–518.

7. Vanham, P. (2017). Global Pension Timebomb: Funding Gap Set to Dwarf World GDP. Retrieved April 11, 2018, from www.weforum.org/press/2017/05/global-pension -timebomb-funding-gap-set-to-dwarf-world-gdp

8. Jolls, C., Sunstein, C. R., & Thaler, R. (1998). A Behavioral Approach to Law and Economics. *Faculty Scholarship Series*, *Paper 1765*, 1471–1498 (part I).

9. Ipsos MORI. (2015). Major Survey Shows Britons Overestimate the Bad Behaviour of Other People. Retrieved April 11, 2018, from www.ipsos.com/ipsos-mori/en-uk/major -survey-shows-britons-overestimate-bad-behaviour-other-people

10. Credit Suisse Research Institute. (2017). Global Wealth Report 2016. Retrieved April 11, 2018, from www .credit-suisse.com/corporate/en/articles/news-and-expertise/the -global-wealth-report-2016-201611.html

11. Kurt, D. (2018). Are You in the Top One Percent of the World? Retrieved April 11, 2018, from www.investopedia.com /articles/personal-finance/050615/are-you-top-one-percent-world .asp

12. Credit Suisse Research Institute. (2017). Global Wealth Report 2017. Retrieved April 11, 2018, from http://publications .credit-suisse.com/tasks/render/file/index.cfm?fileid=12DFFD63 -07D1-EC63-A3D5F67356880EF3

13. Ponting, G. (2017). How Rich Are You? Retrieved April 16, 2018, from www.clearwaterwealth.co.uk/blog/2017/11/7/how -rich-are-you

14. Credit Suisse Research Institute. (2017). Global Wealth Report 2017. Retrieved April 11, 2018, from http://publications .credit-suisse.com/tasks/render/file/index.cfm?fileid=12DFFD63 -07D1-EC63-A3D5F67356880EF3

15. Gimpelson, V., & Treisman, D. (2017). Misperceiving Inequality. *Economics and Politics*, *30*(1), 27–54. https://doi .org/10.1111/ecpo.12103

16. Ariely, D., Loewenstein, G., & Prelec, D. (2003). 'Coherent Arbitrariness': Stable Demand Curves Without Stable Preferences. *The Quarterly Journal of Economics*, *118*(1), 73–106. https:// doi.org/10.1162/00335530360535153

17. Citizens Advice. (2015). *Financial Capability: A Review of the Latest Evidence*. Retrieved April 11, 2018, from www .citizensadvice.org.uk/Global/Public/Impact/Financial%20 Capability%20Literature%20Review.pdf

CHAPTER 4: INSIDE AND OUT: IMMIGRATION AND RELIGION

1. Citrin, J., & Sides, J. (2008). Immigration and the Imagined Community in Europe and the United States. *Political Studies*, *56*(1), 33–56. https://doi.org/10.1111/j.1467-9248.2007.00716.x; Wong, C. J. (2007). 'Little' and 'Big' Pictures in Our Heads Race, Local Context, and Innumeracy About Racial Groups in the United States. *Public Opinion Quarterly*, *71*(3), 393–412. https:// doi.org/10.1093/poq/nfm023

2. Hainmueller, J., & Hopkins, D. J. (2014). Public Attitudes Toward Immigration. *Annual Review of Political Science*, *17*(1), 225–249. https://doi.org/10.1146/annurev-polisci-102512 -194818

3. Blinder, S. (2015). Imagined Immigration: The Impact of Different Meanings of 'Immigrants' in Public Opinion and Policy

Debates in Britain. *Political Studies*, *63*(1), 80–100. https://doi
.org/10.1111/1467-9248.12053

4. Migration Watch UK. (n.d.). An Independent and Non-
Political Think Tank Concerned About the Scale of Immigration
into the UK. Retrieved February 2, 2018, from www.migration
watchuk.org/

5. Citrin, J., & Sides, J. (2008). Immigration and the Imagined
Community in Europe and the United States. *Political Studies*,
56(1), 33–56. https://doi.org/10.1111/j.1467-9248.2007.00716.x;
Hainmueller, J., & Hopkins, D. J. (2014). Public Attitudes Toward Immigration. *Annual Review of Political Science*, *17*(1),
225–249. https://doi.org/10.1146/annurev-polisci-102512-194818

6. Grigorieff, A., Roth, C., & Ubfal, D. (2016). Does Information Change Attitudes Towards Immigrants? Evidence from Survey Experiments. Retrieved April 11, 2018, from www.lse.ac.uk
/iga/assets/documents/events/2016/does-information-change
-attitudes-towards-immigrants.pdf

7. Campbell, A., Converse, P. E., Miller, W. E., & Stokes, D.
E. (1960). *The American Voter*. New York: John Wiley and Sons.
https://doi.org/10.2307/1952653

8. Nyhan, B., & Reifler, J. (2010). When Corrections Fail:
The Persistence of Political Misperceptions. *Political Behavior*,
32(2), 303–330. https://doi.org/10.1007/s11109-010-9112-2

9. Ibid.; Wood, T., & Porter, E. (2016). The Elusive Backfire
Effect: Mass Attitudes' Steadfast Factual Adherence. *SSRN Electronic Journal*. https://doi.org/10.2139/ssrn.2819073

10. Ibid.

11. Duffy, B., & Frere-Smith, T. (2014). Perceptions
and Reality: Public Attitudes to Immigration. Retrieved
April 11, 2018, from www.ipsos.com/ipsos-mori/en-uk
/perceptions-and-reality-public-attitudes-immigration

12. Ipsos MORI. (2018). Attitudes to Immigration: National Issue or Global Challenge? Retrieved April 11, 2018,

from www.slideshare.net/IpsosMORI/attitudes-to-immigration
-national-issue-or-global-challenge

13. Bell, B. (2013). Immigration and Crime: Evidence
for the UK and Other Countries. Retrieved April 11, 2018,
from www.migrationobservatory.ox.ac.uk/resources/briefings
/immigration-and-crime-evidence-for-the-uk-and-other-countries/

14. Ibid.

15. Doyle, J., & Wright, S. (2012). 'Immigrant Crimewave'
Warning: Foreign Nationals Were Accused of a QUARTER of
All Crimes in London. Retrieved February 2, 2018, from www
.dailymail.co.uk/news/article-2102895/Immigrant-crimewave
-warning-Foreign-nationals-accused-QUARTER-crimes-London
.html

16. Tversky, A., & Kahneman, D. (1974). Judgement Under
Uncertainty: Heuristics and Biases. *Science*, *185*(4157), 1124–1131.
https://doi.org/10.1126/science.185.4157.1124

17. Ariely, D., Loewenstein, G., & Prelec, D. (2003). 'Coherent Arbitrariness': Stable Demand Curves Without Stable Preferences. *The Quarterly Journal of Economics*, *118*(1), 73–106. https://
doi.org/10.1162/00335530360535153

18. Allen, C. (2012). Muslims & the Media: Headline Research Findings 2001–12. University of Birming-
ham. Retrieved April 11, 2018, from www.birmingham.ac.uk
/Documents/college-social-sciences/social-policy/IASS/news
-events/MEDIA-ChrisAllen-APPGEvidence-Oct2012.pdf

19. Ito, T. A., Larsen, J. T., Smith, N. K., & Cacioppo, J.
T. (1998). Negative Information Weighs More Heavily on the
Brain: The Negativity Bias in Evaluative Categorizations. *Journal of Personality and Social Psychology*, *75*(4), 887–900. https://
doi.org/10.1037/0022-3514.75.4.887; Ito, T. A., & Cacioppo, J. T.
(2005). Variations on a Human Universal: Individual Differences
in Positivity Offset and Negativity Bias. *Cognition and Emotion*,
19(1), 1–26. https://doi.org/10.1080/02699930441000120

20. Cao, Z., Zhao, Y., Tan, T., Chen, G., Ning, X., Zhan, L., & Yang, J. (2014). Distinct Brain Activity in Processing Negative Pictures of Animals and Objects—the Role of Human Contexts. *Neuroimage, 84.* http://doi.org/10.1016/j.neuroimage.2013.09.064

21. Benson, K., & Gottman, J. (2017). The Magic Relationship Ratio, According to Science. Retrieved February 2, 2018, from www.gottman.com/blog/the-magic-relationship -ratio-according-science/

22. Duffy, B. (2013). Public Understanding of Statistics Topline Results. Retrieved April 11, 2018, from www.ipsos.com /sites/default/files/migrations/en-uk/files/Assets/Docs/Polls /rss-kings-ipsos-mori-trust-in-statistics-topline.pdf

23. Fechner, G. T. (1860). *Elemente der Psychophysik.* Leipzig: Breitkopf & Härtel.

24. Ibid.

25. Huxley, A. (1928). *Proper Studies.* Garden City, NY: Doubleday, Doran & Company.

CHAPTER 5: SAFE AND SECURE

1. *The Guardian.* (1950). From the Archive, 18 March 1950: The Flogging Debate. Retrieved February 1, 2018, from www .theguardian.com/theguardian/2011/mar/18/archive-flogging -debate-1950

2. Ibid.

3. Ibid.

4. Hanlon, G. (2014). Violence and Punishment: Civilizing the Body Through Time by Pieter Spierenburg (Review). *Journal of Interdisciplinary History, 44*(3), 379–381. https://muse.jhu.edu /article/526377/summary

5. Pew Research Center. (2013). Gun Homicide Rate Down 49% Since 1993 Peak; Public Unaware. Retrieved April 11, 2018, from http://assets.pewresearch.org/wp-content/uploads /sites/3/2013/05/firearms_final_05-2013.pdf

6. Beckwé, M., Deroost, N., Koster, E. H. W., De Lissnyder, E., & De Raedt, R. (2014). Worrying and Rumination Are Both Associated with Reduced Cognitive Control. *Psychological Research*, *78*(5), 651–660. https://doi.org/10.1007/s00426-013-0517-5

7. Mitchell, T. R., Thompson, L., Peterson, E., & Cronk, R. (1997). Temporal Adjustments in the Evaluation of Events: The 'Rosy View'. *Journal of Experimental Social Psychology*, *33*(4), 421–448. https://doi.org/10.1006/JESP.1997.1333

8. Hallinan, J. T. (2009). *Errornomics: Why We Make Mistakes and What We Can Do to Avoid Them*. London: Ebury Press.

9. Full list of Perils of Perception studies on page 247.

10. Harcup, T., & O'Neill, D. (2001). What Is News? Galtung and Ruge Revisited. *Journalism Studies*, *2*(2), 261–280. https://doi .org/10.1080/14616700118449

11. Ibid.

12. Dunbar, R. (1998). *Grooming, Gossip, and the Evolution of Language*. Cambridge: Harvard University Press.

13. Trump, D. J. (2017). Just Out Report: 'United Kingdom Crime Rises 13% Annually amid Spread of Radical Islamic Terror'. Not Good, We Must Keep America Safe! Retrieved April 11, 2018, from https://twitter.com/realdonaldtrump/status /921323063945453574?lang=en

14. Nelson, F. (2017). 'Amid' Is a Word Beloved by Fake News Websites, to Conflate Correlation and Causation. UK Crime Is Also Up 'Amid' Spread of Fidget Spinners. Retrieved April 11, 2018, from https://twitter.com/frasernelson/status/92133508933 3723136?lang=en-gb

15. Trump, D. J. (2017). Remarks by President Trump in Roundtable with County Sheriffs. Retrieved February 6, 2018, from www.whitehouse.gov/briefings-statements/remarks-president -trump-roundtable-county-sheriffs/

16. No author. (n.d.). Illusory Truth Effect. Retrieved April 11, 2018, from https://en.wikipedia.org/wiki/Illusory_truth_effect

17. Vedantam, S. (2015). How Emotional Responses to Terrorism Shape Attitudes Toward Policies. Retrieved April 11, 2018, from www.npr.org/2015/12/22/460656763/how-emotional-responses-to-terrorism-shape-attitudes-toward-policies

18. ul Hassan, Z. (2015). A Data Scientist Explains Odds of Dying in a Terrorist Attack. Retrieved February 1, 2018, from www.techjuice.pk/a-data-scientist-explains-odds-of-dying-in-a-terrorist-attack/

19. Pinker, S. (2018). The Disconnect Between Pessimism and Optimism—on Why We Refuse to See the Bright Side, Even Though We Should. Retrieved February 1, 2018, from http://time.com/5087384/harvard-professor-steven-pinker-on-why-we-refuse-to-see-the-bright-side/

20. The White House. (2016). Remarks by President Obama at Stavros Niarchos Foundation Cultural Center in Athens, Greece. Retrieved April 16, 2018, from https://obamawhitehouse.archives.gov/the-press-office/2016/11/16/remarks-president-obama-stavros-niarchos-foundation-cultural-center

CHAPTER 6: POLITICAL MISDIRECTION AND DISENGAGEMENT

1. BBC News & Paxman, J. (2013). Boris Johnson's *Newsnight* Interview. Retrieved February 6, 2018, from www.bbc.co.uk/news/av/uk-politics-24343570/boris-johnson-s-newsnight-interview-in-full

2. Duffy, B., Hall, S., & Shrimpton, H. (2015). On the Money? Misperceptions and Personal Finance. Retrieved April 11, 2018, from www.ipsos.com/ipsos-mori/en-uk/money-misperceptions-and-personal-finance

3. Franklin, M. N. (2004). Voter Turnout and the Dynamics of Electoral Competition in Established Democracies Since 1945. Retrieved April 11, 2018, from https://doi.org/10.1017/CBO9780511616884

4. Ibid.

5. Downs, A. (1957). An Economic Theory of Political Action in a Democracy. *The Journal of Political Economy, 65*(2), 135–150. https://doi.org/10.1017/CBO9781107415324.004

6. Delli Carpini, M. X., & Keeter, S. (1991). Stability and Change in the U.S. Public's Knowledge of Politics. *Public Opinion Quarterly, 55*(4), 583–612. https://doi.org/10.1086/269283

7. Somin, I. (2016). *Democracy and Political Ignorance: Why Smaller Government Is Smarter.* Stanford: Stanford University Press.

8. World Economic Forum. (2017). The Global Gender Gap Report 2017. Retrieved April 11, 2018, from www3.weforum.org /docs/WEF_GGGR_2017.pdf

9. Kaur-Ballagan, K., & Stannard, J. (2018). International Women's Day: Global Misperceptions of Equality and the Need to Press for Progress. Retrieved April 11, 2018, from www.ipsos .com/ipsos-mori/en-uk/international-womens-day-global -misperceptions-equality-and-need-press-progress

10. SKL Jämställdhet. (2014). Sustainable Gender Equality—a Film About Gender Mainstreaming in Practice. Retrieved April 11, 2018, from www.youtube.com/watch?v =udSjBbGwJEg

11. International IDEA. (n.d.). Gender Quotas Data— Mexico. Retrieved February 6, 2018, from www.idea.int/data -tools/data/gender-quotas/country-view/220/35; International IDEA. (n.d.). Gender Quotas Database—Voluntary Political Party Quotas. Retrieved February 6, 2018, from www.idea.int /data-tools/data/gender-quotas/voluntary-overview

12. Kessler, G. (2016). Donald Trump Still Does Not Understand the Unemployment Rate. Retrieved April 16, 2018, from www.washingtonpost.com/news/fact-checker/wp/2016/12/12 /donald-trump-still-does-not-understand-the-unemployment -rate/?utm_term=.ec1d66e9a8d7

13. Horsley, S. (2017). Donald Trump Says 'Real' Unemployment Higher Than Government Figures Show. Retrieved February 6, 2018, from www.npr.org/2017/01/29/511493685

/ahead-of-trumps-first-jobs-report-a-look-at-his-remarks-on-the-numbers; Kessler, G. (n.d.). Fact Checker. Retrieved February 6, 2018, from www.washingtonpost.com/news/fact-checker/?utm_term=.a54148f4ef99

14. Trump, D. J. (2016). President Elect Donald Trump Holds Rally Des Moines Iowa, Dec 8 2016. Retrieved February 6, 2018, from www.c-span.org/video/?419792-1/president-elect-donald-trump-holds-rally-des-moines-iowa

15. ABC News. (2017). Transcript: ABC News Anchor David Muir Interviews President Trump. Retrieved April 11, 2018, from http://abcnews.go.com/Politics/transcript-abc-news-anchor-david-muir-interviews-president/story?id=45047602

16. d'Ancona, M. (2017). *Post-Truth: The New War on Truth and How to Fight Back*. London: Ebury Press.

17. Guo, J., & Cramer, K. (2016). A New Theory for Why Trump Voters Are So Angry. Retrieved February 6, 2018, from www.washingtonpost.com/news/wonk/wp/2016/11/08/a-new-theory-for-why-trump-voters-are-so-angry-that-actually-makes-sense/?utm_term=.4cf2a7a177ea

18. Lenz, G. S. (2012). *Follow the Leader? How Voters Respond to Politicians' Policies and Performance*. Chicago: University of Chicago Press.

19. Duffy, B. (2013). In an Age of Big Data and Focus on Economic Issues, Trust in the Use of Statistics Remains Low. Retrieved April 11, 2018, from www.ipsos.com/ipsos-mori/en-uk/age-big-data-and-focus-economic-issues-trust-use-statistics-remains-low

CHAPTER 7: BREXIT AND TRUMP: WISHFUL AND WRONGFUL THINKING

1. d'Ancona, M. (2017). *Post-Truth: The New War on Truth and How to Fight Back*. London: Ebury Press.

2. Duffy, B., & Shrimpton, H. (2016). The Perils of Perception and the EU. Retrieved April 11, 2018, from www.ipsos.com/ipsos-mori/en-uk/perils-perception-and-eu

3. Evans-Pritchard, A. (2016). AEP: 'Irritation and Anger' May Lead to Brexit, Says Influential Psychologist. Retrieved February 6, 2018, from www.telegraph.co.uk/business/2016/06/05/british-voters-succumbing-to-impulse-irritation-and-anger

4. Kahan, D. M., Peters, E., Dawson, E. C., & Slovic, P. (2017). Motivated Numeracy and Enlightened Self-Government. *Behavioural Public Policy*, *1*(1), 54–86. https://doi.org/10.1017/bpp.2016.2

5. Kahan, D. M. (2012). Ideology, Motivated Reasoning, and Cognitive Reflection: An Experimental Study. *SSRN Electronic Journal*, *8*(4), 407–424. https://doi.org/10.2139/ssrn.2182588

6. Wring, D. (2016). Going Bananas over Brussels: Fleet Street's European Journey. Retrieved April 16, 2018, from https://theconversation.com/going-bananas-over-brussels-fleet-streets-european-journey-61327

7. Simons, N. (2016). Boris Johnson Claims EU Stops Bananas Being Sold in Bunches of More Than Three. That Is Not True. Retrieved February 6, 2018, from www.huffingtonpost.co.uk/entry/boris-johnson-claims-eu-stops-bananas-being-sold-in-bunches-of-more-than-three-that-is-not-true_uk_573b2445e4b0f0f53e36c968

8. The European Commission. (2011). Commission Implementing Regulation (EU) No 1333/2011 of 19 December 2011 Laying Down Marketing Standards for Bananas, Rules on the Verification of Compliance with Those Marketing Standards and Requirements for Notifications in the Banana Sector. *Official Journal of the European Union*. Retrieved April 11, 2018, from http://eur-lex.europa.eu/LexUriServ/LexUriServ.do?uri=OJ:L:2011:336:0023:0034:EN:PDF

9. Duffy, B., & Shrimpton, H. (2016). The Perils of Perception and the EU. Retrieved April 11, 2018, from www.ipsos.com/ipsos-mori/en-uk/perils-perception-and-eu

10. Murphy, M. (2017). Question Time Audience Member Says She Voted for Brexit at Last Minute Because 'A

Banana Is Straight'. Retrieved February 6, 2018, from www
.independent.co.uk/news/uk/home-news/question-time-woman
-banana-is-straight-audience-member-brexit-vote-last-minute
-eu-referendum-a7560781.html

11. Ibid.

12. Norgrove, D. (2017). Letter from Sir David Norgrove
to Foreign Secretary. Retrieved April 11, 2018, from www
.statisticsauthority.gov.uk/wp-content/uploads/2017/09/Letter
-from-Sir-David-Norgrove-to-Foreign-Secretary.pdf. For further detail on official statistics relating to the UK's financial
contributions to the EU, see Dilnot, A. (2016). UK Contributions to the European Union, UK Statistics Authority. Retrieved
April 11, 2018, from www.statisticsauthority.gov.uk/wp-content
/uploads/2016/04/Letter-from-Sir-Andrew-Dilnot-to-Norman
-Lamb-MP-210416.pdf

13. Dilnot, A. (2016). UK Contributions to the European
Union, UK Statistics Authority. Retrieved April 11, 2018, from
www.statisticsauthority.gov.uk/wp-content/uploads/2016/04
/Letter-from-Sir-Andrew-Dilnot-to-Norman-Lamb-MP-210416
.pdf

14. BBC News. (2018). £350m Brexit Claim Was 'Too Low',
Says Boris Johnson. Retrieved February 6, 2018, from www.bbc
.co.uk/news/uk-42698981

15. Farage, N. (2017). Farage: Why I Didn't Refute
'£350m for NHS' Figure Until After Brexit. Retrieved February 6, 2018, from www.lbc.co.uk/radio/presenters/nigel-farage
/farage-didnt-refute-350m-nhs-figure-after-brexit/

16. Stone, J. (2016). Nearly Half of Britons Believe Vote
Leave's False '£350 Million a Week to the EU' Claim. Retrieved
April 16, 2018, from www.independent.co.uk/news/uk/politics
/nearly-half-of-britons-believe-vote-leaves-false-350-million-a
-week-to-the-eu-claim-a7085016.html

17. Fisher, S., & Renwick, A. (2016). Do People Tend to Vote
Against Change in Referendums? Retrieved February 6, 2018,

from https://constitution-unit.com/2016/06/22/do-people-tend
-to-vote-against-change-in-referendums/

18. Bell, E. (2016). The Truth About Brexit Didn't Stand a
Chance in the Online Bubble. Retrieved February 6, 2018, from
www.theguardian.com/media/2016/jul/03/facebook-bubble
-brexit-filter

19. Menon, A. (2016). Facts Matter More in This Referendum Than in Any Other Popular Vote, but They Are Scarce.
Retrieved April 11, 2018, from http://ukandeu.ac.uk/facts
-matter-more-in-this-referendum-than-in-any-other-popular-vote
-but-they-are-scarce/

20. Salmon, N. (2017). Donald Trump Takes Credit for In-
venting the Word 'Fake'. Retrieved April 16, 2018, from www
.independent.co.uk/news/world/americas/donald-trump-takes
-credit-for-inventing-the-word-fake-a7989221.html

21. Silverman, C., & Singer-Vine, J. (2016). Most Americans Who See Fake News Believe It, New Survey Says. Retrieved
February 6, 2018, from www.buzzfeed.com/craigsilverman/fake
-news-survey?utm_term=.dqxK8oRXO#.teYG32pl1

22. Ibid.

23. Flynn, D. J., Nyhan, B., & Reifler, J. (2017). The Nature
and Origins of Misperceptions: Understanding False and Unsupported Beliefs About Politics. *Political Psychology*, *38*(682758),
127–150. https://doi.org/10.1111/pops.12394

24. Paulhus, D. L., Harms, P. D., Bruce, M. N., & Lysy,
D. C. (2003). The Over-Claiming Technique: Measuring Self-
Enhancement Independent of Ability. Retrieved April 11, 2018,
from http://digitalcommons.unl.edu/leadershipfacpub

25. Stone, J. (2015). The MP Tricked into Condemning a
Fake Drug Called 'Cake' Is to Chair a Committee Debating New
Drugs Law. Retrieved April 16, 2018, from www.independent
.co.uk/news/uk/politics/the-mp-tricked-into-condemning-a
-fake-drug-called-cake-has-been-put-in-charge-of-scrutinising
-drugs-a6704671.html

26. Robin, N. (2006). Interview with Stephen Colbert. Retrieved February 6, 2018, from https://tv.avclub.com/stephen-colbert-1798208958

27. Suskind, R. (2004). Faith, Certainty and the Presidency of George W. Bush. Retrieved April 11, 2018, from www.nytimes.com/2004/10/17/magazine/faith-certainty-and-the-presidency-of-george-w-bush.html

28. Andersen, K. (2017). How America Lost Its Mind. Retrieved February 6, 2018, from www.theatlantic.com/magazine/archive/2017/09/how-america-lost-its-mind/534231/

29. Surowiecki, J. (2005). The Wisdom of Crowds. *American Journal of Physics*, 75(908), 336. https://doi.org/10.1038/climate.2009.73

30. The Onion Politics. (2017). Fearful Americans Stockpiling Facts Before Federal Government Comes to Take Them Away. Retrieved February 6, 2018, from https://politics.theonion.com/fearful-americans-stockpiling-facts-before-federal-gove-1819579589

CHAPTER 8: FILTERING OUR WORLDS

1. Manyinka, J., & Varian, H. (2009). Hal Varian on How the Web Challenges Managers. Retrieved February 6, 2018, from www.mckinsey.com/industries/high-tech/our-insights/hal-varian-on-how-the-web-challenges-managers

2. Ipsos MORI. (2013). Margins of Error: Public Understanding of Statistics in an Era of Big Data. Retrieved April 11, 2018, from www.slideshare.net/IpsosMORI/margins-of-error-public-understanding-of-statistics-in-an-era-of-big-data

3. Manyinka, J., & Varian, H. (2009). Hal Varian on How the Web Challenges Managers. Retrieved February 6, 2018, from www.mckinsey.com/industries/high-tech/our-insights/hal-varian-on-how-the-web-challenges-managers

4. Williams, J. (2017). Are Digital Technologies Making Politics Impossible? Retrieved February 16, 2018, from https://ninedotsprize.org/winners/james-williams/

5. Pariser, E. (2011). The Filter Bubble: What the Internet Is Hiding from You. *ZNet*, 304. https://doi.org/10.1353/pla.2011.0036

6. Rashid, F. Y. (2014). Surveillance Is the Business Model of the Internet: Bruce Schneier. Retrieved April 11, 2018, from www.securityweek.com/surveillance-business-model-internet -bruce-schneier

7. Heffernan, M. (2017). Speaking at Ipsos MORI EOY Event 2017. London.

8. Muir, N. (2018). If These Algorithms Know Me So Well, How Come They Aren't Advertising Poundstretcher and Wetherspoons? Retrieved February 6, 2018, from www.thedailymash .co.uk/news/science-technology/if-these-algorithms-know-me -so-well-how-come-they-arent-advertising-poundstretcher-and -wetherspoons-20180111142199

9. Habermas, J. (2006). Political Communication in Media Society: Does Democracy Still Enjoy an Epistemic Dimension? The Impact of Normative Theory on Empirical Research. *Communication Theory*, *16*(4), 411–426. https://doi .org/10.1111/j.1468-2885.2006.00280.x

10. Epstein, R., & Robertson, R. E. (2015). The Search Engine Manipulation Effect (SEME) and Its Possible Impact on the Outcomes of Elections. *Proceedings of the National Academy of Sciences of the United States of America*, *112*(33), E4512–21. https:// doi.org/10.1073/pnas.1419828112

11. Graham, D. A. (2018). Not Even Cambridge Analytica Believed Its Hype. Retrieved April 11, 2018, from www .theatlantic.com/politics/archive/2018/03/cambridge-analyticas -self-own/556016/

12. Wardle, C., & Derakhshan, H. (2017). Information Disorder: Toward an Interdisciplinary Framework for Research and Policy Making. Retrieved April 11, 2018, from https:// rm.coe.int/information-disorder-toward-an-interdisciplinary -framework-for-research/168076277c

13. Silverman, C. (2016). This Analysis Shows How Viral Fake Election News Stories Outperformed Real News on Facebook. Retrieved February 6, 2018, from www.buzzfeed.com /craigsilverman/viral-fake-election-news-outperformed-real -news-on-facebook?utm_term=.nwQB7N9by#.pi8BYrng0

14. McGhee, A. (2017). Cyber Warfare Unit Set to Be Launched by Australian Defence Forces. Retrieved April 11, 2018, from www.abc.net.au/news/2017-06-30/cyber-warfare-unit-to -be-launched-by-australian-defence-forces/8665230

15. Arendt, H. (1951). *The Origins of Totalitarianism.* New York: Schocken Books.

16. Wardle, C., & Derakhshan, H. (2017). Information Disorder: Toward an Interdisciplinary Framework for Research and Policy Making. Retrieved April 11, 2018, from https:// rm.coe.int/information-disorder-toward-an-interdisciplinary -framework-for-research/168076277c

17. Stray, J. (n.d.). Defense Against the Dark Arts: Networked Propaganda and Counter-propaganda. https://doi.org /https://medium.com/tow-center/defense-against-the-dark-arts -networked-propaganda-and-counter-propaganda-deb7145aa76a

18. Obama, B. (2017). President Obama Farewell Address: Full Text [Video]. Retrieved February 6, 2018, from https:// edition.cnn.com/2017/01/10/politics/president-obama-farewell -speech/index.html

19. Carey, J. W. (n.d.). A Cultural Approach to Communication. Retrieved April 11, 2018, from http://faculty.georgetown.edu /irvinem/theory/Carey-ACulturalAproachtoCommunication.pdf

20. Strusani, D. (2014). Value of Connectivity: Benefits of Expanding Internet Access. Retrieved April 11, 2018, from www2.deloitte.com/uk/en/pages/technology-media-and -telecommunications/articles/value-of-connectivity.html

21. Constine, J. (2017). Facebook Changes Mission Statement to 'Bring the World Closer Together'. Retrieved April

16, 2018, from https://techcrunch.com/2017/06/22/bring -the-world-closer-together/

22. Zephoria. (2018). The Top 20 Valuable Facebook Statistics—Updated April 2018. Retrieved April 11, 2018, from https://zephoria.com/top-15-valuable-facebook-statistics/

23. Foer, F. (2017). Facebook's War on Free Will. Retrieved April 16, 2018, from www.theguardian.com/technology/2017 /sep/19/facebooks-war-on-free-will

24. Today in Focus podcast. (2018). www.theguardian.com /news/audio/2018/dec/17/2018-a-terrible-year-for-facebook -podcast

25. Reuters Staff. (2018). Americans Less Likely to Trust Facebook Than Rivals on Personal Data. Retrieved April 11, 2018, from www.reuters.com/article/us-facebook-cambridge -analytica-apology/americans-less-likely-to-trust-facebook-than -rivals-on-personal-data-idUSKBN1H10AF

26. Abbruzzese, J. (2017). Facebook and Google Domi- nate in Online News—but for Very Different Topics. Retrieved April 17, 2018, from https://mashable.com/2017/05/23/google -facebook-dominate-referrals-different-content/#BcTajPpdbiqk

27. Trafton, A. (2014). In the Blink of an Eye. Retrieved February 6, 2018, from http://news.mit.edu/2014/in-the-blink -of-an-eye-0116

28. Langston, J. (2017). Lip-Syncing Obama: New Tools Turn Audio Clips into Realistic Video. Retrieved February 6, 2018, from www.washington.edu/news/2017/07/11/lip-syncing -obama-new-tools-turn-audio-clips-into-realistic-video/

29. Lee, D. (2018). Deepfakes Porn Has Serious Conse- quences. Retrieved April 11, 2018, from www.bbc.co.uk/news /technology-42912529

30. Bode, L., & Vraga, E. K. (2015). In Related News, That Was Wrong: The Correction of Misinformation Through Related Stories Functionality in Social Media. *Journal of Communication*, *65*(4), 619–638. https://doi.org/10.1111/jcom.12166

31. Wardle, C., & Derakhshan, H. (2017). Information Disorder: Toward an Interdisciplinary Framework for Research and Policy Making. Retrieved April 11, 2018, from https://rm.coe.int/information-disorder-toward-an-interdisciplinary-framework-for-research/168076277c

32. Sippitt, A. (2017). Interview Conducted by Bobby Duffy with Amy Sippitt at Full Fact. London.

33. Paul, C., & Matthews, M. (2016). The Russian 'Firehose of Falsehood' Propaganda Model: Why It Might Work and Options to Counter It. https://doi.org/10.7249/PE198

34. Soros, G. (2018). Remarks Delivered at the World Economic Forum. Retrieved February 6, 2018, from www.georgesoros.com/2018/01/25/remarks-delivered-at-the-world-economic-forum/

35. Naughton, J. (2018). The New Surveillance Capitalism. Retrieved February 6, 2018, from www.prospectmagazine.co.uk/science-and-technology/how-the-internet-controls-you

36. Ibid.

37. NPR Morning Edition. (2017). Italy Takes Aim at Fake News with New Curriculum for High School Students. Retrieved April 11, 2018, from www.npr.org/2017/10/31/561041307/italy-takes-aim-at-fake-news-with-new-curriculum-for-high-school-students

38. BBC Media Centre. (2017). BBC Journalists Return to School to Tackle 'Fake News'. Retrieved April 11, 2018, from www.bbc.co.uk/mediacentre/latestnews/2017/fake-news

CHAPTER 9: WORLDWIDE WORRY

1. DiJulio, B., Norton, M., & Brodie, M. (2016). Americans' Views on the U.S. Role in Global Health. Retrieved April 11, 2018, from www.kff.org/global-health-policy/poll-finding/americans-views-on-the-u-s-role-in-global-health/

2. Rosling, H. (2006). Hans Rosling: The Best Stats You've Ever Seen. Retrieved February 6, 2018, from www.ted.com/talks/hans_rosling_shows_the_best_stats_you_ve_ever_seen

3. Gapminder. (n.d.). Retrieved April 16, 2018, from www .gapminder.org

4. Rosling, A., & Rosling, O. (2018). Lecture at the London School of Economics and Political Science, April 2018.

5. BBC News. (2013). Hans Rosling: Do You Know More About the World Than a Chimpanzee? Retrieved February 6, 2018, from www.bbc.co.uk/news/magazine-24836917

6. Vanderslott, S., & Roser, M. (2018). Vaccination. Retrieved April 11, 2018, from https://ourworldindata.org/vaccination

7. CBC News. (2015). Child Vaccines out of Reach for Developing Countries, Charity Warns. Retrieved February 1, 2018, from www.cbc.ca/news/health/child-vaccines-out-of-reach-for -developing-countries-charity-warns-1.2919787

8. Roser, M. (2017). Newspapers Could Have Had the Headline 'Number of People in Extreme Poverty Fell by 137,000 Since Yesterday' Every Day in the Last 25 Years. Retrieved April 11, 2018, from https://twitter.com/maxcroser/statu s/852813032723857409?lang=en

9. Pinker, S. (2018). The Disconnect Between Pessimism and Optimism—on Why We Refuse to See the Bright Side, Even Though We Should. Retrieved February 1, 2018, from http:// time.com/5087384/harvard-professor-steven-pinker-on-why-we -refuse-to-see-the-bright-side/

10. Pinker, S. (2011). *The Better Angels of Our Nature: Why Violence Has Declined*. New York: Viking Books.

11. Loewy, K. (2016). I'm Not Saying That David Bowie Was Holding the Fabric of the Universe Together, but *Gestures Broadly at Everything*. Retrieved April 12, 2018, from https://twitter .com/sweetestcyanide/status/752831763269967872?lang=en

12. Duffy, B. (2017). *Is the World Getting Better or Worse?* Retrieved April 11, 2018, from www.ipsos.com/sites/default/files/ct /publication/documents/2017-11/ipsos-mori-almanac-2017.pdf

13. Psychology and Crime News Blog. (n.d.). If I Look at the

Mass I Will Never Act. If I Look at the One, I Will. Retrieved February 1, 2018, from http://crimepsychblog.com/?p=1457

14. Kristof, D. N. (2009). Nicholas Kristof's Advice for Saving the World. Retrieved February 1, 2018, from www.outsideonline.com/1909636/nicholas-kristofs-advice-saving-world

15. Ibid.

16. Small, D. A., & Verrochi, N. M. (2009). The Face of Need: Facial Emotion Expression on Charity Advertisements. *Journal of Marketing Research*, *46*(6), 777–787. https://doi.org/10.1509/jmkr.46.6.777

17. Small, D. A., & Loewenstein, G. (2003). Helping a Victim or Helping the Victim: Altruism and Identifiability. *Journal of Risk and Uncertainty*, *26*(1), 5–16. https://doi.org/10.1023/A:1022299422219

18. Post, S. G. (2005). Altruism, Happiness, and Health: It's Good to Be Good. *International Journal of Behavioural Medicine*, *12*(2), 66–77.

19. Wallace-Wells, D. (2017). When Will Climate Change Make the Earth Too Hot for Humans? Retrieved February 1, 2018, from http://nymag.com/daily/intelligencer/2017/07/climate-change-earth-too-hot-for-humans.html

20. Mann, E. M., Hassol, J. S., & Toles, T. (2017). Doomsday Scenarios Are as Harmful as Climate Change Denial. Retrieved February 1, 2018, from www.washingtonpost.com/opinions/doomsday-scenarios-are-as-harmful-as-climate-change-denial/2017/07/12/880ed002-6714-11e7-a1d7-9a32c91c6f40_story.html?utm_term=.cca57c62761d

21. Roberts, D. (2017). Does Hope Inspire More Action on Climate Change Than Fear? We Don't Know. Retrieved February 6, 2018, from www.vox.com/energy-and-environment/2017/12/5/16732772/emotion-climate-change-communication

22. The Climate Group & Ipsos MORI. (2017). *Survey Results Briefing: Climate Optimism*. Retrieved April 11, 2018,

from www.climateoptimist.org/wp-content/uploads/2017/09 /Ipsos-Survey-Briefing-Climate-Optimism.pdf

CHAPTER 10: WHO'S MOST WRONG?

1. Rivlin-Nadler, M. (2013). More Buck for Your Bang: People Who Have More Sex Make the Most Money. Retrieved April 12, 2018, from http://gawker.com/more-bang-for-your-buck -people-who-have-more-sex-make-1159315115

2. Ibid.; Lamb, E. (2013). Sex Makes You Rich? Why We Keep Saying 'Correlation Is Not Causation' Even Though It's Annoying. Retrieved February 6, 2018, from https://blogs .scientificamerican.com/roots-of-unity/sex-makes-you-rich-why -we-keep-saying-e2809ccorrelation-is-not-causatione2809d-even -though-ite28099s-annoying/

3. Vigen, T., Spurious Correlations. Retrieved February 6, 2018, from www.tylervigen.com/spurious-correlations; Vigen, T. (2015). *Spurious Correlations*. New York: Hachette Books.

4. Full list of Perils of Perception studies on page 247.

5. Meyer, E. (2014). *The Culture Map*. New York: PublicAffairs.

6. Schlösser, T., Dunning, D., Johnson, K. L., & Kruger, J. (2013). How Unaware Are the Unskilled? Empirical Tests of the 'Signal Extraction' Counterexplanation for the Dunning–Kruger Effect in Self-Evaluation of Performance. *Journal of Economic Psychology*, *39*, 85–100. https://doi.org/10.1016/j.joep.2013.07.004

CHAPTER 11: DEALING WITH OUR DELUSIONS

1. Bell, C. (2017). Fake News: Five French Election Stories Debunked. Retrieved April 12, 2018, from www.bbc.co.uk/news /world-europe-39265777

2. d'Ancona, M. (2017). *Post-Truth: The New War on Truth and How to Fight Back*. London: Ebury Press.

3. European Commission. (n.d.). Public Opinion— Eurobarometer Interactive. Retrieved April 16, 2018, from http:// ec.europa.eu/COMMFrontOffice/publicopinion/index.cfm

4. Mance, H. (2016). Britain Has Had Enough of Experts, Says Gove. Retrieved April 16, 2018, from www.ft.com/content/3be49734-29cb-11e6-83e4-abc22d5d108c#

5. LSE Public Lectures and Events. (2012). In Conversation with Daniel Kahneman [mp3]. Retrieved February 6, 2018, from https://richmedia.lse.ac.uk/publiclecturesandevents/20120601_1300_inConversationWithDanielKahneman.mp3

6. Ibid.

7. Tversky, A., & Kahneman, D. (1974). Judgement Under Uncertainty: Heuristics and Biases. *Science, 185*(4157), 1124–1131. https://doi.org/10.1126/science.185.4157.1124

8. Dobelli, R. (2014). *The Art of Thinking Clearly: Better Thinking, Better Decisions.* London: Sceptre.

9. Hawkins, S., Yudkin, D., Juan-Torres, M., & Dixon, T. (2018). Hidden Tribes: A Study of America's Polarized Landscape. More in Common. https://hiddentribes.us/pdf/hidden_tribes_report.pdf

10. Pew Research Center. (2017). The Partisan Divide on Political Values Grows Even Wider. www.people-press.org/2017/10/05/the-partisan-divide-on-political-values-grows-even-wider/

11. Original source: www.people-pss.org/interactives/political-polarization-1994-2017/

12. Marshall, A. G. (2015). *Wake Up and Change Your Life: How to Survive a Crisis and Be Stronger, Wiser and Happier.* London: Marshall Method Publishing.

13. Greenspan, S. (2009). *Annals of Gullibility: Why We Get Duped and How to Avoid It.* Westport, CT: Praeger.

14. Taber, C. S., & Lodge, M. (2006). Motivated Skepticism in the Evaluation of Political Beliefs. *American Journal of Political Science, 50*(3), 755–769.

15. Davis, E. (2017). *Post-Truth: Why We Have Reached Peak Bullshit and What We Can Do About It.* Boston: Little, Brown.

16. Pennebaker, J. W., & Evans, J. F. (2014). *Expressive Writing: Words That Heal.* Enumclaw, WA: Idyll Arbor.

17. Safi, M. (2018). India Backs Down over Plan to Ban Journalists for 'Fake News'. www.theguardian.com/world/2018/apr/03/india-backs-down-over-plan-to-ban-journalists-for-fake-news

18. Michael-Ross Fiorentino, M. (2018). France Passes Controversial 'Fake News' Law. www.euronews.com/2018/11/22/france-passes-controversial-fake-news-law

19. Stolton, S. (2018). EU Code of Practice on Fake News: Tech Giants Sign the Dotted Line. www.euractiv.com/section/digital/news/eu-code-of-practice-on-fake-news-tech-giants-sign-the-dotted-line/

20. Read Across the Aisle. (n.d.). A Fitbit for Your Filter Bubble. Retrieved April 16, 2018, from www.readacrosstheaisle.com/

21. Wardle, C., & Derakhshan, H. (2017). Information Disorder: Toward an Interdisciplinary Framework for Research and Policy Making. Retrieved April 11, 2018, from https://rm.coe.int/information-disorder-toward-an-interdisciplinary-framework-for-research/168076277c

22. Sippitt, A. (2017). Interview Conducted by Bobby Duffy with Amy Sippitt at Full Fact. London.

23. Shermer, M. (2016). When Facts Backfire. *Scientific American, 316*(1), 69. https://doi.org/10.1038/scientificamerican0117-69

24. Ackerman, B., & Fishkin, J. S. (2008). Deliberation Day. In *Debating Deliberative Democracy* (pp. 7–30). https://doi.org/10.1002/9780470690734.ch1

25. Mulgan, G. (2015). Designing Digital Democracy: A Short Guide. Retrieved April 12, 2018, from www.nesta.org.uk/blog/designing-digital-democracy-short-guide

26. Lakoff, G. (2010). Why 'Rational Reason' Doesn't Work in Contemporary Politics. Retrieved February 6, 2018, from www.truth-out.org/buzzflash/commentary/george-lakoff-why-rational-reason-doesnt-work-in-contemporary-politics/8893-george-lakoff-why-rational-reason-doesnt-work-in-contemporary-politics

INDEX

vaccines, 36–41, 38 (fig.), 47, 99, 197–198, 238
Varian, Hal, 171
VoCo, 187
voting, 46, 133–135, 134 (fig.), 137, 174
Vraga, Emily, 187

Wakefield, Andrew, 37, 39, 41
'Walk It Back' (The National), 165
Wall Street Journal, 235
Wallace-Wells, David, 204, 205
Washington Post, 142, 146, 204
wealth inequality, 85–90, 87 (fig.), 91
weapons of mass destruction, 99
weight, 9, 25–29, 26 (fig.), 32, 114, 233, 238
Wells, H. G., 10, 11
what we're told effects, 13–16, 17–18, 20, 39, 70–71, 190, 224 (fig.)

Wheeler, McArthur, 216–217
willpower, lack of, 81–82
Wisdom of Crowds, The (Surowiecki), 166
wishful thinking, 153, 154, 165–169
women's suffrage, 137
    See also gender equality
Wood, Thomas, 100
Word of the Year, 7, 13, 163
World Bank, 41
World Economic Forum (Davos), 85, 138, 189
World News Tonight (television program), 143
World Values Survey (WVS), 43, 45–46
WTOE 5 News, 161

Yale Law School, 153

Zuckerberg, Mark, 175, 182–183

Bobby Duffy is director of the Policy Institute at King's College London. Formerly, he was managing director of the Ipsos MORI Social Research Institute and global director of the Ipsos Social Research Institute. He lives in London.